D1708889

WORKING STIFF

The Anthology of Professional Wrestling Literature & Art

Edited by Josh Olsen ■ Foreword by Box Brown

gimmick
press

Working Stiff
The Anthology of Professional Wrestling Literature & Art
Edited by Josh Olsen

Copyright © 2015 Josh Olsen
All rights reserved.
All works contained within remain the intellectual property of their creators.
Published by Gimmick Press

Cover art and layout by Katie MacDonald

ISBN-13: 978-1519478894
ISBN-10: 1519478895

Table of Contents

Foreword

Wrestling as art is a fairly new concept in some ways. Even though the outcomes had been predetermined since the early 1900s, not a soul in the business would admit to it. Would a snake oil salesman call his business an artform? Hardly. Yet it is an artform.

In recent years with the breakdown of kayfabe and the apocalyptic state of the WWE monolith, we've seen a rise in the artistic side of pro-wrestling. Not just in the storylines and characters but in the method and practice. We see wrestlers honing their crafts the way we artists hone our own crafts. The wrestlers' bodies and actions are their canvases and notebooks.

These artists are deconstructing the medium and pushing the genre to places Lou Thesz would fear to tread. Wrestling can be seen as both a medium and a genre the same way superhero comics can. The works found herein are of the pro-wrestling genre. The works of the wrestler we see on TV and in live arenas are in the pro-wrestling medium.

Growing up many of the people around me didn't understand wrestling. I struggled to explain it to them but didn't have the words. Too often the appeal of wrestling is not self-evident to a casual viewer. There are times when we, even as avid fans, cringe at what we're looking at. My parents didn't know what to think. Even my friends asked why I cared about that fake stuff. As if sitting through a baseball game is more legitimate than watching Bobby Heenan and Gorilla Monsoon fumble their way through Prime Time Wrestling. Why was I setting the VCR a week in advance to record WWF Superstars while I was away on vacation? It's just a bunch of guys slapping each other around, isn't it?

Clearly no. It isn't just guys slapping each other around.

When I was a child I could have taken this book and given it to my detractors as a gift with a note that read: "Know wrestling know me."

...

Box Brown is an Ignatz Award winning cartoonist, illustrator and comic publisher from Philadelphia. His book *Andre the Giant: Life and Legend*, released in 2014, spent three weeks on the *New York Times* Graphic Novel Best Sellers List. He launched the comics publishing house Retrofit Comics in 2011.

Preface

I'm a lifelong fan of professional wrestling. Granted, my viewership may wax and wane, depending upon my enthusiasm for the current product, but I remain a steadfast and vociferous consumer of the professional wrestling genre, in all of its varied formats. I'm a collector of professional wrestling trading cards, comic books, and VHS cassettes. I'm a player of professional wrestling video games. I'm a frequent viewer of professional wrestling movies, be they critically acclaimed documentaries and films such as *Beyond the Mat* or *The Wrestler*, or popcorn fare like *No Holds Barred*. I'm a reader of professional wrestling books, such as Mick Foley's epic *Have a Nice Day*, Scott E. Williams' controversial *Hardcore History*, or David Shoemaker's *The Squared Circle*, one of the few books that I've ever read, reread, and then listened to on audiobook. In recent years, I've evolved into a big fan of audiobooks, and more so than that, I'm a rabid listener of podcasts, with most of my favorites being about or created by professional wrestlers.

Colt Cabana's *The Art of Wrestling* was, for lack of a better term, my gateway drug. I began listening to *The Art of Wrestling* immediately after Colt appeared on episode 334 of *WTF with Marc Maron*, back in November of 2012, so almost exactly three years ago, from this writing. At the time, I had become more or less a casual professional wrestling fan. I occasionally watched *RAW* with my then-8 year-old son, who was really into Rey Mysterio and CM Punk, I infrequently attended Detroit-area events, and I would pay for autographs from the likes of Virgil, every time I saw him at the Motor City Comic Con, but my awareness of the current state of professional wrestling was pretty limited. However, that all changed after I first listened to Colt Cabana. Colt, and his podcast, reignited my passion for professional wrestling, and listening to *The Art of Wrestling* got me excited to actually watch professional wrestling again. But this time, I wasn't just watching WWE, I was paying attention to the indies, as well, so when I attended local promotions, like Detroit's XICW or the Squared Circle Revue, there was an added sense of excitement, because I had listened to Colt's interviews with the likes of Jimmy Jacobs and Truth Martini and Zach Gowen, among others, and so suddenly I was paying closer attention to the names on the rosters, because I was invested in their stories, and in their lives, as well as their in-ring performances. I wanted to learn about who came from where, as well as where they're going. Colt's podcast introduced me to Tyler Black and Claudio Castagnoli and Kevin Steen, before they were Seth Rollins and Cesaro and Kevin Owens. Through *The Art of Wrestling*, I learned about ROH and CZW and PWG and ICW. Colt Cabana's *The Art of Wrestling* is almost single-handedly responsible for resparking my interest in watching professional wrestling, and introducing me to alternative and independent wrestling promotions, but *The Old School Wrestling Podcast*, with Black Cat and Dre, deserves an equal amount of credit for introducing me to alternative and independent professional wrestling writing and art.

The format of *The Old School Wrestling Podcast* is quite simple and straightforward. Co-hosts Black Cat and Dre (real names redacted), two Chicago-area family men with a lifelong for passion for professional wrestling, watch and discuss various "old school" professional wrestling pay-per-views and events. The show is zero frills, and frankly there are numerous other professional wrestling podcasts that follow a somewhat similar format, but what *The Old School Wrestling Podcast* has over its competitors is the affable personalities of its co-hosts, as well as its community of creative listeners. A number of *OSWP*'s most vocal supporters are prolific writers and artists, themselves, and one of the show's recurring guests is Robert Newsome, creator of *The Atomic Elbow*, a truly excellent professional wrestling zine. I'm proud to say that *Working Stiff* features the work of several contributors to *The Atomic Elbow*. *The Atomic Elbow* is where I first saw Scott Stripling's tale of a post-apocalyptic, biomechanically enhanced Arn Anderson, and it's where I first saw an excerpt from Box Brown's then still in-progress *Andre the Giant: Life and Legend*, a graphic novel I would eventually assign to my students at the University of Michigan, for the duration of four sections of composition that I unofficially transformed into "Pro Wrestling 101" (to the chagrin of my *former* employer). Along with *The Art of Wrestling* and *The Old School Wrestling Podcast*, *The Atomic Elbow* is most definitely another inspiration behind the creation of *Working Stiff*, but that's not just because it's a zine that features professional wrestling themed reviews, interviews, comics, and art. One of the little things that I immediately loved about *The Atomic Elbow* is that when a copy arrives in the mail, the envelope typically contains, in addition to the zine, an assortment of flyers, stickers, and trading cards. As a matter of fact, this was an idea that I loved so much that I started doing it with my own books, as well.

I don't often write about professional wrestling, my role is typically of the consumer and the fan, but my previous two books, *Six Months* and *Such a Good Boy*, were full of pop culture musings and nostalgia, and so I thought that it was only fitting that I, too, began sending out trading cards along with copies of my books. At first, the cards consisted of whatever I had extras of, be it baseball cards, Garbage Pail Kids, Wacky Packages, or professional wrestling cards, but as my supply of dupes ran low, and I became more and more passionate about professional wrestling, I began to send out more and more 1985 Topps WWF, and fewer 1989 Topps baseball, and a funny thing happened. All of a sudden, people wanted to talk to me about wrestling. They wanted to share their stories and their memories. Maybe they came of age in the Attitude Era. Maybe their dad used to take them to Florida Championship Wrestling. Maybe their local, family dentist was Ric Flair's father. I was very moved and inspired by these stories, and I thought to myself, somebody ought to write a book about this. That was my initial idea, to compile a collection of interviews or stories about people's various professional wrestling memories, but the concept for that book is still available

(I think), because of what happened on February 13, 2014. It was the night before Valentine's Day, but it was also Friday the 13th. I was in Toledo, Ohio, at Black Kite Coffee, at a poetry reading organized by Michael Grover. As I had been doing for several months, by then, I was handing out professional wrestling trading cards, along with copies of my books, and when it was Matthew Sradeja's turn to read, he said that he wanted to share something in honor of the cards that I was distributing. His concise, but no less impactful poem was entitled "Andre the Giant," and that was the moment that everything clicked into place, and I came up with the idea for *Working Stiff*, an anthology of professional wrestling themed literature and art.

The process of compiling and editing this book has been more rewarding, challenging, time-consuming, and downright enjoyable than I ever could have imagined. I've read and reread the contributions to *Working Stiff* more times than I can keep track of, and yet, I still find them all just as amazing as the first time I read them. In a sense, the creation of this book was a selfish venture. After all, if somebody else had already compiled a professional wrestling themed anthology, chances are I wouldn't have penned that initial call for submissions. Instead, I would have simply bought somebody else's book. But obviously that wasn't the case. As far as I could find, back in February of 2015, using my finely tuned librarian research skills, there was no professional wrestling themed anthology, and so, I decided to make one. In short, this is the book that I wanted to read, made possible because a collection of professional wrestling-loving writers and artists trusted me with their work, and for that, I'll forever be grateful.

Josh Olsen, Editor

Acknowledgements

Thank you to everyone involved in the creation of this book. Thanks to Katie MacDonald, for shooting the cover and handling layout duties. Without you, this book would be little more than an idea. Thanks to Box Brown, for his foreword. Thanks to the editors of the various publications in which many of the following pieces first appeared. Thanks to all of the wonderful contributors included in these pages. Without your work, and your patience, and your faith in this project, none of this would have been possible. Thanks to you, the reader. And, finally, thanks to everyone who ever laced up a pair of boots and took a bump.

"It's still real to me, dammit."

Pepper Gomez

Rick was no stranger to the pink belly
to hand cuffs, the riding crop
& now Roz was into this new bought
bunk bed & puppy wrestling fun game
in the spare bedroom freshly painted
Flamingo Dream for the four girl pups
Kylee, Krista, Kirsten, & Kendall
with a Hot Pink scarf loosely tied
to the ceiling light fixture
for the Stairway to Hell Ladder Match
with no disqualifications
& Rick on his back naked loosely tied
to chairs with scarves of blue & purple
riding on a wave of vodka & Xanax
a black target painted on his belly
now covered with paw prints & fur swirls
as Roz was squirming on the bottom bunk
with the gaggle of Bassett puppies
dipping them in trays of Easter egg coloring dye
for the drop on Rick prone & down for the count
until Lady Roz began mounting the ladder
for the top bunk with the single boy pup
to snatch & capture the championship belt scarf
& she made it up there breathing heavy
"Rick, don't move a muscle."
"I'm here for you, honey bunny."
Rick saw the boy pup dangling over him
dipped in blue & sporting the pink scarf
& he was barking, barking, barking.
"Pepper Gomez," Rick said.

1

Bobo Brazil

rocked the CoCo Butt
his feared finishing move
ask Leaping Larry Chene
after his missed Flying Headscissors
ask Killer Kowalski
after he lost his grip on The Claw
ask Dick The Bruiser
after his Top Rope Knee Drop went wide
ask 2 Tag Team midgets
Fuzzy Cupid & Sky Low Low
ordered out of the dressing room
on a slow dull night at Cobo Hall
for comic relief in an undercard snoozer
to sprint into the ring to taunt
to circle dance around the dazed Bobo
down on his knees dog tired
(his opponent tangled in the turnbuckle)
but in the right position for midget height
to deliver the CoCo Butt to their sweet spot
ask them all who delivered their first concussion
who set in motion early onset dementia
search out their graves or scattered cremains
& Ask the Dust about Bobo Brazil
who checked out after suffering a series of strokes.

Channeling Ox Baker, 1995-2003

"You will hate me." – T-shirt, screen-printed, by Ox Baker. 1970s.

I like to hurt people, but am no great
heart-puncher. I play football and know
the way to a man's heart is to square
the shoulders and put my head
through his chest. I like to hurt people
even when I am hurt, even when I am
barely functional with headaches, so I hold
my knife up at the dinner table and say
that I know where each artery is and the best
way to cut them. I can't articulate this
to the therapist. I can't articulate. So she asks
me to talk to my father. But this is not how
we speak: he likes to hurt people, too;
our shared language is pain. In school,
I whip a classmate with my house key,
held at the end of a long chain. He begins
taking karate some afternoons. I see him
in the neighborhood wearing his gi. I understand
his purpose, though I am not afraid
of him and will beat his ass. I wish
I hadn't, that our fight had gone any way
other than its anti-climax. I wake up often
with the image of him pinning my arms back,
bearing my breast to the sky. Just once,
I'd like to sleep long enough to allow his fist
to hammer my heart. But I am the great heel
of childhood; here, there is no closure.

For Hulk Hogan, Who, By His Own Reasonable Estimate, Has the Largest Arms in the World

In a bookstore, I saw Atlas figure on the covers of innumerable
paperbacks and thought of you. Brother, the burden those arms
must carry. The work of lifting giants, quelling earthquakes, mauling
t-shirts, and cupping the noise of the mob to an ear is yours;
you asked for it then and you ask for it now. Your arms I imagined
variously: the jack lifting a car over my father's body, the cranes
in my mother's factory, twin pythons that could devour my problems
were I able to scream your name loud enough. I screamed,
but I won't see you in the flesh until that flesh, no longer taut,
is incapable of its former glories. Until then, I invent my own encounters
and spin those. Here is one: Once, I claimed to have met you
at a Big Boy restaurant, pouring syrup on a stack of pancakes.
When you took my hand in yours, it disappeared. Then you did.
Cup your ear, Hulk. Tonight, when I call out, come. Lift me.

For Jake "The Snake" Roberts, on the Occasion of Making an Unlikely Out in Centerfield During a Charity Softball Game

Like every catch before or since, yours is a matter of geometry
and probability. To say this is to admit that I believe in miracles.

Pro-wrestling is this: the work of death and resurrection. I watch
to see your throat cut. To see you rise, diminished. Again, again.

In your documentary's climax, you are smoking crack in the bathroom.
You show me this to articulate that some men prefer ruin.

Again the gambler crows that he has twenty-two. The game
is blackjack. Few are born to cast lots, but who does this stop?

For Brutus "The Barber" Beefcake, Who Was Unable to Cut Hair

It should have been obvious: hedge shears cannot navigate
the part in a man's hair with any accuracy, are useless

in matters relating to the crew cut, the mop top, the short regular,
or the balding. It was the bowtie, maybe, or the tassels on his biceps,

alternating red and white like a barber pole, or his zeal for the mullets
of other men. My barber never smells of baby oil, never uses

anything larger than kitchen scissors. Her shop is open; a building
tangible, lived in. Beefcake's was a prop, a sugarpane window

disgruntled wrestlers hurled each other through. He often stood
back from fistfights, hiding among his empty antiseptic jars, ducking

behind his flophouse barber chair. His eyes were those
of a desolate man. They're the eyes I have, sometimes,

when fifteen dollars is the price I pay for a woman
to massage my scalp, when this is my only means of contact.

In Retrospect, the Fan Who Started the First "You Fucked Up!" Chant Feels Pretty Bad About the Whole Thing

"How Ignorant thou art in your pride of wisdom!" — Mary Shelly, Frankenstein

Unlike the incident in Nassau
where Bahamian fans—convinced
all Samoans possessed indestructible
heads—dropped a cinder block
on The Barbarian from a balcony,
his chant was innocuous,
a way of letting the wrestlers
know he was in on the act,
that he knew a missed suicide
dive was a sign of life. But the Chant,
drunkenly croaked to life,
quickly outstripped its creator,
overtaking a gleeful crowd
all too happy to flaunt their
secret knowledge. The Chant
grew, was audible on televised
events when luchadores slipped
from the top turnbuckle, while
injured men writhed with torn
ligaments. The privilege of wrestling
fandom being anonymity,
those chanting went home
safely, knowing wrestlers
couldn't seek retribution. The creator,
however, went sleepless some nights,
had visions of quadriplegic grapplers
being carted away while the Chant
rose up from those in the know.
The Chant, he realized, was worse
than The Barbarian's cinder block,

10

worse even than a wrestler's
own knowledge of failure. The Chant
is unaware of the blurred line between
theatricality and crisis, cannot tell
a real paramedic from one too muscular
for his uniform. It is blind
to the handshake deal between wrestler
and fan: one agrees to the plausibility
of hold and counterhold, the other
to pretend this sequence mostly painless.

This Is Fluid

Fighting, in imitation of the greats. Trying to remember just how the moves went. Leaping from the turn-buckle, bodies colliding like trains in black and white silent films, to the canvas, to the canvas, but really I'm sure it was eleven year old arms stabbing at each other in awkward elbowed throws, catching glances, although, to be sure, there was blood and bruises on our pale faces, his remaining so light, mine darkening to Mexican brown by mid-summer, tinged by the sun, the red fluid weaving in streaks under my nose, across my lips, painting each other's shoulders. Bruises around eyes like bad make-up.

But this is memory.

When my mother told me she had cancer, that the surgery was already scheduled. I imagine this: We're on TV under dramatic lights when she confesses in tears, which I mirror, but I keep my strength, because goddamn in this world a man can only shed tears for his mother, and I hold her, my powerful arms wrapping around her suddenly weakened body. Somewhere, there is cheering, a crowd surrounding a stage.

But my memory also says this: I've called my mother for some other reason; it's been too long, and I'm hours away by car, down a backward-flowing river. I'm telling her good news, something about her grandson or a new job or a good day at work, when she tells me, almost casually, about the cancer. About the surgery. About the likely chemo. In this version, I reply, simply, "Oh." In this version, my voice is dry, or wet. The sound I make is a cough or a suck. What follows is a conversation, I'm sure. I'm sure, but I don't recall. But no wailing. No dropping the phone. No pleas of why god why. There is no crowd cheering.

In this version, after I hang up the phone, I don't hold my mother, but I take my dog for a walk around this shitty small town and think about hitting things, slamming my fist through windows, into parked cars, into the stupid fucking face of that guy who has the audacity to be standing in his goddamn driveway on the day my mother tells me she has cancer. In this version, I hit no one. I bag up my dog's shit and go home, tell my wife what I know, and go on with my day.

I hit Eric as hard as I can because he made contact with me, and it hurt. This is the way it happened, so often. It's a game. All of us watched pro wrestling, the WWF (before lawsuits). Jimmy Supafly. The Ultimate Warrior. Junkyard Dog. These were our superstars, our celebrity crushes. I loved them and wanted to be them. My brother, Kevin, was one of us. Eric, Tim, and Andy, too. And me. Most of the time, it was in Andy's yard, because it was a corner lot and flat. And his parents didn't seem to care. We'd pull out old jump ropes to mark the edges of the ring, but it didn't take long for those to move, for the play to expand the space. We had rules, of course. No one was supposed to get hurt. We all knew the moves, the suplexes and piledrivers and stomps that never landed. We played well for hours, unless it was me and Eric, the two most even in size and age. For some reason, our competition turned to violence, real violence, with spit and blood, much like our friendship, which soon became fluid and then jagged as he found friends better at sports more accepted, more tangible, less acted.

When we started, I'd stalk a jump rope ring, holding my clawed hand out in imitation of Baron Von Raschke, Master of the Iron Claw (sorry, Von Erich). We'd laugh. In some version of this, I am Von Raschke; I am the crowd pleaser, the entertainer, the athlete, the professional. In another version, so much closer to the truth, I'm a skinny suburban kid playing games. We engage, Eric and I, throwing each other around, playing the moves, pretending to be dazed until the last moment, allowing ourselves to be pinned until just before the count of three. And then a shot hits, a fist to face or neck or shoulder, and anger rises. The other hits back, and again. We bleed.

I imagine my mother's surgery, the Iron Claw machine moving forward, tearing into her breast to grab that tumor and squeeze it into submission or simply rip that fucker out, the tainted blood oozing across surgical fingers. I imagine the cancer as some baby alien from a sci-fi movie, misshapen and grotesque. I imagine it growing limbs, disproportionately long arms and legs, wiggling, and hanging from the cold metal. Its face forms in my mind, but only slightly, for a moment—a bulging mass like a cauliflower ear.

Eric drops me. It could be a trip, punch, push, who knows, but I'm down, face-first. He carves an elbow into my back, which just barely registers, and then he hits me on the ear, first right, then left, his hands curled so knuckles and nails strike first. Repeat. My brain jiggles for a moment or so before it registers what he's doing. His fists are hard, small baseballs. I let him do it again; I let him hit me, pummel my ears again and again, until a feel and hear a pop. I finally turn and grapple him. We wrestle a bit, continuing on with the play, but it's the final act. We both wipe away the blood, he from his lips and forehead, me from my nose and ears, and we laugh.

Sometimes, it's hard to find the right end to our stories.

The Junkyard Dog would have pinned his opponent, a clean ending. The ref's hand would slap the canvas three times. Arms would be raised. The crowd would cheer or boo. But I don't get a referee to tell me when the fight is done, when the story has come to an end. My mother is not surrounded by thousands of screaming fans; the cheering section is small, and victories less clean, less final. Yes, there is an ending, a grand finale, but what brings us there is ever-changing; the ending may be absolute, but the process is fluid. No one will let me know when the story ends—no countdown, no slapping of the mat—but, to be sure, it ends.

So I imagine this: I'm in a hospital bed, the rigid sheets pulled halfway up my torso, and the bed is in the middle of a ring. I'm almost alone. Thousands are in the stands, looking down upon me, but in the ring it's just me and a man in vertical black and white stripes. He watches me, closely, as my breath goes staggered and then almost, almost gone. He raises his hand over the hospital bed. My breath is gone. My chest shudders, goes still. He gently slaps the bed. Then again, and again.

flowers at dreamland

i had a dream last night
it was a beautiful dream

terry funk and i are making a phone call
i am punching through a folding chair
"don't fucking touch her again"
terry's breath hissing through the space in his teeth

my daddy was a wonderful person
but he understood life

terry funk and i are sitting in a crowded apartment in kaifeng
it's 3 am and everyone else is sleeping
we stare at each other until i blink
when i open my eyes he is gone

terry, why do you do that stuff?
for the hell of it, dad

it is christmas eve, and i watch terry funk on television
they cut him out of the wire
all blood and torn tights
he's smiling

are you saying i'm not good enough?
you are.

when terry funk breaks my nose
he is staying in our guest room
finally, i think. finally

Be a Man

Track 1 – "Intro"

Macho Man, whose voices are these? There is a din you wear like a feathered boa, a soft scaffolding, a city made of noise. You've dropped one act and replaced it with another. I want to laugh at you, you made-up muscular clown. I want to see through your artifice and stare into your maudlin aches. I want to be confounded by you, to walk the streets of the place you live and wonder if the footprints I see pressed into the pavement belong to you, or if you are a less clever architect building walls from a kit, painting them as you've seen others painted before, spreading stucco across black space on an intercontinental scale as phony as the slur you speak to bring me into your dreamworld.

Track 2 – "I'm Back"

Where did you go, Randy? I listen to your plumage bloom and let your fresh colors ooze between my ears. Once when I was a child my mother dyed her hair blonde. It's difficult to color her with correct language. Many of her hairs were still naturally blonde. Others had turned gray. She opened the box for the dying kit and with my cousin's help put on the plastic cap, pulling strands through the pinprick eyelets that gridded her head like lineless points of longitude. They lathered and rinsed, restoring vigor. I did the same, already towheaded, emphasizing my vigor. I wore my new dyed top of yellow-white like a helmet or a second skull. This means nothing to you now, you ghost, nor did it then. Perhaps you were aware of me inasmuch as you were aware that people existed whom you would never know. Yet here you are with me, posthumously. When my father turned 40, my mother bought him trick birthday candles. When he blew them out, the flame would flicker and disappear, then come back to us, twisting as strong and orange as ever.

Track 3 – "R U Ready"

I don't think we're ready. My dad retired last week. I remember, in Punta Gorda, sometime in the days before hurricane Charlie hit, as though it rode your crashing elbows, Randy, my grandfather looked at me for the last time. Wide and blue, how my father, or my older brother would look if either were so old and bewildered. You could hold a photograph of each of them from a similar point in their lives. The age of 18, let's say. You could place them on the table and layer their faces, one on top of the other, and find that they match almost perfectly. In Punta Gorda, the patients in the Alzheimer's ward played with colorful bending tubes and plastic keys. They stroked the backs of fake kittens. So long as their hands were busy. Hold my hand, Randy, and explain to me what it's like where you are now. Ease my fear. Calm me. Squeeze my face. Blind me to the three of them as they stare back at me in Punta Gorda, eyes streaked with light, jaws trembling as though to speak, stuck in the muck of muteness. Or if I do see them, Randy, allow me to smile in return and accept the finishing move of time, slammed on my back with my limbs tangled in spotlight, hoping that the profundity of my trepidation over what comes next, though seen, will not be recognized.

Track 4 – "Hit the Floor"

My grandmother died in Billings. She told my mother her plans to pick tomatoes from plants that withered 50 years ago. She commanded things to my uncle, who was back in Minnesota, creeping his truck along the country roads, breathing sun into his nose, the flesh plane where squamous cells would stem and take root, the nose that two years later would curdle down its length. A doctor sliced it off his face. I hear you, Randy, lurking in the shadows like history. In Billings, as she died, my grandmother told Fred, my uncle, to feed the hens. Birds, I presume, who stuck their beaks into the dirt to guzzle feed. Who are these men, Randy, that speak for you at the outset of your song? The ones that haunt the air like ghosts? My mother tried her best not to split apart, to become ravaged like a barn in a whipping green squall that punctures July or August. She tried to explain to her mother that Fred wasn't there, the tomatoes weren't there. Your persona, Randy, is something to reach for. In the face of oblivion, there you are, revealing your mad eyes to what's inevitable, daring it to face you. To grab you and pull on your limbs as you ride it like a wave through time, or a writhing body. My uncle couldn't take care of himself. The umbilical cord, when he came out, wrapped him in a chokehold as strong as nature. After his nose was off, and he preferred white gauze to the prosthetic made for him by an artist who specialized in such things, because his fingers were too clumsy to apply the glue, my mother would be the one to change his bandage. I saw her once, holding the strip between them on the couch my grandmother called the Davenport, her eyes solid and impenetrable as battened shutters as she stared at the hole in his face. She leaned closer and pressed tape to his cheeks. It was very quiet. Maybe the TV was on. The sound of tape tearing. One strip. Another strip. She never once revealed the storm that thrashed the depths inside her.

Track 5 – "Let's Get it On"

Macho Man, I get your gist of locked limbs and fluid exchanges. I see back to the times I crawled like your

17

promiscuous elbows across heaving supine flesh that smelled of strawberries or patchouli or cake. How can I not connect you to the Marvin Gaye song, the tune that accompanies all the clichéd parodies of human love that play on screens? I'm not sure if this is what you allude to, if you allude to anything. It makes me sad that bodies fail. I like to enter your name in the YouTube search bar and watch your face contort into impressions of madness while your threats to Tito Santana, Jake the Snake Roberts, or Hulk Hogan, your ultimate foil, leap from your tongue, soaring at my inner ears in waves the top rope launched. Elizabeth at your side, pressed against you. Her gold dress sparkling in the hot light and her hair teased in long flips, her shy uncertain smile. It's all kayfabe, maybe; I'm uncertain of how well you know her, though I can speculate. She agrees with your insane threats. Her voice is as frail and weak as her will. She curls inward, shrinking in your voice, the thing that might control her better than any script. I wonder, when you dropped your persona, and you were you, Randy Poffo, your body away from the camera, if you loved your wife? Did she scream when your heart stopped in Seminole, Florida and your Jeep crashed into a tree, and there you were, slumped dead over the wheel, or if she joined your body in silent proneness, in those first moments your legend outlived you? I look at myself each morning in the full length mirror. I trace the lines in my body and wonder how they will change with time. My parents claim they are vegan but eat meat whenever I'm around them. They were scared into dieting through a support group at the hospital, where they watched videos of doctors pulling strings of plaque like tapeworms from human valves. My father bemoans steak. To him, it is medium-rare poison. When my brother and I were children, let's say seven years old, our mother and father avoided telling us how we were conceived when we asked them, telling us instead they used a book. I didn't know that adults were capable of running, that their full-grown weight hadn't already ruined them. I've never been authentic. In these bedridden moments I recall, Macho Man—in my college house, in the nighttime shadows of my friend's driveway in Saint Paul, on the bathroom floor, my mouth pressed to a different mouth, some that said my name, others that didn't care to know it—I construe things in a specific way—I envision us sharing a posture: we are on our backs as we're thumped by another, stuck in the pinning position. Hands holding us both down against our upward thrusts. Your quest for a title spanning intercontinental lengths, ample as libido, your endless self-promotion that comes off you like a boozy wake in gravel words and neon tights. This is loneliness, I think, and it is parody. I can see us both, staring into the lights, aware of ourselves as bodies, wondering if it's the end of anything.

Track 6 – "Remember Me"

I drive along the north bend of Lake Calhoun, Macho Man. Like a season you conjure yourself from the blueness of night's air and breaking waves, and you rise from the dead. I remember when the Israelis flew their jets over the Gaza Strip and rained bombs for several weeks in an operation called "Days of Penitence." My mother drove Fred home from chemo therapy and he ate stew with us. After our meal, I turned on the TV and felt my guts twist while watching the news of conflict. Fred came in the room and keeled over and vomited on the ottoman. His wracked system couldn't handle beef and carrots. I've heard a story repeated again and again of Fred coming home late one night and vomiting behind the garage. My grandfather woke and found him beneath the clothes line and asked him if he was drunk. It must have been those bad hamburgers, Fred told him. I remember my mother sopping up vomit with a cloth, the rancid stink and the stain it left. Macho Man, we spelunk together into the difficulties of human history. How many of us have died, documented on camera with our faces charred and limbs missing, or silently in hospital beds, evaporating through the seams of our robes like steam?

Track 7 – "Tear It Up"

I spent years pointlessly dreading the draft. How about you, Randy Poffo? Did you dread such things as napalm or white phosphorus? Neither you nor I ever wore fatigues and stormed the desert, kicking in doors and interrogating shepherds with black hoods and cameras and soaked rags. When I was eight years old I wrote a note to my dead grandfather wishing him well on his new voyage. I wrote that I'd see him again someday. He lay on his back with the door open to his casket, the pine vessel he rode into oblivion. I peered over the side at his Silly Putty face and his white hands painted and folded over his frozen torso. His limbs were purple when he died, Randy, the color of an outfit you might wear to a championship bout. My mother took the note from me and slid it in his breast pocket. Maybe it's still there, tucked in the sagging space that was his chest. I don't know how well such a parcel can withstand time if it's sealed, then buried, or if its message can be decoded, transmitted across the ethereal waves from this life to the thing that comes next. Can you tell me, Randy, or am I too late once again? I keep my Selective Service card inside my wallet. Now and then I pull it out and feel waves of dread fill the room up to my chin like a sneaking choke hold. It disturbs me that I can't understand the intercontinental sorrow suggested by this card. In 2004, the year I turned 16, my father, a sailor during Vietnam, was convinced the draft would return, and that it would remain the official policy for years to come. So was I. If I ever received my notice, he told me, I was supposed to tear it into shreds, or burn it, as if that would engulf the looming scape of time.

Track 8 – "Macho Thang"

The beat beneath you is stilted, Macho Man. How do you keep your footing in this shattering nightclub of sound? I picture you before me flexing your body among bodies in the strobing pulse, constituting time and space as your limbs take paths and linger successively like wings that spread and fade. My eighth grade science project was ripped off in the judging phase, Macho Man. Can you believe that? It was as if the kid who won did so because he had a manager who snuck up behind me and smashed my skull with a folding chair. I had climbed a ladder and counted to three, then dropped balls of various densities before a flashing strobe light, while my dad snapped the camera shutter closed. The images we made recorded the falling objects in each phase of their downward trajectories, ball upon ball, reinforcing the math of Galileo, as if his numbers were not already held in footings poured by God. That same year, I cracked a rib playing football at school. My dad flushed the pain killers I was prescribed out of fear that I would become addicted and crave them during math class or band, perhaps the way you injected yourself, if you injected yourself. I believe you know a thing or two about ladders, Macho Man, leaping professionally from them with your elbow extended before a strobe of flashing blubs. How many moments of your life were captured by people you would never know? I looked at the photos from my science project several years ago, though not while you were still around, and ogled the balls in their recorded routes. Are your motions the same as these, Randy, captured by cameras in a wake of effects, dissolved by time like the old flesh features of a skinless skeleton, a thinning echo of things no longer here?

Track 9 – "Be a Man"

This could be it, Macho Man, your title track. The words flake off you in landslide sheets, a shed past, or an abandoned memory. Here we are, Randy, confronting the old versions of ourselves, two slight waves approaching zero in the universe. I'm certain of it. I search your name the way I search symptoms on my skin and see you how you once were, standing beside the Hulkster, who these days lives in Tampa mere minutes from your final launch. Mean Gene Okerlund holds the mic between you, two megapowers afraid of blowing up the earth in a single nuclear promo. Is this what your slogan suggests, locking arms with intercontinental challengers in tests of mortal strength? Should I aspire to madness, to take off my shades and view the world through your staged psychosis? Sometimes I wonder which of my actions are most important. My dad spent months on a nuclear submarine in the North Atlantic, teaching himself guitar while he and his crew chased Russians through the depths per the dictum of mutually assured destruction. I watch your hand meet Hulk's, a convergence of madness and mania. The dead alternatives sleep beneath my pillow like lost teeth. I examine them in dreams and somber moments as if reading a script I found in my grandfather's dusty drawer. How easy it would have been ten years ago to exist in fatigues, bewildered and wandering the dusty waves of Mesopotamia alone, high on opium or pills, soaking sun into my blue eyes and my nose until I lie on my back to rest, far from the closest battalion. Tell me what it is, Randy, to cross your hands over your chest, contemplating your liminal stare into the blue canopy of the universe. Tell me how it feels when the canopy fades and you cannot decipher yourself from the extraneous details of sand and goats, and your skin slowly is replaced with air, the empty cloth sagging between your white ribs.

Track 10 – "Get Back"

I don't always realize when I'm talking to myself. The language of the mind is often found in scraps, as the unconscious likes to impress itself on objects. An empty shotgun shell in the wet grass, or a dented kettle, or an elbow pad stained with sweat. I like to think it's me you implore, Macho Man, but I know it isn't, although I hear my heals scrape along the path yours once stepped. Maybe you are on the other side of me, and we are separated only by some strange dimensional partition that cannot be crossed until the conditions are proper. The street outside is empty but will be filled with cars soon. I stop sometimes when I go to the pantry for a snack. My breath catches like it will never return as I glimpse my empty shoes, pointed at odd angles like passing boats. In these suspended moments I suddenly understand the subtext you have written, that my shoes are identical to how they would be if I were to spontaneously combust, or fade like a moment from half a century ago. I wonder, when I eventually stare into my father's eyes at his end, will I see my grandfather, too, or just my father, assuming he precedes me? What will we do with his shoes, the inserts left with impressions of his feet? I feel the urge sometimes to go on walks but rarely do I go on walks. The roads are wet and it looks like more rain is soon to follow. Come back, Randy.

Track 11 – "Feel the Madness"

If someone forced me to diagnose your calculated raving, Macho Man, I would simply tell them you are sad. I might elaborate and explain that you are breathing life into a self that died years back and cannot be resurrected. And so you take the skin you once wore and drape it across your shoulders like a pathetic boa. A decade ago, my older brother lived with Fred, separated from him in sleep by my grandmother's empty bedroom. Not all violence is staged, Macho Man, as you know. There is such thing as true delirium, or rage, or drunkenness. Fred got out of bed one night and stumbled down the hall with inebriated steps as stilted as your verse. He saw my brother in the kitchen and launched forward as if diving from the top rope, throwing his fist at my brother's alarmed eyes, which were certainly streaked in fear as he examined those of our uncle, which must have been deranged and inscrutable. My grandmother's oxygen machine was still in the house, coiled in plastic tubes. My mother and father have always been mystified by her luck after the many nights she spent smoking in bed, corrupting her lungs with arsenic and tar as the machine pumped her full of artificial breaths. It must be some primordial urge, Macho Man, compelling you, like the rest, to flaunt your past as if we can sense it with the same intensity as you once did. You might as well be feeding dead hens or weeding a garden that's been paved. I look at this new you, Randy, confused by this face I can remember but do not know.

Track 12 – "What's That All About"

Spare me, Randy, of your mournful ode to the incomprehensible. Mostly, I remember only what I want to remember, or what I think I need. The falafel restaurant in Saint Paul where on some days I ate happily alone, the seasonal release of a specific beer infused with pumpkin and nutmeg. Like a diseased nose I excise from the past such things as smashed bottles and broken condoms, or the blurred memory of waking up in a stranger's living room after I was found on my back, shaking on the sidewalk outside a closed convenience store, pants undone. Fred's obituary described his love for pickup trucks and his black lab though omitted other crucial facts like his ornery refusal to bathe, or his nightly highballs mixed to toxic levels, or his clumsy inability to glue the prosthetic nose to his face and look less monstrous. How monstrous do I appear? There are sensations that run through me, clogging my elbows and settling in my stomach like broken waves, which I can't name. Sadness, perhaps, or maybe chagrin, or self-pity. Explain things to me, Randy. If I have placed myself on a trajectory to suffer shock and crash my car into a tree, please let me know, because I'm getting tired of your iambic charade.

Track 13 – "Gonna Be Trouble"

Here is your madness, Macho Man. It is reflected in me. Can you sense it? It spans the longitudinal waves of your voice, which echoes through the black universe, sheathing me like a chrysalis of sound. People sometimes fail to recognize me when I go home. They aren't used to my short hair and diminished biceps. I once saw a father choke a child who wasn't his own as punishment for poor sportsmanship. A bench full of padded children sat shocked and silent. We didn't know what to do. Maybe, Randy, we were grateful it wasn't any of our dads doing it, or maybe we wished he would go further and seal the child's lungs closed and remove him from our realm of sweat and skates, our passions were so blind and biased. Children can be monsters that way. This was a while ago, back when you still donned the neon cowboy hat and the tasseled coat, when you made your living with your clownish elbows, when you still made a living. Sit with me, Randy. Embrace what you are at the expense of what you were. I could lift far more at sixteen than I can now. Be a voice, Macho Man. Be an echo. Reverberate through the emptiness between stars and celestial bodies. Spell yourself for an audience of vacuums and dust.

Track 14 – "Perfect Friend"

Hand me your cup, Randy. I wish to dip it into this ancient flow of voices and drink. It's here that our missions meet. Tell me, Mr. Poffo, how did you cope with disconnection? Is it enough simply to recall? Is it too much to implore the effaced likes of you? To whom am I speaking? Can you hear through your persona? I have seen photographs of my father in his high school singlet with his hands crossed behind his back in a line of fit wrestlers. I remember when my grandfather was my father's age. Certainly the consciousness must transform with the body through time. My friend drank a liter of rum one night and went insane, Macho Man. He could have cut a promo with you and Hulk Hogan. He could have placed his hand in yours and feared for the safety of a world. He held a snow shovel in the kitchen, facing me, daring me to tempt him. If you were there, Macho Man, would you have crept behind and smashed his head with a chair? Maybe I saw you in his smile, his senseless mood as old as DNA. His brother grabbed him and applied a choke hold, then suplexed him to the hardwood, cracking his scalp in the process. There were screams. My friend's voice pooled in my ears like a sea of blood and has been heavy since, pleas of, "Kill me, kill me." My grandmother died in Florida, Randy, a lot like you. She washed her windows alone, felt a flutter, and lay on her back in the grass and sun as her pacemaker failed. I am beginning to get your madness, Macho Man. I am beginning to understand. Perhaps it is the voices on which you ride, the structure holding your recorded words, which still grieve loss years after you yourself have perished. This is the tune you sing Macho Man, Randy Savage, Randy Poffo, one in which the dead mourn the dead, reunited in your nothingness.

Thank You Daniel

In the reality where Daniel Bryan's neck didn't break,
close to the one we live in,
the one where the other third graders and I argued
about who cut the rope when Owen fell.
A reality where we couldn't see through
the fuzz of fiction.

In that other world, would Bryan still be my favorite?
Or is it the breaks
from seeing him fail again and again
that show me the bit of self
that makes me chant.

At the WWE Christmas Party

they're in the spirit of giving
after taking so much offense.

This is what I imagine:
Vince McMahon loves taking shots
at Daniel Bryan's beard
and gives him the ugly sweater prize
even though Daniel is in a t-shirt.

The odd couples, the freaks, the tag teams
stand in arrangements no one would expect,
like Hacksaw caught with Iron Sheik
and a seatful of blow.

And it's not a wrestler who breaks the ice
of the dance floor,
but a nameless sound guy
louder than them all.

Road to WrestleMania

"America, if you had a soul then God would look down and spit in it." - Rusev, 3/14/15

Franklin, you got shitty drunk. Yeah, but shit, was it fun. Those little kids
were so into the hero. Shit. We were into the hero. "He pooped his pants!"

"He pooped his pants!" We chanted. "Feed his legs." Ryback: that wrestler
has such tiny legs but really his legs are monstrous and it's just an issue

of perspective because the man is built like an upside-down isosceles.
No neck. Once, again, "He pooped his pants." "Cena sucks." " U.S.A.

U.S.A. U.S.A." Afterwards we missed the turn to the pizza place. Yeah,
we shat the bed on that one. I felt so guilty during the national anthem.

Then there was that Dad. That dad, he hit his baby. Baby got in a head-butt,
though. Franklin, *their children will grow to be failures.* That's what Rusev

the anti-American heel said tonight. I'm watching it right now. I hope
you are, too. Funny thing is that Rusev is from Bulgaria and he waves

a Russian flag. Sure, Bulgaria was on the bloc but never a satellite.
Pinko-commie-ruskies! His signature is a camel clutch. It has to be.

Camel clutch is metaphor for xenophobia. Camel clutch is synecdoche
for brown person. "He pooped his pants. He pooped his pants."

Franklin, we're friends. I know this because during the intermission (separately)
we bought the exact same two things at the concessions stand for $34.99.

We could have bought like 4 beers with that money or maybe dinner
for that family. Hot dogs can be dinner. Oh yeah, those half-brothers

(both stars) fought like full brothers and it was awesome. We're awesome.
Then the Miz called us all losers, called the city of Milwaukee losers.

You screamed so loud. "I'm getting my Ph.D.!!! I'm getting my Ph.D.!!!
I'm not a loser. You are!" I don't think that heel has as many degrees

as we do. At least he knew it was Milwaukee. The other guy called us
Minneapolis then Milwaukee. But fuck, man. We are Milwaukee. We

got 6 degrees between the two of us. Soon we'll have 8. At that moment
I knew we were friends. I admit it's nice to know that you are equally

proud of getting a Ph.D. I'm arrogant. We'll win, America can't.
Remember when Sherman Alexie asked a room full of grad students

if they had ever shat themselves as adults and we raised our hands? Other
than Sherman we were the only two. Sherman scolded the rest, told them

they couldn't be real writers if they couldn't admit the universality of that truth.
Friend, it got shitty when that lady kept screaming. Taking that moment away

from those kids. Those kids. What were we doing there? We're grown-
men, grown-ass-men getting Ph.D.'s in America. I'm glad you told her off.

I just wish you'd done it half as much. Hey Franklin. There is so much racism,
sexism, and homophobia in wrestling. It's okay, though, I know it's fake.

Sons of Adam

"He had no name, we wrestled, yes." - Ilya Kaminsky

My belt buckles
as I walk to you,
brother. My gut

thuds flat. I turn
buckles toward
your corner of the ring.

Call the coroner,
I've been dreaming
of forty unwashed

doves. My hands fall, sing
hellfire and brimstone
to your tombstone.

They called you Cain

(you roll back
your eyes). I erupt
flame. I'll bring

my boot to your boot
(they're the same
size). Eye to eye. Slam

after slam, choke
after choke, I can
just feel your fire.

Fight me brother,
in this inferno, in this
squared circle

or in the netherworld:
bursting into fire,
drowning in purple

lined caskets, unmarked
graves. Fight me, brother.
Let's look for blame.

Load Up the Spaceship with the Rocket Fuel

The first time I watched an Ultimate Warrior promo as an adult I thought, how the fuck did this speak to me as a kid? I would venture to say Warrior was my favorite wrestler as a ten year old girl. He's certainly the one that towers over anyone else in my memory, but I would stop short of calling myself a true fan. I was casual in my devotion, like someone who shows up for Mass every Sunday, but doesn't quite remember every parable.

I watched WWF All American Wrestling, on Sunday mornings, with the same regularity as Ducktales afterschool. A little strange considering I was not athletically inclined nor interested in being so. I was interested in the books I buried my face in all weekend, not the park. I can't remember a skinned knee or getting dirty from play.

Physicality was anecdotal in my family. Fighting was relegated to people who existed in the fringes of family lore—the grandaunt who once beat up a fruit-seller, my father's father who was a major in the Dominican Army and died in a bar fight. By and large, I came from bookish, humble people. My grandmother had beautiful handwriting. My grandfather had been a civil engineer for a sugar refinery and liked to solve math problems for fun. My father's Master's degree is in Museum Studies. I followed suit as a quiet, obedient child as are many children who choose to slip away to another world through the imagination.

It would have made so much more sense if I, the consummate good girl, would've cheered for Hulk Hogan with his All-American image. Bret Hart's technical skill should have won over the equally proficient student in me. Even Randy Savage would have made more sense. His style was familiar, growing up against the backdrop of late 80s Dominican aesthetic in New York City where louder, brighter, and shinier were better.

But Ultimate Warrior? He was more raw than wholesome. More brute force than deftness. More frenetic energy than pomp. His theme song, a din of smashing cymbals. His signature moves included a gorilla press which involved essentially hoisting a man above his head and dropping him unceremoniously onto the mat. And Warrior's ring entrance was nothing short of maniacal. A 275 lbs. man with a bodybuilder's physique tearing through an arena to the ring, the ropes of which he shook as if in the grip of an electrocution.

My soft spot for pro-wrestling must be an extension of the fondness I have for other symbols of my preadolescence: cherry frio frios on sweltering August days, Aquanet hairspray, Arnold Schwarzenegger movies. I never went to a live wrestling show, never asked my grandmother to buy me an Ultimate Warrior action figure. So how could I have been a fan of a man who shouted into a camera and threatened his opponent with, "Laughter is not the key for the disease that you have to contend with!" How did I hear him snarling whole strings of unintelligible sentences and say yes, this resonates with me? Clearly, the adrenaline of it all had made me deaf.

It did not, however, make me blind. And that is how wrestling spoke to me, through the eyes. And what I saw in The Ultimate Warrior was future me. Not physically, of course, but in the fighting spirit I would have to adopt to be a writer. In the obstacles, from self-doubt to rejection to systematic guardians of Literature, lined up like opponents that fill the trajectory of a career. In the way you have to believe in yourself, beyond logic, almost delusionally to pursue an art you love. Not with casual devotion, but with the fervor of fanaticism.

Sometime in the mid-90s, I abandoned the WWF. After years of loathing Rick Rude and his arrogant gyrating, anticipating each time Damien would slither out of Jake the Snake's bag, and The Undertaker hushing me into funereal silence. I suspect the timing coincided with real boys being more accessible than the men on my TV. But I didn't leave the wrestlers completely bereft. I tagged in a partner, someone fresh and full of enough energy to carry the mantle into a new era. My grandmother.

Maria Mercedes Gomez was born January 3, 1929. Billed from Puerto Plata, a northern coastal city in the Dominican Republic, but also from La Romana and the capital of Santo Domingo. She was trained—in the sport of life—by being the second youngest girl out of six siblings. The six illegitimate children out of the nine her father sired but never fathered. Well, there was a murmur of the special interest Maria's father took in her. She would later perform her matriarchal duties as Mercedes Camacho, accompanied by her husband Francisco. Her U.S. debut was in Chicago. She eventually retired in New York. I called her by her ring name: Mami. Her signature moves included un ta' te quieta which was something like a Ric Flair chop that I can tell you made me see stars a few times. The promos she cut in the kitchen as she cooked, promising to wipe you off the map for your transgressions, were terrifying. But out of character, she was playful and self-sacrificing.

Mami had always been a sports fan. And yes, I know what Roland Barthes says in his essay, "The World of Wrestling," that "wrestling is not a sport, it is a spectacle." Wrestling is devoid of the unplanned outcomes at the heart of competitive sports today, but sports have their roots in spectacle. The very origin of the word sport is not in competition, but in "pleasant pastime." It is a shortening of the word disport, meaning "activity that offers amusement or relaxation." The national anthem, the crack of bats, and Harry Caray leading the fans in singing "Take Me Out to the Ballgame" during the 7th inning stretch were as much a part of the spectacle of the Chicago Cubs games my grandmother loved as the game itself. In New

York, Mami adopted the Yankees. After I grew up and moved out, I'd return home to watch the Superbowl with her. Before her stroke, she looked further, internationally, waking up at four o'clock in the morning to watch World Cup games.

There is a moment when you see your parents as people, when they break kayfabe. Parent is just this character they play. They had a whole other reality before you came along. And they contain a world inside of them now, parts of which don't include you. The revelation feels like treachery. All my life, Mami had been Mami. The person who woke me up for school, who reminded me to put my bookbag where it belonged, who kissed me goodnight. She revolved around me like the sun around earth. Until one day, my father corrected my geocentric view. As a young woman, Mami had been a good swimmer. Forget the swimming for a moment. Mami had been a young woman! Coarse black hair with no trace of grays, taut skin, robust body. Laughing on a beach, racing against her friends. Not just a good swimmer, my father said. "She was a fish." Once she was in the water, no one could catch her.

What surprised me then was not my grandmother watching wrestling, but her affinity for Stone Cold Steve Austin. Affinity is a light way of putting it. My grandmother loved Stone Cold with the ferocity Latina women her age reserve for the protagonist of a telenovela. She used to call me to remind me to bring orange juice for my daughter who she babysat, to ask how the fettuccine con salsa béchamel recipe turned out. And to give me a play by play of how Steve Austin had exacted revenge on Vince McMahon that week.

One day, I committed the cardinal sin against any wrestling fan. I was watching Monday Night Raw with Mami, sometime during the Monday Night Wars. Vince and Stone Cold were fighting ringside. Vince turned around, right into a crisp chair shot to the head from Austin.

"Mami, you know this is fake, right?"

Rather than launch into the explanations that I do nowadays about the physical tolls on wrestlers' bodies, the danger being comparable to stunt work, or asking if I knew that my favorite novel was fake, my grandmother said, "Bring me that folding chair over there. Let me hit you with it and you tell me how fake it feels."

I never tested Mami's belief in Steve Austin again.

But how did a sixty-eight year old grandmother, avid knitter, in Easy Spirit sneakers feel championed by a shaved head, blue-eyed, beer chugging anti-hero from Texas? She certainly couldn't relate to Stone Cold as an immigrant or a woman. His being a personification of the Attitude Era—marked by great matches, rivalries and factions, but also a generous dose of low-brow jokes, racial stereotypes and sexual objectification of women—should've seemed crass to someone like Mami.

Perhaps in Austin's antagonist Mr. McMahon, Mami saw a bit of her adversaries as a woman in

Caribbean society in the 50s. The oligarchy, the patriarchy, cronyism. Her financially comfortable father who sicced the police on his illegitimate kids while sending the others to private schools abroad. The father of her two children who threatened to bring every one of his army buddies into court to testify against her, to dishonor her, if she dared to take him for support.

Strange as it sounds, I suspect Mami saw her younger self in Stone Cold. When she dove into that water with the confidence he swaggered toward the ring with after that instantly recognizable sound of shattering glass. So much better than the competition. So good, all you could do was submit to their mastery and watch. Her, shrinking as the distance from the shoreline grew. Him, growing larger as the audience swelled. Until her limbs grew tired. Until he retired. Two people who didn't need to be couth to win. Who won because they weren't.

It isn't necessary to remember every match, belt exchange, and storyline to remember the feeling. And the feeling is what matters. The feeling is what makes you a fan. And what did I feel watching The Ultimate Warrior? An air of invincibility. That you could win or lose and remain unbowed. That you were the first person who needed to be convinced of your worthiness as champion. Sometimes the only person. That this belief will propel you when your opponents win.

Fighting was not, in fact, anecdotal in my family. It was central. Inescapable. Necessary. Fighting was an opportunity to right wrongs. And if it didn't completely right them, it eased the helpless feeling of being at life's mercy. Even if you were taking the loss, you got a few good moves in.

Stories are a way of slipping away from your life, but they're also a way of drawing closer to yourself. And the stories in those books I read as a kid were no different than the stories I watched unfold in the ring. I shouldn't have been surprised by my grandmother's favorite wrestler. Or mine. We don't always champion the characters who are a reflection of us as we are, want to be, or are expected to be, but the ones we will have to become to continue our stories.

No Holds Barred: The Dookie-Free Review

Directed by Thomas J. Wright
Written by Dennis Hackin
Release Date: 2 June 1989
Running Time: 93 minutes
MPAA Rating: PG-13

The late 1980s was a golden age for wrestling. I was a mere four years old when this film came out, so I have no memory of it. But I do remember Hulk Hogan. He was a giant behemoth of a man, larger than life on the TV that I still controlled with a couple of knobs embedded on the side of the set. Watching him take on greats like "Macho Man" Randy Savage, Jake "The Snake" Roberts, and The Ultimate Warrior was like watching Godzilla take on Ghidorah - all bets were out the window and the fate of my little world was in the balance. I needed to see Hulk win. Because if he lost, then America lost. The greatest hero in the world would have lost. And I might have thought that evil had the power to triumph over 24-inch pythons.

Say it ain't so.

I had seen other movies with the Hulkster in them, namely *Suburban Commando*. So when this film was brought to my attention, I knew within the first five minutes of it that I needed to talk about it. This is a movie that embodies that Vonnegut-esque outlook I had about wrestling back in the day, a time when body slams and suplexes were beautiful and nothing hurt (when they landed). When supermen clashed with supermen in the most raucous and theatrical way possible, grunting and groaning as they struggled to assert dominance.

Did I mention I like Jane Goodall, too?

But back to the film. Hulk Hogan is Rip, the man with no last name. Star of the World Wrestling Federation, he is pressured to come wrestle for a man named Brell and his organization, the World Television Network. Being a faithful and loyal guy, Rip declines. Unfortunately, that's where things start to get ugly, as Brell uses his cronies to try and muscle Rip into converting.

I'm going to stop here and deconstruct the last paragraph, because it actually sounds like what happens in movies sometimes. However, this is *No Holds Barred*, and *No Holds Barred* is so much more than a movie. It's a trainwreck. A glorious, glorious trainwreck. One that if I was clinically depressed and on the edge of suicide, I would watch again and again until my stomach caved in from laughter, realizing that I was put on this earth to celebrate the name of Rip. To revel in his overly macho absurdities and the cheesiness of his one-liners that only make sense to the people he interacts with, because they've drank the Kool-Aid as well. To uncontrollably giggle at the way Rip seems to overcome adversity by hyperventilating and bugging his eyes, and how he reacts to stimuli in his environment by not just grunting, but by pursing his lips and exhaling, like an overly amorous chimpanzee.

Remember when I called Rip the man with no last name? Well, that was a lie. No one in this film has a last name, other than cameos from other well-known wrestling personalities like "Mean" Gene Okerlund or Jesse Ventura.

I always find it odd that I never saw the "Mean" in Mean Gene. I always wanted to rub his head and give his mustache a quick combing in a therapeutic fashion, the way a mother runs her hand through her newborn baby's hair, because that's what I think Mean Gene's mustache must feel like.

Damnit, I got distracted by that puppy dog Mean Gene once again, when I told myself I wasn't going to let it happen. Sorry. Back to the story, folks.

Right, so no one in the film has a last name, and it's probably better for it. No one will want to be tracked down to answer for this. Except maybe Brell. Brell is the villain of this movie like a train running over someone is a weight loss method. Played by Kurt Fuller, a man who plays pretty much the same role in any movie he's in, he's reached his slimy, antagonistic peak here. Brell is a character who takes every single stereotype about a nasty network executive and then adds a twist of sociopath to it for no reason, despite the fact that all of his actions are easily traceable to him, and on any sane plane of existence would get him and his entire organization shut down and thrown into prison. But this is a world where no holds are barred, and no logic is left un-borked.

Speaking of logic borking, it's time to speak about the last and most outrageous piece of this *No Holds Barred* puzzle: Zeus. A man so intense one of his eyes lost focus and instead looks inward to focus his rage. A man so dedicated to his name that no, he does not wear a toga. No, he has not named any of his moves after thunder and/or lightning. No, he does not speak Greek. What has he done to incorporate the name of the virile, lightning-bolt-chucking, super-masculine Greek god of thunder into his image? Shave Z's into the side of his head, of course. He also gave himself a unibrow and shaved half of his right eyebrow off, so I guess that kinda looks like a lowercase cursive Z? I mean, whatever. He grunts, he screams, and he acts like he kills things while wearing the stupidest outfits imaginable.

He's got some kind of back story told to us by a person seemingly introduced just to spout exposition. Supposedly he killed someone in the ring, went to prison for it, and was released before his time was up. But we're never given a reason why someone so obviously psychotic would have ever been given an early release. Maybe the parole board was a bunch of deaf-blind people.

So after a series of overtly-illegal events, including kidnapping, assault, attempted murder, domestic abuse, and botulism (probably), Rip is finally forced to confront Zeus in a battle that Vince McMahon, owner of the WWF, would never actually allow in real life: a no-rules, battle-to-the-finish showdown. Sounds right up his alley, right? Well, you would be correct, except for one little thing - it's happening on someone else's network. No way that would ever happen in a million years. People can kill themselves, but it better be happening on Poppa Vince's show.

In the end, Zeus is defeated, Brell is electrocuted in the least believable way possible, and Rip is still beloved by millions as a man of the people, and a kicker of people's butts. Nothing has changed, and two people are dead.

Yay.

This movie. Wow, this movie. When I reached the end, I truly believed I needed to stand and applaud, because I have never seen anything more nonsensical, more pandering, and more contrived than this film. But what can you expect when a literal "Hack" wrote this movie? Don't believe me? It's right there at the top folks, read 'em and weep tears of laughter. This is a quintessential Hulk Hogan movie, because it is literally Hulk Hogan being Hulk Hogan for an hour and a half and loving every minute of it.

It's like baby's first movie. Like watching a bunch of six-year-olds doing a Christmas Play while from the pews, their parents cheer them on. And you know what? By the time it's all over, you damn well better stand up and applaud with the rest of those forced to watch this pile. Because there's nothing left to do but revel in the unparalleled insanity you just witnessed. You have looked into the abyss, and it has stared back at you, its lazy eye and awkward monobrow growling and screaming, driving you mad...

AND THEN ALL THAT'S LEFT IS THE RAGE, BROTHER! IT'S TIME TO GET OUT THERE AND WIN! WIN IT ALL! WIN EVERYTHING! TAKE NO PRISONERS AND MOST IMPORTANTLY, LEAVE NO HOLDS BARRED!

WOOOOOOOOOOOOOOOOOOOOOOOOOOOOO!!!!!!!!!!!!

Editor's Rating: FOUR OUT OF FOUR STARS, BROTHER!

Finishers

The year was 1986, and The Road Warriors were the greatest tag team in professional wrestling. In the glow of a fifteen-inch television screen, they set up for their tandem finisher, the Doomsday Device. Animal, built like a fire hydrant on steroids, lifted up onto his shoulders a dazed, puffy-haired man in a singlet, so that the guy rested in an upright, seated position. Hawk, leaner than his partner, but little less muscular, leapt from the top rope, right arm extended. For a second, the camera flashed to the victim's face as it switched from a slack jaw to sheer terror. Hawk connected with the clothesline, sending the poor guy ass over teakettle in a full backward flip before he landed in a heap on the mat.

At nine years old, Slawson and I lived with one foot in the alternate universe of pro wrestling. We watched Hawk soar above the ring and we flexed our fledgling muscles back at him after impact.

Slawson reached into a bag of Cheetos and devoured a handful. He sucked the cheese dust from his fingers, leaving them glossy, glazed with sticky orange residue. I sipped from my can of Diet Mountain Dew. It never tasted as good as the original formula, but Slawson's mom had started buying only diet sodas in an effort to control her son's swelling pudge. Slawson said our teacher told his mom that other kids were picking on him for it—pretending to lose their balance as he walked by, as if the earth shook beneath his weight.

Saturday evenings, the real world was forgotten. Slawson had his eyes fixed on the screen. "That's us one day. World tag team champions."

I wasn't stupid. I was the kind of kid who got picked last in gym class with good reason. The kind nobody bothered picking a fight with because what do you have to gain from punking out the littlest kid in the class? I didn't think I'd ever make it to the National Wrestling Alliance or the World Wrestling Federation. Not really.

On the TV screen Hawk wrapped up his post-match soliloquy over the mic and slapped Animal's bare chest, a symbolic passing of the baton. "Ain't that right, big man?" Animal began his rant.

Outside, daylight faded. I would need to run home at the end of the show to beat my curfew of the streetlights coming on. But inside, in the glow of the TV screen, the prospect of becoming a wrestling champion seemed somehow possible. Like still thinking Santa *might* squeeze down the chimney—not three hundred sixty-four days out of the year, but just on Christmas Eve.

And so I pointed a finger at the television screen as Arn Anderson and Tully Blanchard moved into frame to pose a challenge, promising a shoving match, maybe a brawl to build to their upcoming match with the Road Warriors. "You better watch out, Horsemen." I crushed the soda can in my hand, squeezing the last bits of yellow-green bubbling syrup out over the brim, onto the space between the knuckles of my thumb and forefinger. "We're coming after you."

The Hart Attack was a modified, safer variation on the Doomsday Device. Jim Neidhart lifted a guy, not on his shoulders, but up to just above his waist. Bret Hart jumped, not off the top rope, but rather from a running start, to deliver a clothesline.

It's a move Slawson and I delivered to his old, oversized teddy bear easily a hundred times in the build up to recreating our own main event scenes in his basement.

In junior high, Hulkamania was running wild, but Slawson and I favored "The Macho Man" Randy Savage. He was the wild-eyed high flyer and the innovator. Plus, he had Miss Elizabeth.

We laid down the couch cushions in Slawson's basement and reenacted matches, taking turns playing The Macho Man. October 13, 1988, I was cast as Butch Reed. That meant I got most of the offense in, but it also meant Slawson got to rally in the end—stomp his foot while he jabbed my chin and then jump off the sofa to deliver the flying elbow drop. I hated taking that elbow from him. He never meant to hurt me, but there was just too much of him to guarantee he wouldn't really land on top of me. And try as he did—two showers a day—it was tough for a sweaty fat kid to keep the BO off of him.

Slawson posed with his left thumb beneath his waistband, right index finger spinning in the air, then pointed outward to his older sister's discarded Barbie Doll. Post-match, whoever played Savage would prop the doll on his shoulder to make believe it were Miss Elizabeth, wearing that same white dress she did at the end of WrestleMania 4, when she stood by her man for four straight tournament matches. When Savage let her hold the world title, we knew that was true love. He not only wanted to have the belt, but to share it with her. And unlike our mothers and sisters and the girls at school, she understood the importance of the gold.

Before Slawson could leap, his dad showed up, stepped right over me and smacked his son upside the skull for being a knucklehead and trying to kill his best friend.

I remember that day because we had gone through the motions with particular vigor then, knowing that the next night, October 14, 1988, was a break from *WWF Superstars* on the TV screen and from play-suplexes. Mr. Slawson had the night off from his job tending bar, and he would drive us two hundred miles west to Niagara Falls to catch the WWF live.

When we got to the arena, there was a line out the door to get in, lurching forward inch by inch, a motley collection of people with neon t-shirts that emblazoned with names like The Ultimate Warrior and Brutus "The Barber" Beefcake. We must have waited an hour to get through the door, and once we were through, there was an unbelievable shuffle of people inside, zigzagging between arena gates and bathrooms and merchandise stands.

"Stay close. Don't wander off," Mr. Slawson said. "Look out for each other."

We did. He bought us Pepsis and hot dogs slathered in mustard and relish, the way Slawson liked them. I preferred mine with only the thinnest streak of ketchup, but didn't say anything.

When we got through the arena entrance, the show was already underway, and everything fell into place. A hundred rows of seats, positioned at a slant so we could see over the heads of the people in front of us. Spotlights hanging in the rafters, focused on the wrestlers below. Focusing the entire world on that ring.

It felt foreign and almost eerie to take in the sound of bodies slamming on the mat in the absence of the TV commentators telling us what to watch for. So I told the story to myself. Conjured my best imitation of play-by-play man Gorilla Monsoon in my head. *Look at Duggan's face. This bearhug might be too much for ol' Hacksaw.*

I watched closely as the ring crew carried out the four walls of the steel cage—grids of blue metal with big square gaps through which the fans got a clear view of the ring, and that allowed the wrestlers to climb. All of my excitement drained with the monotony of the crew fastening each wall of the cage together, and shaking it to be sure it would hold. My head felt heavy and bobbed as the process stretched on to fifteen minutes, then twenty.

Then the music hit. The maniacal laughter into the *Money, money, money, money, mon-eee-eeeey* of the Million Dollar Man's intro.

Next, "Pomp and Circumstance." The arrival of Randy Savage and Miss Elizabeth.

The match was underway. Five thousand fans stomping their feet, clapping their hands, all but praying at The Macho Man's alter. Slawson and I had our eyes glued on the ring.

The battle raged for fifteen minutes. DiBiase locked in his Million Dollar Dream sleeperhold. Savage sagged, but at the crowd's urging, fought up to his knees, to his feet, and hit DiBiase with elbows to the ribs to get free. A series of jabs. Then he went up to the top rope for the double axehandle. Then the flying elbow. All that was left was for The Macho Man to climb up and over the cage to secure the win.

Mr. Slawson wanted to hit the road ahead of the crowd, while folks watched Savage re-ascend the cage to pose with the title and while Miss Elizabeth clapped politely from the ground.

Slawson had other ideas. He called ahead, talking to his father's back, ahead of me, on the walk toward the doors. "I heard all the wrestlers are staying at the Ramada. And they always go to the bar in the lobby after a show."

"We've got a three hour drive." Mr. Slawson said.

"Let's just go for an hour. Just one hour. We'll see who shows up."

"They're not going to let a couple kids in a bar."

Slawson pouted, head down, feet shuffling. He had to realize his old man was right, but *goddamnit*, he wanted it. Who's to say The Big Boss Man or Akeem wasn't going to meet up with Slawson, take him under his wing, be the first one to tell him *not* to lose weight, and that if he kept chasing his dreams, he might be the next great super heavyweight?

I watched him closely to see if he was going to cry. The guys in gym class had made him cry *bad* a week earlier, when he couldn't get to the volleyball in time. Eric Chudy in particular walked right up into his ear and called him a *worthless lard ass*. The gym teacher had Chudy sit out the rest of the period. Slawson cried. Silent. Arms at his side, not even bothering to wipe off his face or cover up. When it kept going, the teacher said he could sit out, too, if he wanted, so he ended up sitting alone on the opposite side of the gym from Chudy.

Slawson didn't cry on the way out of the arena, though. Or in the parking lot. Or in the car. He stayed quiet, staring straight ahead, while his dad and I made belabored small talk about how my grades were, before he turned on conservative talk radio and didn't speak another word until we were back on our street.

The New Age Outlaws are on the shortlist of the best tag teams of the late 1990s. The funny thing is, for as long as "The Badass" Billy Gunn and "The Road Dogg" Jesse James tagged up, they never really developed a tandem finishing maneuver, sticking instead to their singles moves—Gunn's Fame-asser standing leg drop; Road Dogg's pump-handle slam.

But perhaps that's a sign of the times. The so-called Attitude Era was always more about big personalities, stunts, and sexy storylines than grappling. The Outlaws got over on charisma, their trademark dialogue—commanding fans who weren't down with them to suck it—more memorable than anything they ever did after the opening bell. I bet Slawson and I would have loved the Attitude Era if it had lined up with our high school years, when we would have been the target demographic.

But when we were in high school—when we got our driver's licenses and our first jobs, Slawson pushing carts in the grocery store parking lot, me selling knock-off Slinkies out of a mall kiosk—mainstream wrestling bottomed out. You had freaking Doink the Clown and his midget sidekick Dink running around dousing people with buckets of water. You had four-hundred-pound Bastion Booger shaking his ass before he sat on jobbers.

I tuned out.

And I saw Slawson less. Homework got harder and I started seeing a girl named Trina. Visiting Slawson's house went from a daily occurrence to something I did once every other week or so, and we didn't sit together at lunch half the time because he always had to go talk with the school counselor. He would never tell me what they discussed.

But it was Slawson, of course, who discovered Crash Pro Wrestling, an indy promotion that ran shows on alternating Saturday nights at the Play All Day skating rink in the next town. CPW personnel laid down cheap carpeting over the floor and a series of folding chairs. Space enough for a couple hundred people, though the night I went there were a lot of empty seats. I bought a red and white striped cardboard carton of popcorn. Slawson bought two and a hamburger, burnt black as a hockey puck.

He was getting fatter and had dark rings under his eyes. He told me he hadn't been sleeping well, but quickly added that his mom got him some pills that ought to help.

The Killer Kid, who couldn't have been more than two or three years our senior, lost his footing trying to balance on the top rope and fumbled into an awkward roll on the mat, only to get up, lock in an armbar, and act as though the preceding fifteen seconds had never happened.

Slawson cupped his hand and hollered, "You fucked up!"

He wasn't the only one. A half dozen men, most of them older than us yelled similar sentiments. A mousy woman with curly black hair and glasses, seated in the front row wearing a black Bret Hart shirt with a silver facsimile of his signature on the back, craned her neck, cupping her hands over her son's ears as she glared at the lot of them.

There were a lot of guys like the Killer Kid who missed their punches or cracked skulls with one another and backed away holding their foreheads. And then there was Trent Givens.

Givens had lost almost all of his matches in the WWF, but in this skating rink, in front of this crowd, he was a superstar. He ran roughshod over Johnny Gargantuan, a three hundred pounder with some muscle, but a lot more flab. Gargantuan took the advantage for a couple minutes, hitting a knee and forearms and holding down Givens in a rear chinlock. But Givens punched his way out and finished things off with a bodyslam and a fist drop off the second rope.

"I know it ain't the WWF." Slawson crumpled the tin foil wrapping from his burger and stuffed into one of the empty popcorn containers. The show was over "The guys here are on their way up, or on their way down. But either way, they're doing it because they love it, not for the money or the glamour."

I looked around me. Spilt Budweiser seeped into the carpeting. The crust from a slice of pizza sat on a chair, ragged with teeth marks. Fluorescent lights flickered above us. "No shit, Slawson."

"Come on, let's go meet Trent Givens."

I figured he meant to stake out some hotel lobby, but instead, we only walked to the opposite end of the rink to find a row of card tables peddling bootleg WWF t-shirts and old magazines, plus two autograph tables. Shams Hellwig sat at one, flexing so his bicep tattoo of a crucifix bulged. He was probably the best received indy wrestler of the night. The other table was for Givens, twice the other guys' size and twice the line, with a dozen people waiting.

Johnny Gargantuan wandered past in his black unitard. "Slawson, you miserable puke, you made it out again."

"Wouldn't miss it, big man."

Gargantuan barked—maybe a sneeze or a laugh or a sigh.

Slawson patted his back on the way past. "Don't let the act fool you. He's a hell of a nice guy."

This was Slawson's world. He had stumbled through some portal and come out of it amidst the fabric of professional wrestling, practically part of the act. But this act was grittier. Dirtier. Sadder. Like stepping through your wardrobe and finding all the snow is yellow and the lion isn't anything more than a mean old housecat who hisses at people.

We got to Trent Givens. He had his hair tied back in a ponytail now, revealing forehead scars you couldn't see from afar. A cardboard placard sat in front of him.

Autographs $8

Photos $14

I couldn't fathom shelling out for a fucking Trent Givens signature, but Slawson had a ten dollar bill ready.

"I don't have any change, buddy."

"It's all right, you can keep it, champ." Slawson grinned and laid flat an old WWF magazine, opened to a photograph of Haku poised over Givens with a nerve hold on his trapezius. Afterward, Slawson told me all the wrestlers always charged oddball amounts like that and never brought change. The promoters paid them performance fees, but autographs and merch were how they really made ends meet.

Givens signed over the words in the magazine in big, swooping black Sharpie. "You and your friend gonna be wrestlers?"

"Na. I'm not tough enough," Slawson said. "But I'll be a fan for life."

It was the first time I had heard Slawson admit he wouldn't end up a wrestler. But then, he was still going to shows like this, paying two hours of grocery store wages for a famous jobber's signature. I wondered what the hell he was doing with his life.

Slawson drove us back and he talked. I studied street signs. Now that I had a license, I was just starting to discover routes and shortcuts beyond driving the main drag through town.

Perhaps it's because I wasn't really listening that I missed the transition, or maybe my failure to listen made him shift. Either way, he went from describing the technical proficiency of Scott Jacobs's superplex to talking about killing himself.

"I was thinking about the ultimate tandem finisher." He looked straight head, both hands on the wheel. "Get on an overpass like that Thruway entrance in Syracuse—the one by the university. I'm thinking you dive off that so that you'd crack your skull or break your spine from the fall. But on top of that, you time it just right so an eighteen wheeler is going to smash into your body on the way down. There's no kicking out of that."

"Shit, Slawson. What made you think of that?"

Neither one of us said anything for a while.

"I got some tapes from Japan." Slawson made a turn, one block from my place. "*Puroresu*. Really good shit. And my dad's working nightshifts again. Want to stop by and have a beer?"

One of the oldest tropes in wrestling sees a good guy getting roughed up, only for other good guys to storm the ring and save him. The cavalry. It's exciting to see, but it also introduces the question of why nobody comes out for the save on other occasions, when one of the good guys takes an especially bad beating.

Do the supposed good guys who don't help out—these passive, bystander fucks—feel regret at their own inaction?

"I think I've hit my limit for wrestling tonight." I looked out the window. "And I'm supposed to call Trina when I get back."

"Right," Slawson said. "Trina."

He didn't say another word. Just dropped me off at my place, and to be fair, I didn't thank him for the ride or for telling me about the show.

I didn't say a lot of things to Slawson around that time. Like that I wanted to hang out with Trina over him because she had started giving me handjobs, or like if he lost twenty pounds and stopped wearing wrestling t-shirts to school, maybe he could get some, too.

He didn't wait for me to get in the house to back out of the driveway and I didn't look back. Without a word, we understood that was the last time we were going to a wrestling show together.

Sweet and Sour: a finishing maneuver used by Lance Cade and Trevor Murdoch. Their pairing never garnered a team name, but the Internet unofficially dubbed them The Redneck Whirling Dervish. Portly

Murdoch ran from one corner and clipped his opponent's knee. Musclebound Cade charged from the opposite corner and nailed the victim with a clothesline. It's not much of a spectacle. The move fits those underachieving days of tag team wrestling.

Slawson and I didn't have any emotional goodbyes when I left for college. I saved that for Trina, even though she dumped me a week after prom. We sat on her porch and talked in hushed voices because her father was on the other side of the screen door, watching baseball. She told me I was a good guy. I said let's keep in touch. We hugged and her hair smelled like honey.

Trina and I didn't keep in touch, but around Thanksgiving time, Slawson got my phone number at college from my mom and called to ask if I was coming home for the holidays. I was surprised by how happy I was at the prospect of seeing him. We grabbed jalapeno burgers the day before Thanksgiving and ended up talking for two hours and making plans to hang out again on the weekend. That Saturday, it was like old times at his place, eating Combos and Doritos, drinking diet soda and, after his parents had gone to bed, beer. I went back to school, but when I came home for Christmas, there was an unspoken understanding that things were the same as they'd been years before. I'd come over in the afternoon and didn't have to ring the doorbell. Slawson's mom brought us snacks without us asking. We played blackjack. I talked about life at college. Emphasized the positives—the hot redhead who lived two doors down, taco bar Tuesdays in the dining hall. Left out the negatives—my floundering grades, the fact that I hadn't made any real friends yet or so much as held hands with a girl at school.

Slawson told me community college sucked. "Two years, and I'll have my Associate's. Maybe I can get an office job then."

My last night before I went back to school, Slawson told me he wanted to give me something. He handed me a box, two inches high, a foot by a foot around, covered in blue wrapping paper with a pattern of snowmen waving their arms at me.

"Slawson, I didn't get you anything," I said. "You didn't have to do this."

"I know, I know. It's all right."

I shook my head and tore the wrapping paper. Inside it, a generic white cardboard box from some department store. I peeled back the tape and found the picture frame inside.

Billy Gunn—before he'd found a home with the New Age Outlaws—up in the air, leg extended, his faux-brother Bart Gunn holding a jobber in his arms, horizontal, in sidewalk slam position. The two of them played a cowboy duo, and labeled this move the Sidewinder. Over the surface of the picture there was blue and black ink, autographs from each of the Smoking Gunns.

"I caught the guys at separate signings—you know they broke up last year, right? Both of them looked surprised to see the picture." Slawson rubbed his eye and I was worried he was going to get weepy on me. "I think it meant something to them."

I lifted the picture from the box. It was in a sturdy frame, not a dollar store plastic job, but the kinds our parents would keep old photographs in, and I half wondered if he had displaced some heirloom to find a home for this piece of memorabilia.

"I was thinking about you and me hanging out again after we stopped talking and after you went away to school, and I wanted to give you a little something to remember the run we had." He was turning a little red in the face and avoided eye contact. The next words came out wooden, like he'd been practicing them. "I figured you could look at this picture and know if you ever got in trouble, I'd be waiting in the corner for you to tag me back in."

"It's beautiful, man." I reached out to put a hand on his shoulder the way I never had before, the way I had seen older men touch one another. He must have thought I was going for a handshake because he leaned back to sort of reach out his hand to me, but we were in all the wrong position, and ended up collapsing into a hug neither of us had really bargained for. He still smelled, but not as bad as he used to.

"I'll hang it in my room at home," I said. "So when I come back on breaks, I can always remember the good old days."

Slawson's cleared his throat. "I figured you'd bring it to school with you."

I forced a smile. "Well, you know what people think of pro wrestling." I stopped myself and looked down at my shoes, stained in clouds of melted snow. "The guys at college would probably draw moustaches on the guys."

"The Smoking Gunns had moustaches."

I looked at the picture. Of course he was right.

"Look, I love it, Slawson."

"I heard you." He nodded quickly. He had his hands balled into fists and for a split second I thought he might take a swing at me. "You take care, all right?"

I thought of all the things I probably should have said. Like you should come visit me at school, or let's go out and grab a slice, or let's get a couple of your old man's tall boys out of the fridge, or *goddamnit* let's pop in that old VHS of WrestleMania 2 and watch The British Bulldogs beat up The Dream Team.

I told him to take care of himself, too, and got out. Kept my gloves off and got near frostbitten just so I could hold onto Slawson's present and make sure I didn't drop it in the snow on the way home.

The Triple Powerbomb: a finisher executed by the three-man team of The Shield. Roman Reigns jacked up dudes so they sat on his shoulders, before he slammed them down, shoulders first to the mat. Ambrose and

Rollins got on either side, hands on the victim's chest to add the additional force of two extra men's strength to the slam.

I watched The Shield over a decade out of college, after I had succumbed to the magnetic draw that wrestling always has on its most devout believers, regardless of how long they've been away. I thought Slawson would have liked them.

Slawson had faced his own triumvirate of threats. Insomnia, sleeping pills, and depression. He tried to commit suicide that next summer, while I stayed away from home working a camp counselor job. From what my dad told me, Slawson's mom saw his bedroom light still on when she went to the bathroom at three in the morning and opened his door to check on him. She saw the pill bottle right away. The attempt ended in a schmozz of EMTs pumping his stomach and carting him to the hospital.

That same day, two of the ten-year-old boys in my care got into a scrap. The kind of situation that starts with roughhousing and ends with tears. I took the boy who got his lip bloodied to the nurse's office where a white-haired woman asked him what had happened and dabbed Neosporin over the cut.
Along the walk back to our bunk, I felt like I ought to say something to the boy. Teach him some profound lesson. Nothing came to me.

When I was in bed that night, I thought about all the things I might have said. Probably because Slawson was still fresh on mind—because I was thinking about calling him the next day—my mind turned to wrestling.

I thought about tag team partners working together, and that I might draw some metaphor about how these boys shouldn't fight—they should look out for each other like were on the same team.

Maybe I'd break down the mechanics. There's a basic formula for most every tag match. The good guys control the early going, but, inevitably, the bad guys take command. They cheat and they double team one of the heroes until he can hardly take anymore. But then the good guy breaks free and tags in his fresh partner, who runs wild.

That's the formula wrestlers have used for nearly a century. The problem is that, just as old as that rule, there is the exception. The times when the fresh man waiting in the corner chickens out, feels slighted, or reveals himself to be aligned with the villains. The weakened wrestler scratches and claws for the sweet reprieve of the tag. His partner short arms him or leaps backward off the mat altogether to head to the locker room early. He leaves his teammate, exhausted and beaten, to fend for himself against overwhelming odds.

On Being a Fat Wrestler

When #GiveDivasAChance was trending on Twitter it was almost a relief to see the problem surrounding women in the sports entertainment world being acknowledged on a larger scale. For those of you who don't follow the world of the WWE, you may not know that their commentators constantly acknowledge throughout their programming what's trending in regards to the WWE on Twitter, in an effort to be on the ball and seem plugged in and interacting with their fans.

To no one's surprise, this hashtag was grossly overlooked.

The Divas is the name of the women's wrestling division within the realm of the WWE, and a name like that is just the tip of the iceberg in terms of how they view women. On top of that, the title belt is a big, pink butterfly, and a fair amount of their employed wrestlers are fitness models. Don't fit their designated aesthetic? Aren't stereotypically "pretty" enough? Well then skill be damned, you aren't getting your shot on television.

This hasn't always been the case, considering they used to employ larger female wrestlers, such as Bull Nakano from Japan, but the women have always played second fiddle to their male superstars. Their matches will be bumped entirely from a show if a men's match runs overtime, they only get one dedicated match per show, some male superstars have entrance themes that run longer than an entire Divas match, and most of the storylines are entirely centered around looks or being the love interest to a man and petty schoolyard romance dramas. These women aren't being allowed to highlight their skills that they have busted their asses to develop. Unless you can be viewed as a sex object, you aren't worth promotion in their eyes.

This has trickled down and affected the indie wrestling circuit as well. Growing up as a woman, I was always seen as an outsider in the boys club of wrestling fandom. Thankfully, my dad was happy that one of his children was actually willing to watch it on TV with him on visits, and we would make a big deal about renting a Pay Per View together. At the time there was a small amount of women being represented, but they were always tough. Even Chyna, whose entire gimmick was that she was ugly and big, was allowed to fight the men. I got the itch in me as a kid to want to fight. But I never thought I'd be welcome in this world, so I shelved my desires.

In case you aren't aware, I am a fairly fat individual, so it's already a bit of a hassle to be taken seriously when it comes to fitness and participating in sports activities. Add that to being queer and a lack of masculinity, and you end up with a winning, or losing, combination in terms of acceptance.

I ended up getting involved backstage at local wrestling promotions instead. I learned how to set up a ring, picked up tips and tricks from other wrestlers, and got a better feel of what it was like to be in that environment live. Sadly, I rarely saw any female performers participating in said shows. Fast forward to 2014, and I caught wind that there was a small feminist promotion called the League of Lady Wrestlers; they started as a performance art collective in Dawson City out in the Yukon but had one Toronto show called the Hogtown Throwdown. I immediately reached out and expressed my interest in being involved in any facet, pitched my character to them, and was shortly added to their roster after. It was like instant gratification; I didn't have to worry about my appearance, or desirability, or sex appeal, or gender identity, or sexuality. And so on and so forth.

Doughnut Messaround is my name, and playing up the fat card is my game. Other wrestlers in my league play on typical stereotypes—such as Dykemaster 3000, a butch dyke who has a manager in a giant penis suit named Dick; Ladyboy, a gender-bending character in drag who is quite the ladies' . . . lady; Cuntzilla, a swamp monster with vagina dentata; and many more.

Just as quickly I was accepted into a league with a bunch of amazing feminist women, and all seemed okay in the universe, there was the realization that we needed to train with professionals. Of course, these professionals are cis hetero men who don't seem to be properly equipped to handle having women in their spaces. We were given private lessons apart from the rest of the students so that we could train as a league, but it wasn't enough for me. I decided to reach out and look into training full time; I had gotten a taste for the ropes and I wanted more. Training was three days a week, but it was a strain financially to meet. Never fear: "We have a discounted rate for female students." I inquired as to why this was, whether or not the training was less intense or less frequent, but was just told that was how it was. Normally, I'd be one to fight against gender inequality, but this is one of the few times it worked in my favour, so I kept my lips zipped.

My first day of classes arrived, and when I showed up, everyone seemed shocked to have me there and immediately jumped into a mix of mansplaining what wrestling is and flirting with me. There was a lot of condescension in terms of my ability. Whenever I'd have trouble with a move, instead of being met with a solution or an attempt to teach, they would share one of the following responses: "Well, you're too fat to pull it off" or "Girls always seem to have trouble with that move." My favourite being "Women are allergic to leapfrogging." This was all said with a completely deadpan look on their face. No one thought they were being cheeky; they truly believed that women and fat people were less adequate.

The funny part about this is that there are plenty of fat men, and women, in wrestling, and they are more believable in cases due to their size factor being an advantage. My in-ring experience was written off because it wasn't "real wrestling." It seems their deciding factor on whether or not it was real was the lack of men involved, since it was done in a professional ring and with the same moves they were using.

What was even more upsetting was how the women who would come to the gym to help out would feel toward female wrestlers. Complaints would be raised by me that local promotions didn't include women and they would retort, "Well, no one wants to pay to see women fight." Obviously, the right market is not being tapped, considering the Island Rumble, which was my first-ever match, sold out to a crowd of 300 people well in advance of the show itself, with many demands to release more tickets.

I wonder how much of being excluded since I'm a fat girl is from social stereotypes in sports, and how much is from the fact that the primary example we have for us in the media doesn't support women. The problem exists everywhere, and we need to start somewhere to fix it. Until then, my dreams of falling down and getting beat up for a living will only be fulfilled emotionally as opposed to physically. I can support my feminist league by providing alternative narratives to smash the patriarchy, wear queer-as-all-get-out shirts to the gym, and yell at the top of my lungs on the Internet, holding out hope for someone bigger taking notice.

Remember, I may be fat, slow, and a dyke, but I can still throw down, knock you over, and make you cry and tap out of even the simplest Boston Cream or Camel Clutch. I'm still wrestling and I refuse to lose weight to conform to your narrative of what you feel the public will buy into as a pro wrestler.

Work

50

This being a Tuesday. I remember because it'd been the morning after *Raw*'d had to go and cancel the kayfabe funeral service they'd planned for Mr. McMahon that night.

In its place a real tribute to Chris Benoit, aka the Crippler, or sometimes the Canadian Crippler, and occasionally just the Rabid Wolverine. He'd gone and choked himself to death sometime over the weekend. Bodies of him and his wife and kid being discovered that afternoon a few hours before McMahon's funeral'd been set to air.

Uncle Rog's reading all about it in paper behind me, while I'm flipping eggs and trying fill in all the stuff the news always leaves out. Pretty much all the important shit.

For example, shoot is what they call it when reality starts getting in the way of a work. Or sometimes they have what they call a worked-shoot, which is where everything gets a little confusing.

Like how all the wrestlers'd had to break kayfabe for the night to talk about what a great guy the Crippler'd been. Real wrestlers' wrestler. Consummate professional. Never no-showing. Never taking unnecessary risks. Always protecting guys from getting hurt.

Yah, real hero, Rog says. He's got the paper laid out across the cutting board. Tracing the words with the tip of this eight-inch carving knife. The way he's got that carving knife in his hand pretty much every hour of every day of every shift I've ever worked with him.

49

Maybe top five wrestling technicians of all time. What CM Punk says.

Weeks earlier, Benoit's bashing the guy's head in with a steal chair, getting disqualified. He's locking that

Crossface in good and tight, almost snapping the guy's neck in two. Not letting up no matter how many times the ref calls for the bell.

What they always say in wrestling: steal chair. Never: folding chair. Never just: chair. Always: *steal* chair.

Then suddenly the Crippler's dead. Nobody knows why, nobody knows how, and Punk's breaking down blubbering about what a loss it is. What a terrible, tragic, senseless loss it is. For everybody.

Of course the details being a little fuzzy at that point. As of when they go on air that night, the police haven't released much more than the name: Chris Benoit, professional wrestler, wife, and son.

By this morning the papers are saying Benoit'd choked himself to death, but only after first putting the Crippler Crossface on his wife then kid. Strangulation, the police call it. What Rog is underlining with the tip of his carving knife. What Rog is huffing and puffing about.

Whether you find this all fitting or just ironic, I say, probably a matter of perspective.

48

First day I ever worked here, Rog's reading the paper with that knife as his place holder same as this morning, same as every morning he preps for lunch and dinner.

So I walk up from behind him to introduce myself. Mumble: Hey, I'm the new breakfast guy.

He snaps around on me, sticks that thing an inch from my jugular, says, You wanna get stabbed, kid? You got a death wish? That it?

Son, in this kitchen you don't never walk behind a man with a knife in his hands unless you ready to die. You hear me?

Same thing at least once a week for all the years I been here: walk behind him, don't say nothing. Mind my own business. Only to have that psycho spin around and stick that thing in my face. You gotta death wish, boy? You wanna get stabbed?

Cut your goddamned tongue out, maybe you speak up then, eh?

47

Anyway, best friend a guy could ever have. That's what they all say about the Crippler. Rick Flair, Arn Anderson, Dean Malenko, Chris Jericho, Chavo Guererro, Edge, Punk, everybody.

Good family man, too. Always showing off pictures of his kid. Always calling home after matches.

46

Shit, Rog says. Probably WWF just messin with people's heads again. These meatheads thinkin it's the real fuckin deal, whackin off to it. Rog making like he's jerking off the handle of his knife all over the omelet bar.

WWE, I say. World Wildlife Fund sued them for name infringement.

Uncle Rog, he's rereading lines from the story over and over and shaking his head. Bulllllllll... shit... he's telling me.

Bulllllll... shit.... he's saying again.

Scripted, I mumble. Not fake,

There's a fan right beside the flattop, big vent right above. I could probably tell Rog I wanna take that carving knife, turn it sideways, and jam it up his candy ass. Even if he was listening, which he ain't.

You smell what the Rock is cooking? I mutter it into the vent above my head.

Bull shit, Rog says.

Predetermined, I say. A *work*.

45

Raw originally being scripted to have the whole roster paying final respects to Mr. McMahon all night. Saying what a good boss he'd been. Really tearing up about the tragic accident from the week before, saying if they'd only known how real things could get. How everything was gonna turn out.

Mr. McMahon, who'd only the week before been back feuding with his arch-nemesis again, the Rattle Snake Stone Cold Steve Austin, when Stone Cold'd finally taken his feud a bit over the edge. Blammo! Blows up Mr. McMahon's limo in the parking garage on live TV to end the episode.

Which, all this leading up to this week's big televised funeral, where old Stone Cold at some point would come out and read a little bible verse of his own. Call it Austin 3:16.

Proceed to desecrate all the flowers, that shiny coffin. Maybe shower Mr. McMahon's shiny bronzed corpse with a couple shook up Steveweisers. Shake his head in Mr. McMahon's cold dead face, flip him the double birdies. Call him names. *Say What?* about thirty times and wait for him to say something back. Be real disrespectful about it.

Which'd be when Mr. McMahon would've had enough. Come back to life Undertaker-style. Reach up out of the coffin and grab Stone Cold by the throat. Maybe even pull him down in that coffin with him— trapdoor or something. Real creepy.

But also, world wrestling entertainment at its finest.

Instead, Mr. McMahon has to drop the whole thing, come out and explain the unfortunate irony. Talk about what a loss it is for the wrestling world. Say what a consummate professional the Crippler has always been.

Send his condolences to the family, really emphasize that part, the condolences to the family. The family. And what a great family man Chris always was. Call him by his first name. His Christian name.

Bull fucking shit, Rog says, he's shouting, spitting, pouting. Waving the tip of that knife at the back of my head with little regard for my safety.

44

Rog who's officially Sous Chef Rog to Uncle Wayne's Head-Chef Wayne, officially, though I'm fairly certain neither of them has any actual culinary training. Unless you count all meth that Rog's cooked in his life.

Rog being in charge most of the time when Auntie Carol ain't around. Less for Wayne to worry about, more time for Wayne to sit on his fat ass.

Earn the big bucks, as he calls it. Usually'll pat his belly a little after saying that, then lean back in his swivel chair, put his hands behind his head, and close his eyes for a bit.

Making the big decisions, he says, with a big yawn.

Like hiring Rog and every one of Rog's little meth-head minions. *Reformed* minions, as Wayne is quick to point out.

Never miss a shift, Wayne says. Not Rog, not Sissy, not a one of them minions that Rog's recommended.

Too much to lose, Wayne says. Probation and all that. Not like some flake college kid, no-shows the first time he gets his hands on a fake ID.

He's always looking straight at me when he says it.

43

Me being an Auntie Carol special.

Auntie Carol's nephew being married to the wrestling coach's daughter, whatever you might call that relationship.

Me needing an actual job to pay for school so I don't have to do this the rest of my life. Or worse. End up sitting on a couch and sucking off the government teat like my ma, my step-dad, my fat-assed step-sister.

Course there's my fake job as a wrestling manager but not the kind of fake wrestling job that gets paid the big bucks or any bucks at all.

Me, just to be part of a team, part of a family. Me, for the love of the sport. The fame and glory.

42

I'm like five-four, maybe a buck fifteen on a good day. Too tall to be a dwarf, too skinny to be a midget. Too scrawny and fragile to be worth a damn in a singlet, let alone sequined tights.

But that doesn't stop me from helping out the team. Wipe the mats, fill the water bottles. That type of thing. The manager, though sometimes the guys'll call me the ball boy when they're trying to get under my skin.

As in: Hey ball boy, fetch me some fresh water.

Or: Coach, can we get that ball boy over here to wipe these mats for once. They stink like piss.

Or: Hey ball boy, you wanna give deez a wipe down too? What's that? Deez nuts?

But I don't let it bother me.

The closest I'll ever come to being a wrestler. The wrestling manager. Even if it's not the Classy Freddie Blassie kind.

41

It'd only taken me about a week of flipping eggs here, I come to find out I'm the only one works in restaurant who ain't never bought drugs from, sold drugs for, and/or a bit of both from Uncle Rog.

Once a day I got big Sissy coming up behind me while I'm grilling up a side of bacon. Sniff my neck a couple times, scrunch up her face. Then sniff some more. My ears, my hair, my face and chest.

I smell bacon, she says. Then to back Rog: You smell bacon, Rog?

Smells like bacon to me, Sissy, he says. Then: Better give that one there a little pat down. That there's an Auntie Carol hire.

To which Sissy starts grabbing and stroking the insides of my ankles, my thighs, the outsides of my hips, ribs, armpits. Sticks her finger in and around my mouth like she's checking for cavities.

Finishes it all up by reaching up between my legs, getting a good handful, goosing it a couple times, then sliding on back up through the bony craters of my ass cheeks.

Can't be too careful, Sissy tells Rog when she's done with me. All the places they be stashing wires these days. Finishes it all off with good hard pat on the rump.

This is my life. What I get for wanting to make something with my life. Earn my own way. For not wanting to be a leach on society like everybody else I grew up with.

40

I'm tossing a couple juicy sausage links on the flat top. Hundred percent pork. Fatty as hell. Listening to the grease sizzle a little as it spills out. Going to town chopping them up with the side of my spatula.

You telling me these jokers go on national teevee, kiss the man's ass for three hours after he's killed his wife and kid?

What kind a man? Rog keeps muttering. He's marching back to ask Uncle Wayne in the office. What kinda man, Chef? he asks Uncle Wayne.

Wife, maybe. Sure I can figure that, but some little kid? Real tough guy. Killin his goddamn little kid. Just cut your dick off, motherfucker. Do the world a favor. Bleed to death. Ain't that tough enough for you?

If I didn't already know everything I know about Rog—how much meth he's cooked and sold in his life, how many knee-caps he's smashed, how many lives he's threatened over a few missing pills—I might think he's actually torn up about all this.

39

For the record, Uncle Rog is not my uncle, the same way Uncle Wayne is not my uncle, the same way Auntie Carol ain't my auntie, old senile Grandma up at the host station ain't my grandma. Same way big Sissy out waiting tables sure as shit ain't my big sister.

But like it says out there on the sign: *Andersons Family Restaurant: Real Good Food, Real Good Family Atmosphere.*

And as Uncle Wayne puts it, since we're never gonna be confused with real good food, then we're obliged to put on a convincing show for the second part.

Keep that woman from chewing the rest of my ass off, Wayne says.

Just look at my sad sad ass, Jermy, he says and pulls up the back of his chef coat. There ain't no more ass for that woman to chew off.

Auntie Carol being *that woman*, not being an Anderson herself, but being Wayne's wife—actual wife— and as Rog puts it, the one wearing the big-boy pants in the relationship. The balls of steel, the designated swinging dick.

In charge of the whole thing and making a point to pop her head in the restaurant a couple two three times a day just to make sure we're maintaining the façade.

Far as I know, there ain't one actual Anderson among us.

38

Auntie Carol comes back, pokes her head in to remind me, the way she does every day.

Don't forget, Jeremy. She's tapping her watch. Twelve o'clock sharp, she says. Makes that squinty-eyed smile at me, all cheeks, no teeth.

Egg whites only of course, she says. Eight-six onions and peppers. Sub turkey sausage.

Calls back over her shoulder: You know how your Auntie Carol's watching her cholesterol.

Then heads out to kiss a little customer ass on her way back down to the basement. Manager's office, aka the torture dungeon.

We don't have turkey sausage. We've never had turkey sausage so long as I've been here. But that's never stopped her from asking for it, so it's never stopped me from pretending to give it to her.

Yes ma'am, I say after she's left.

Anything you say, ma'am, I say. Grab my junk good and hard, with a little pelvic thrust thrown in there for good measure.

37

Sometimes Coach'll let me tussle a little at practice, maybe roll around with the flyweights, have me try to get out from under their holds and pins.

You could say that's my specialty I guess. Squirming.

My patented finishing move—if I were an actual rassler—how to wiggle my way out from under the body slams of even the biggest strongest fattest sweatiest of heels.

Just call me the Worm.

If I were an actual midget I think I could for sure make it as a wrestler, at least as a midget who'd interfere with all the matches. Get people to chase me.

And then run away. Never let anybody catch me. Get them all counted out while my normal-sized wrestler buddy would just stand in the ring and yell, Run Wormy run!

If only I were a little shorter, fatter.

36

Uncle Wayne, days he's feeling extra family-like, he'll sneak up from behind me while I'm at the grill. Throw different submission holds on me. Full Nelsons, Cobra Clutches, sometimes just your good old fashioned sleeper hold.

I'll teach you to rassle, he'll tell me. Pick me up and shake me around like a rag doll. You ready to tap, boy? he'll ask. A moment later: You ready for night-night?

The other day he goes and drops his wallet in front of his office door. Jermy, he tells me. Be a pal and get that for old Uncle Wayne? he says. He's rubbing his back, making like he's big Sissy and seven months pregnant.

Back's killing me, he says.

Only, when I go to bend over and pick it up for him, he's straddling the back of my neck with them sweaty-assed thighs of his. Hoisting me up backwards, hanging me upside down for a pile-driver.

And he may've protected my head like a seasoned pro when he kicked his legs out and flopped back on the tile floor, but still.

Rog over there reading the newspaper same as usual and doing nothing but egging him on.

Yah, Chef, he says. Teach that boy some manners.

Nobody ever seems to worry too much if my eggs might be burning or if Wayne really might be cutting off my windpipe, or in danger of dropping me by mistake, maybe breaking my neck the way Owen Hart once broke Stone Cold's neck. Put him on the shelf for a whole year. Almost ended his career for good.

You know what happens to guys who break other guys' necks by for-real pile driving them too hard by accident? They end up dying a couple years later when nobody checks to see if the harness is secure before they try to repel down to the ring from the top of the arena.

Nobody seems to think Wayne's various finishing maneuvers are abusive or inappropriate for a family restaurant.

35

Me and my fat-assed step-sister, we used to wrestle a little bit back when we were kids.

What'd usually happen, me and Dee-Ann, we'd have the front of the house to ourselves, under the condition that we were not under any circumstances to bother my ma while she's back in her bedroom all day watching her stories.

Dee-Ann's old man, first thing in the morning, Dale'd get up off the couch and head out to the bars for the rest of the day to pretend to be looking for a job so the old lady wouldn't kick his lazy ass out once and for all.

Which'd usually end up with Dee-Ann—three years older and at least fifty pounds heavier—coming up from behind me while I'm playing with my rubber wrestling guys, then sitting on the back of my head Yokozuna-style and bouncing up and down.

You wanna wrestle, eh? she's whispering in between bouncing on my head. You ready to tap out, yet?

C'mon wormy, she's whispering. I thought you were a big tough wrestler guy.

Your wrestling guys are pretty gay by the way, she's whispering.

Your butt is gay, I'm whispering from under her fat-assed butt.

It's all fake you know?

Nuh-uh.

Is too.

Goes on and on about how her dad knows Sergeant Slaughter and he drinks with him all the time and Sergeant Slaughter tells her dad all about how they're all actually friends and they all hang out and get wasted together after all the matches. Talk about how gullible all those stupid little boys are who think it's real and play with their gay wrestling dolls.

Nuh-uh, I say. Is not.

Yeah-huh, she says.

34

Rog's back behind me waving that knife around again. Well, I'm waitin, Jermy? Waitin for you to explain this wrestling shit to me.

You's the wrestler, ain't you?

I actually stop what I'm doing, turn around, and say it loud and clear as I can: Roids, man, shit. Then: The bigger the muscles, the tinnier the wiener, I say. The fuck should I know? I'm actually facing him when I say it, staring down the tip of that knife.

Shit, I say. Maybe he got jealous. I'm back to mumbling now. Back to flipping my eggs, rolling Auntie Carol's omelet nice and tight like a burrito.

Maybe he caught his old lady checking out his kid's dingaling during bath time, I say. Shit, I just cook the eggs.

That's right, Rog says. I clean forgot. You's one of them leotard fairies, ain't you? One of them—he cups his hands and makes a farting noise—fudge packers.

33

They really wanted to get all the kids around here off the drugs, they'd have a blown up picture of Rog up there on that Meth billboard I pass by every morning on my way to work.

Shit, put him in a commercial, something, anything where they could show all them kids Rog's stringy-assed mullet, where it begins and ends with all that forehead stretching longer and longer in-between.

Those six, seven missing teeth, all the ones I've been able to count anyway. That sunken spot in the bottom corner of his jaw where his gums'd started to cave in. The pink scars and purple ravines that cut across his face and forearms. All them jagged blue veins.

His shaking hands whenever he ain't twirling that knife.

Let Rog talk to the kids. Let Rog tell them the type of shit he tells me on a daily basis.

Shoot a close up of those mix-matched bug-eyes of his—one blue, one brown—as he blinks and blinks and twitches and tells me: You smart-assed me like that a few years back, I'da called up ol Sissy, come pay you a little visit. A house call, you know what I mean.

I'da called up old girl one night and I'da told her I got a little job for ya.

Y'know what she'd say? he asks me. She wouldn't say shit, he says. Wouldn't ask *what* for, wouldn't *ask how hard*, wouldn't *ask how much*.

She'd say, What's the address? Hour later, show up at your back door—midnight or noon, rain or shine, sleet or snow. Introduce you to her two little buddies, her boyfriends, she calls 'em. Taller one named Lucky Louie, shorter one named Stan the Man.

And boy, let me tell you right now, you don't never wanna be on the wrong of end of a house call with Sissy's little boyfriends. These little guys, they ain't cute names for vibrators.

Start the conversation by introducing the back of your head to Louie, and finish the conversation by introducing your knee-caps to Stan the man's flat hard head.

Shoot a documentary of Rog just telling all the druggy kids about his relationship with big Sissy, all the shit she's done for him over the years, everything they done together.

32

Dee-Ann says her dad's friend from work, his uncle was in the army with the Sarge. Says her dad's told her all about it and how the Dale thinks it's really pathetic that kids like me play with all these wrestling dolls when it's not even real and all the wrestlers think I'm a joke.

How Dale says that nobody'd ever pay good money to watch a midget like me get thrown around by grown men anyway.

I don't care, I say, still from up under her butt. I hate Dale anyway.

Wanna call up my dad and ask him right now? He'll tell you.

Uh-uh, I say. I hate Dale, I say.

Fine, have it your way then, she says. Starts shifting her weight from side to side until she lets out the loudest wettest, most vibratingest fart ever. Vibrations reverberating against my ear lobes like their coming inside my own head. Literal brain farts.

I struggle and struggle to squirm free. Head butt, bite, turn my head this way and that. Make it at least ten or fifteen minutes of Dee-Ann bouncing up and down and grinding my head into the carpet before I give in and start crying.

Mommy!

Goddamn it Jermy, she's yelling from back in her bedroom. How you ever gonna grow up to be professional wrestler if you start crying every time your sister teases you?

Nobody wants to pay good money to watch a crybaby get thrown around the ring, honey. Suck it up or do something about it, Jermy, but Mommy doesn't want to hear it. Mommy's got stories to watch.

31

It's been raining all morning, God Almighty Himself pissing down on us pretty much since I opened at

five. Sounds like we're all stuck inside some old television with no antenna, nothing by white noise.

Occasionally it'll thunder and rattle the dishes a little, make the lights flicker, but other than that, just another beautiful goddamn summer day here at Andersons' Family Restaurant.

None of this changing much about the good life in the Good Food kitchen. Maybe other than a few fewer bitching customers, a couple more complaints than usual from the regulars—old biddies all of them— wouldn't miss a day rain, sleet, or snow to bitch about my cooking. Tell me my eggs is too runny, my toast ain't burnt enough, my bacon's too limp.

Which is real frickin hilarious, let me tell you. Don't matter how many times I have to hear Sissy come back and tell me.

One time I just went ahead and stuck a handful of uncooked strips down my pants and flapped them around for Sissy and everyone else to see.

How's my bacon now? I keep asking Sissy. It get hard yet?

Right up until Auntie Carol has to poke her sourpuss back there. Squint and squint through them old lady glasses til finally she realizes what's sticking out my fly.

You take that bacon out of your pants right now, mister. This is a family restaurant. I... I... I have half a mind to call your coach up right now and ask him how he might feel about your shenanigans.

Other than that it's the same old windowless dungeon, all these dingy-yellow halogens buzzing like bug-zappers.

Maybe the only other thing's changed, radio reception sucks a little worse than usual, which is why I got my mixtape in. Listening to a little Slim Shady til Carol comes back and tells me it ain't family friendly.

30

Rog says to me, he says, Shit, boy. You wanna know tough?

My old daddy, he says, he used to wrestle bears.

For money, he says.

Mucho dinero. He's rubbing his thumb and forefingers together with one hand, showing me the money, waving that blade around in my face with his other.

Really, I say, What'd all them bears pay with?

Rog up in my ear, waving that blade up and down as if he's sizing me up for a suit, maybe a coffin. Wasn't much bigger than you, my daddy.

Now imagine one of them big mama bears around these parts, he says, hoo-boy.

Boy, you think you seen big Sissy pissed off, shit, you don't want to see no big mama bear after they done took her cubs away and chained her up in the middle of the trailer park.

What I'm imagining is a pregnant Sissy with a spiked dog collar around her neck, chained to the basement of that meth shack Rog still lives in out in the boonies. Where Wayne's made me go pick him up from more than a few times. Rog having his license revoked and all.

Sissy playing the dancing bear, Uncle Rog there with his whip and chains trying to tame that awful beast.

29

Back before Dee-Ann's old man'd took off for good, left Dee-Ann behind along with me and Ma, he did take us to see Sergeant Slaughter one time.

It was this flag match, what they called it. There's Sarge marching to the ring with old red white and blue waving from side to side. Playing this song that's supposed to be vaguely patriotic, but not the national anthem or even Proud to be An American. Aren't any words to it even. Just some uppity drums and horns playing.

Then there's the Iron Sheik, who's already made his way to the ring. What sounded like bag pipes. Has what I'm guessing to be the Iranian national flag.

First thing, before old Sarge gets out there, Sheik grabs the microphone. Iran number one, he says, waves his flag. Then says: USA—spits on the mat, stomps it in.

Whole crowd goes wild. Dee-Ann's dad even gets up and gives him the thumbs down. Calls him a dirty A-rab. Tells Sheik to go back where he belongs.

Then old Sarge gets up there, makes a big deal out of putting his flag up on the side of the ring and saluting it. Then turns to face Iron Sheik, points back at the American flag, and shouts, Nobody spits on these hallowed grounds and gets away with it, maggot.

And that's how it starts.

28

I check the window, see about five plates ready to go out. Check the time on the tickets. Minimum fifteen minutes.

Ring that order bell three times as loud as I can make it sing. Order up, Sissy! It's been fifteen minutes, Sissy.

Ring it a couple more times just for good measure. Come get your food, Sissy, before it gets cold, and I have to remake it for all them ol' biddies because you're too slow and fat and lazy. Mumble that last part up into the air vent for nobody but me to hear.

Still, when I look back Rog is making eyes at me. Says: You ain't never heard the one about sleeping dogs, boy? How about sleeping bears—big pissed off pregnant snoring bears?

When I look back over to the office, I see Wayne leaning back in his swivel chair, staring at the ceiling.

One of these days, I mutter to myself, head over to check out the latest ticket.

27

Trick is, Rog says, first off, don't be dumb enough to get caught up in a no bearhugging match with no pissed off mama bear.

Stick and move, he says. Puts the knife between his teeth and shows me like some old time boxer. His fists way out in front of his body. Float like a butterfly, he says, sting like a bee. All that Mohamed Ali shit.

Shit you not, boy, he says. Seen it with my own two eyes. Says this while taking the knife out of his mouth, grabbing the handle, making a devil sign with his pinky and pointer, and pointing that devil sign at his eyes and then over at mine.

Point is, he says, my daddy he ain't never wear no fruity little leotard to wrestle no bear. My daddy'd come straight home from the factory in his coveralls. Strip down to his civvies. Even things out. Give that mama bear something to tear into in between getting slapped around by a guy half her size and only his fists to make conversation with.

Whatchu think about all that, boy? Huh? Still think this rasslin makes you a big tough guy? Get all hopped up on them roids, shrink your wiener, then take it out on your wife and kids?

Bullllll.... shit! Rasslin.

I ain't actually a wrestler, I shout a minute later, after he's headed back to smoke with Sissy.
You hear me? Just a goddamned manager. That's all, I say.

I get the water, do the laundry, wipe the mats. Can't anybody understand that? It ain't the WWE, I shout. It ain't like I'm some Mouth of the South or Mr. Fuji. I sure as hell ain't no Bobby the Brain.

26

It's not long until Auntie Carol hears me bumping some Real Slim Shady. Pops her head back in: Just what is it you think you are listening to now, mister?

I cock my head and squint as if to try to figure out what's playing. After a bit, I shrug my shoulders and go back mumbling, *Will the real Slim Shady please stand up, please stand up?*

Auntie Carol takes a couple steps closer, cups her hands around her mouth. Shouts that she's telling me for the last time. This is a family restaurant, young man. Shouts that we do not listen to that gangster rap here at our family restaurant.

Says it all slow and marbley in her mouth: *gang...ster.*

Like we're some bootlegging outfit for Capone.

Look hee-ah, see... I say out of the side of my mouth as I walk over to turn off my tape. *I ain't taking no orders from some dame, y'hee-ah?*

Shake my fist in the air like I seen in this old timey movie once. *Y'hee-ah?*

25

Just to prove that her dad wasn't no two-faced liar on top of everything else he was and wasn't, Dee-Ann makes him drive us around all night after the match til we finally track down the hotel bar where old Sarge and his buddies are tying one on at.

But Dale, I keep saying, I didn't even bring my Sergeant Slaughter doll. But Dale...

You don't need no damn doll to get an autograph, son, he mutters. He's scrounging around the bar for a couple of cocktail napkins, then an itty-bitty pencil that somebody's left sitting by the dartboard.

It's a goddamned aut-o-graph, boy, he says. All's he gotta do is sign something.

Dee-Ann's shoving me over toward them one bulldozer step at a time. Go on, worm, Dee-Ann's telling me. We don't got all frickin' night.

Over Sarge's shoulder, I recognize Iron Sheik, right away. Then Wahoo McDaniel next to him. Both hunched over half-full pitchers of beer and half-eaten pizzas.

Mr. Slaughter, Dale finally says stepping out from behind me. Sir, he says and gives this real awkward two-fingered salute more like the boy scouts than the Marines.

It's just my wife's kid here, he says, and grabs me by the shoulder, pulls me over next to him. Well you know.

Everybody's eyes on me now as I look up and look away, hug the napkins and pencil to my chest as tight as I can.

Go on, boy, Dale says and wrenches at my arm again. Ask them man.

The Sarge's all chin and moustache, just like I've seen on TV. But besides that almost unrecognizable without his signature drill instructor hat and aviators.

He sighs a big sigh, then turns almost in slow motion to get a good up and down of me first, then Dale, who's suddenly taking an active interest of the game on the TV back in the corner of the bar behind us.

Mr. Slaughter, I say, hold out my handful of napkins and pencil as far as I can reach. Would you please sign these? I forgot to bring my Sargent Slaughter wrestler doll.

24

Where's Sissy? Auntie Carol wants to know, she's got that sourpuss all puckered up under those glasses of hers.

She's right here, Auntie, I mutter and grab my crotch.

I got my back to her, I'm trying to tune in some CCR or Skynyrd, maybe even some Johnny or Willy or Waylon if nothing else. All two and a half stations we get around here. Anything that won't make me want to stick my head in the deep fryer before noon.

Where's she at?

Where the hell's she ever, I'm muttering. Smoking, sleeping, fucking in dry storage again. Take your pick, lady. Mumble it extra quietly.

Would you turn that crap off for a second? I can't hear a word you're saying.

Smoking! I finally shout. She's out smoking in rain. With Uncle Rog.

Jeremy Schmidt, she says. Only person here knows actual name. Be serious, she says. You know well as I do Sissy's about to have that baby.

Cancer baby, I mutter. Spawn of Satan.

Just tell her I'm looking for her, she says. I got papers for her to sign before she goes on leave.

Paid vacation, that's what Sissy calls it. Only way I'm ever gonna get time away from all you freaks and losers, she says.

Says it's Devon's from the garage down the street. Says she been waiting her whole life to have her a big beautiful black baby.

Yah sure, Uncle Wayne says. Devon's. Winks at Rog when he says it.

Eventually I turn the radio back up, blast some Dirty White Boy. *I been in trouble since I don't know when,* they're singing through the radio fuzz.

I'm in trouble now... I'm singing right along with them. *And I know somehow I'll find trouble again...* My own kind of radio fuzz. *Cause I'm a dirty white boy...*

23

Old Sarge, he takes one last sip of beer shoots another look back at Iron Sheik and Wahoo McDaniel, neither of them looking up from their pizza and pitchers.

Ah Christ, he says, and snatches the napkins out of my hand. Plops the napkin down on an empty spot of the pizza tin in front of him.

Well, who do I make it out to, soldier?

Dee-Ann blurts it out before I can open my mouth: *Worm!* She shouts it and then explodes with giggles. *His name's Jermy the Worm.*

Dale lets out a little titter of his own, before giving Dee-Ann a smack upside the head.

I hear either Sheik or Wahoo let out a big *Ha!* with a mouthful of pizza, then start coughing.

To Jermy the Worm, the Sarge reads out loud as he scribbles unsteadily on the tiny napkin, the wobbly pizza tin. Pencil like a toothpick in that sweaty paw of his.

He takes a long look at it, squints his eyes trying to read his own writing. Looks back at back at Sheik and Wahoo, then back down at me.

Well shit, he says, big smile stretching out across that chin of his. Almost forgot to sign my name, he says.

Except instead of signing his name, he goes and wipes his mouth with it. Smears the pencil scratches over with pizza sauce and slobber.

Looks at it again, squints. Ah Christ, he says, now where are my manners?

22

I'm glancing back at the last plate of eggs been sitting in the window for close to ten minutes now, I'm dinging the bell again and hollering bloody hell for Sissy.

Oh Sissy, I'm yelling in between dings. Your food's getting cold.

Outside it sounds like the rain is coming down even harder. Wherever it is Rog and Sissy have holed up to get a heater and stay dry.

Eventually Wayne wakes up from making all his big decisions, gets up off his ass and waddles over to the

73

kitchen.

Now where the hell Rog and Sissy run off to again?

21

Sheik and Wahoo are doubled over with giggles behind Sarge's broad shoulders, making googly eyes at each other like teenaged girls. Dale and Dee-Ann both tittering quietly behind me.

Sarge craning his head back now, his face all scrunched up as if he's about to sneeze. Except instead of sneezing, he only sniffs and snorts, eventually sucks up pretty much all the snot he can muster, probably all the snot any of us can muster aside from maybe Dee-Ann.

Sarge now holding up the tiny napkin to his nose and letting loose with the biggest wettest, loudest of nose-blows ever known to man. We're talking a nose-blow the sound a vacuum makes when you stick your lips down the hose and see who can suck harder.

One of them nose-blows where you need another whole Kleenex just to wipe up all the overflow snot from the first Kleenex, which is just what he uses the other napkins for that I've handed him.

I can hear Dale cough out the last of his giggles, then edge closer to me. Now you just hold on a second there, mister, he starts to say.

But before Dale can step around me or come up with anything else to say, the Sarge is balling up all the napkins together, wiping excess snot and pizza sauce off his hand and handing it all back to me, my hands out like I'm taking communion or something.

God bless you soldier, he's saying, that big booming baritone of his. He's saluting me a full-on Marine salute, though not actually standing up off his stool or looking in my direction.

Now get the hell outta here why don'tcha. Let old Sarge and his comrades drink in peace.

74

20

Eventually, Grandma comes back and starts eating bacon off the window. Goes at it like an ally cat eating bubble gum off the bottom of a Dumpster.

This food's cold, she says and works at a couple more bites.

You're old, I mumble and turn back to the grill.

You're gonna have to remake this, she says.

You're gonna die soon, I say.

She's moved on to the hash browns. This food's too cold, Jermy.

Like your lifeless corpse.

Where's Sissy?

When I turn back, the old lady's pulling a fork out of her pocket. I yell for Sissy over my shoulder.

Grandma yells her name too: Sissy! Like somebody's just dropped a cement block on that cat's hind legs.

I ring the bell about eight more times. Grandma's looking for you, Sissy! I yell over my shoulder. Auntie's looking for you too, Sissy! I yell. Food's cold Sissy. Nobody wants it now, Sis—

19

When the big one hits, it rattles everything, knocks out the lights completely. Everything goes quiet for a moment, except for the old biddies out in the restaurant, sighing and moaning, me wishing that I couldn't imagine what their sex sounds sounded like.

Ooooh... I say. Scary.

You ever stop talking, boy? It's Wayne come back out from the office, up off his fat ass for the probably second time all morning.

But it's the rapture, Wayne, I say. *Ooooh...*

Jermy, Wayne says, that's enough.

But it's the rapture, Wayne, I say again when the lights still haven't come back on. It's the reckoning, I say. Start banging my spatula on the grill, banging the pots and pans hanging next to it.

Jermy shut your ass, Wayne says. I can hear him stumbling his way over to try and put a headlock on me.

He's coming, Wayne, I start shouting, He's coming, He's coming to take us away!

First Mr. McMahon, then the Crippler, now us. We have to pay, Wayne. Pay for the sins of Rog and Sissy. The birth of their spawn.

18

What it was, me and Dee-Ann'd both gotten a bit older. A couple more years under our belts, a few more pounds for one of us, about fifty or sixty more pounds for the other.

And maybe that was it. Maybe Dee-Ann'd simply lost her youthful vigor, as they say. Maybe she'd simply grown tired of pinning me and sitting on my head and pulling my arms back and sometimes my legs til it seemed every bone in my spine might pop out one at a time. Make those little ping-ping-ping noises the way cartoons make it sound with a rope gets stretched to its breaking point.

Whatever reason, she can't muster up much enthusiasm to hold her submissions anymore. Doesn't even bother waiting for me to give up squirming and call for Mommy.

Ah Christ, she says one day. Rolls off me completely. You pathetic little worm. All this gay wrestling you watch and you still can't even put up half a fight worth my time.

I'm sitting up and rubbing carpet burns off my cheeks and forehead.

Bet you couldn't even pin me if I laid there and gave you a two-count head start.

Yeah-huh, could too, I say.

How much you wanna bet?

Million dollars.

You ain't even got no ten cents.

Yeah-huh, I say. I got almost five whole dollars saved up from cleaning out the couch cushions.

Show me, she says.

You don't have to be an expert on wrestling to know a setup when you see it coming.

17

Don't you be making fun of no rapture, boy. First it's Rog's voice coming from around the corner.

Then it's Sissy from a bit further down the back hallway: What's that spaz saying now?

The lights are on by the time I turn to see them making their way back from dry storage, both of them tucking things in, re-adjusting articles of clothing.

Boy's making jokes about the coming apocalypse, Rog says.

That shit ain't funny, freak-boy, Sissy says. She's trying to tie her apron back on way down underneath all that belly, stretching them sausage fingers out far as they'll go. Some of all that bulge being a baby, possibly the spawn of Satan.

This ain't no time to be joking about no end times, she's saying, patting her belly now with both hands, rubbing them around the lumpy circumference of it all, massaging the baby, pointing that bulging volcano of hell right in my direction.

Mess around and God Almighty'll shoot a lightning bolt up your ass, boy, she tells me. Then to her belly: Nuh-uh, not while me and my little Jayshawn standing in the same kitchen as you you won't.

You mean Rog Jr.? I mutter. I wander off and ring the bell a couple more times. Order up, Sissy, I say. Food's getting cold, Sissy.

Sissy, Grandma's saying still, again, the sound of that dying cat somebody oughta put out of its misery.

Sissy, this food's too cold now. Old lady's got that fork out, mixing the yolks in with the hash browns and bits of bacon. She's talking with half a mouthful of yellow and gold mush spilling out her rotten teeth.

I told Jeremy he's gonna have to remake this. You can't serve this now, don't you think, Sissy?

16

Dee-Ann having herself a pretty substantial set of boobies on her by then. Not that I was some perv or something. Makes it harder to get leverage is all. Hard to get a good grip on anything.

Plus there's all that greasy face to consider, the zits, the zit cream, all that sweaty neck fat only inches away.

Almost worse to deal with than her smothering crotch pins.

But such were the stipulations of our final match.

Me on top for once. Pretty much my whole scrawny body draped across her chest, her lungs going crazy underneath me. My right arm barely holding on to all that thigh of hers as I pull the leg up toward me. Leverage it best I can, considering the weight and strength disparities I'm facing.

One... she says, and takes a deep breath, my body literally rising and falling with each inhale and exhale.

I can see nothing in front of me but those bloodshot whites of her eyeballs, the mounds of reddening flesh twitching ever so slightly atop her cheek bones. That bulging blue vein running from her forehead down to her eyes.

Two... she says, and takes another breath.

15

Problem with you, boy, Rog says. Rolls up the newspaper and taps me on the nose like I'm a puppy that's shit in the house again.

All this rasslin business be messin with your head. Giving you this false sense of security. That mouth of yours always runnin and you ain't got no clue about consequences and repercussions. Real life type shit, let me tell you.

Rog putting down the newspaper and picks back up his knife. Rog shaking that knife at me and telling me about how him and the old lady are going at it one night a few years back. All fucked up, he says, rolls them buggy eyes back in his skull until I can see only the bloodshot whites. Starts like he's humping the oven door.

How he's just managed to pass out for the first time in like a week. How she's just kept on going at it by herself. How pretty soon after he's out cold she starts mixing in the ludes. Gets her hands on a filet knife.

I can smell it on you, she keeps telling him, he keeps telling me. Keeps smelling the crotch of my pepper pants and making stink faces as demonstration.

Smell that lying cheating cunt Sissy on you, he tells me, knife inches away from my junk, finger pointed at my nose. I can't take no more your damned lies, he says, and does a little half-assed Zorro swipe down there.

Baby, he keeps yelling at her, at me. He's scurrying back against the headboard, or in this case the microwave at the end of the line. Cupping my dingaling dear life, he says.

He's acting all this out for me—both parts, himself cupping himself and his old lady swinging that knife around, this bug-eyed look in his/her eyes. Pants on, at this point anyway.

It's yours, he keeps yelling at her, at me. It's you, baby, he pleads with me. It's your own nasty stank-ass cunt, baby. It's all you. Probably ain't washed or douched it in week and a half. God knows how long.

This whole time she ain't stopped reaching and grabbing and lunging for it with one hand, he tells me. Swinging that fuckin filet knife with the other.

14

It's now or never, I think to myself as I lie there atop Dee-Ann's jittery chest. I know what I have to do. You could even say it's predetermined, even if it isn't exactly scripted.

Three! I shout and in one fluid motion, I let her leg slip out from under my forearm, while dropping my elbow—Macho Man style, if not from the top buckle, then at least with the same bony edge to it, right on the money spot, that fragile zipper holding her jeans together for dear life.

All the while I'm posturing up, the recoil of my elbow drop to propel myself forward, my feet driving against the carpet. I can feel her chest, those hot mountainous boobies—desperately trying to erupt underneath me, but not quickly enough.

I have my opening and I'm taking advantage. Her head tilted up just enough, her eyeballs bulging, mouth gaping. I go for it. Those lips, all those crooked teeth. That slimy monster lurking down waiting to be tamed.

I have it locked in. Hard and tight. My body stiff as a board and planked precariously above her with all my weight pressed down through my lips, my probing tongue. Everything around me so very fuzzy and underwater.

13

Rog's got me cornered in the back of the kitchen now, carving knife in one hand, his other grabbing at my junk, my thigh, my butt, my hip, as I cup myself and press back against the cooler. Me not really acting.

And just when I think I got her calmed down, he tells me. I says, Baby give me the knife. And like a real dumbass, I go and reach out for it. Baby, I says, as I let go of myself and put everything out there for her. And just like that, he says. Bam!

Crazy bitch goes all in, he tells me. Lunges at me, at... it.

And sure this ain't my first rodeo, you know? he tells me, taps the side of his head, winks. I manage to block the initial attack.

But see, that ain't never what gets you, boy. Taps his head again. It ain't never the initial thrust, he says, the one you see coming. It's the follow-through, he says. That's the one. Shows me how he blocks her with his forearm, but how the knife keeps going off to the side.

He's pulling his pants down now, standing up like Captain Morgan, one foot pressed up against the side of oven. He's not even hopping or losing his balance, like a regular ballerina. Has that carving knife tucked up in the skin behind his knee. Shows me the inch and a half pink worm running up the inside of his thigh.

What the hell you go and do that for? he's yelling, at her, at me.

Good six inches deep, he says and pats his thigh. Go ahead, he tells me. Touch it. Juiciest part of the inner thigh. The good stuff.

Has his chili-pepper pants all the way down to his ankles now, like he wants me to get down on my knees and ask him to cough.

Go ahead, he tells me again and slaps himself. Touch it.

Grabs me by the hand and pulls my fingers to it. Both warm and scaly at the same time.

Feel that, boy? That there's true love. Somethin you wouldn't know nothin about, now would ya?

All the drugs in the world, he says and pulls back out the knife, pulls up his pants. And did I go and kill the crazy bitch?

Did I kill the bitch, he says again as he turns to walk out the kitchen. Fuckin' rasslin, man.

12

It takes me a second to realize the words aren't coming from where I've pinned Dee-Ann's lips, tongue, throat. How long Dale's been standing just inside the doorway, door swung wide open behind him.

What... the... hell...?

These being the last words I can remember Dale ever saying to me before he took off and left my ma to raise me and Dee-Ann both. I can't tell you what he said next, what I said, where my ma might've been to put in her own two cents.

I remember only Dee-Ann bucking me off and sitting upright. Dee-Ann wiping my slobber off her lips and staring down at her hand, how she couldn't take her eyes off that last bit of saliva coating the inside of her thumb.

Daddy! I remember her saying eventually. Almost crying as she says it.

Daddy! I can remember her saying again. A pitch I've never heard her hit before or ever again.

Please, I can remember her saying, the swiftness of her movements as she seemed to spring to her feet.

Daddy, I remember her saying over and over, it's not what you think, it's not what you think.

11

Come noon and the rain has finally let up. Not that there's a lot of sunshine and rainbows peeking through back in the Good Food kitchen.

It's scary quiet. Pretty much all the old biddies gone home for the day. Lunch crowd just starting to filter in. Uncle Wayne back in the office sitting on his ass, Rog and Sissy nowhere to be found. The usual.

Grandma's back telling me that Auntie Carol told her that she's waiting on her omelet still. She's tapping on her watch and telling me, She's a very busy woman, you know? She doesn't have time for this.

Who's a very busy woman? I say.

You know... she says. Carol.

She say that or you say that? I say. I turn around, point my spatula at her accusingly.

Very busy, she says, then clicks her tongue and shakes her head at me. She's running her wrinkly fingers up and down the window shelf longingly. After a couple passes, she picks up a few crumbs of something on the tip of her finger, examines it, then sticks out that little bloodless tongue of hers. Licks.

How many times I've seen that goddamned little blue tongue since I been working here. Enough to have the nightmares, let me tell you.

Jesus, Grandma, I say. Stop that. Take the spatula and smack the window about two inches away from her. No, I say. Bad Grandma. Get.

10

To make things clear: I may enjoy a good old fashioned fake wrestling match from time to time, bunch of oiled up guys running around in tight-tights and sometimes having to pick each other up with one hand over each other's bulging crotches.

I may even be the guy in charge of walking into a locker room full of naked runty college kids playing grab ass after every practice. The privilege this earns me? To gather up all the dirty, sweaty jock straps and singlets that it's then my job to wash and fold and get back to them by the next day.

I may never've had no girlfriend. I may never've even gotten laid, but this all doesn't mean I'm a fudge packer or some sister fucker. Doesn't mean that there aren't perfectly good reasons. Doesn't mean that if you'd've grown up the way I did and seen half the shit I've seen, heard, felt, and been felt by. Doesn't mean you wouldn't understand perfectly where I'm coming from. That you wouldn't be just as messed up about love and lust and the opposite sex as I am.

9

Well? Grandma's asking me, tapping her watch the same way Auntie Carol does.

Well, what?

Did you make it, yet? she asks.

What?

Carol's omelet.

About eight times now.

Where is it then?

Right there.

Where?

It up my ass, Grandma.

Where?

Go away.

Don't forget, she calls back before finally wandering back to front of the restaurant. Only egg whites, she says. Turkey sausage, she says.

I'll get right on that, Grandma, I say. Grab my crotch again for nobody in particular.

8

There's this one time, I'm just watching some wrestling tapes in living room, minding my own business, choreographing all the moves with my wrestling dolls.

At the same time, I'm having to overhear Dee-Ann go on and on with her newest twenty-something potential future baby-daddy.

What are you wearing, she's saying, this giggly voice I've never heard before.

She's tucked up in the breakfast nook. Only phone we've got, not even cordless, and pretty soon it gets so I can't barely concentrate on the match at hand.

No you...

No you first...

No... Well... Okay...

Nothing...

Like totally...

Yah, silly. Totally totally.

No, totally...

Well come over here then... I'll prove it to you.

Ah... skip work.

I'll make it worth your while...

Don't you love me...?

Don't you want me...?

Ah fuck this, she says at one point.

Hold on a second, babe. I gotta take care of a little pest.

7

Oh Sissy, I yell over my shoulder. I'm making Auntie Carol's omelet again. You better not forget about it this time.

Mumble under my breath: Come back there and shove it up your fat ass, maybe you'll remember then.

One of these days, Wayne calls out from back in the office. I'm telling you, you don't watch out, one of these days one of these here women gonna back there and sit on you, use you like a cheap tampon.

I got my Slim Shady back on now. *Hi... My name is... My name is...*

You hear, me, Jermy?

Chicka-chicka... I'm singing while I separate egg whites for another omelet for Auntie.

One of these days, Jermy?

One of these days, Jermy, I mutter to myself in my Wayne voice. Spread out the whipped egg whites on the flat top, scoop up a spatulaful of greasy fatty regular pork sausage, drop it on top.

Jermy...?

Shake my bony little finger at myself. *One of these women here gonna come sit on your face... Then what'll you have to say for yourself?*

6

My little Iron Sheik doll's got Sarge locked in the camel clutch. Don't you want me, baby? little Sheik's saying.

He's sitting down hard on the Sarge's rubber back, wrenching his rubber head back til it looks like he might rip it clean off.

Don't you love me? Sheik's saying.

Shut up, gaywad, Sarge's saying. Shaking his fists so the ref knows he's not about to tap out. Trying to channel the crowd chanting: *U-S-A... U-S-A...*

I can feel the floorboards shake with each closing step, but I don't bother to look back.

What's she gonna do to me she hasn't done before? I can remember thinking. Remember thinking: This ain't my first rodeo.

When I feel her hands cupping my cheeks first and not her thighs, I know immediately something's wrong.

Maybe this is why I've left my mouth gaping wide open for a surprise attack. It's her stubby nose that I feel next as it bops my own nose, then keeps going. For a second I'm confused. Why's she sticking her nose down my throat, why's it so wet, so slimy? How's she wiggling around and around it like that?

Everything being so dark and wet and confusing, all the light in the room suddenly eclipsed by so much hot flesh pressed up against my face.

Everything so underwater, as if I can hear that slurping and gurgling from inside my own head. As if our bodies have morphed into one.

This monstrous, wet nose worming its way down my through and nearly drowning me. Looking for what, I don't know.

A moment later it's over, she's licking her lips and wiping her face on the inside of her arm. She's reaching down to hammer-fist me in the nuts.

Whispering in my ear: *Gaywad.* Then turning and waddling back to the breakfast nook, back to the phone.

But baby... she's back to whining.

But baby, I'm so hot right now...

5

I wait about ten minutes, ring the bell a good twenty times before I grab the plate myself and go looking for Sissy.

Oh Sissy... where are you...?

Come out, come out wherever you are...

I know exactly where she is of course. Where both of them are and what they're doing.

Sissy, you in there? I yell loud as I can and knock three times on the door to dry storage.

Housekeeping, I say in this high-pitched voice.

Go away, freak, I hear her yell.

I knock again. But Auntie Carol needs her fatty omelet, I say.

Knock couple more times. I'm carrying the plate up above my right shoulder pressed up high on my fingertips. Delivering a little room service.

Well go give it to her then, she shouts.

Knock, knock, I say. Finally start to crack open the door slowly and softly as I can. Without looking in, I reach in the half-opened door hold the plate out. Room service, I say.

Right as I say it, the door flies all the way open, revealing Sissy, more red-faced and out of breath than usual.

What is your problem, boy?

She's hitching up her pants underneath her belly, pulling her shirt down where her apron should be hiding everything. I can't help but see those stretch marks and varicose veins burned into my eyeballs for all eternity.

Back in the shadows I can just make out the outline of Rog draped over a crate of flour bags. His head propped up against the shelf where we keep the potatoes. He's got one hand resting on his bare chest, chef coat completely unbuttoned. With the other he's pinching a doobie, lips puckered up at me, blowing smoke rings.

Go away, freak-boy, Sissy says. Takes my hand with the omelet and serves it back to me. Shoves me back out into the hallway.

Closed for lunch, she says. Slams the door in my face.

4

I wait til I hear Sissy take a few steps back, then knock again. Oh Sissy, I say. Auntie Carol needs you to bring her her omelet. Needs you to sign some papers for her before you go on vacation, I say.

By this time, I'm gently slipping the door open just enough to reach in with the omelet again. She's a very busy woman, I'm saying.

Without looking, I'm gently setting the plate down just inside the door quickly and quietly as I can. I'm closing the door that way too.

Probably saying the next thing a bit louder than I need to. A little excited, a little caught up in the heat of the moment.

I shout over my shoulder, I say, Auntie Carol says she don't want you to sue the restaurant when your cancer baby comes out all deformed and retarded.

3

I'm walking briskly now. I'm listening as the door swings open. Those footsteps, those thundering foot-steps, coming behind me.

What'd you say, freak? Sissy's booming voice echoing down the halls from behind me.

I'm at a trot now back to the kitchen, my feet slipping and sliding on the greasy tile floor as I turn the corner. As I feel my feet go out from under me, as I slip down, then immediately pop back up. All my wrestling training coming back to me.

Whoa, whoa, whoa, what's the big emergency? Uncle Wayne's saying from out of the office. Slow down before you hurt yourself, he's telling me.

You better run, boy! Sissy is yelling from behind, breathing heavy.

I make for the double-doors out to the restaurant, but then there's Grandma and Auntie Carol both standing there cross-armed and scrunching up their pruny faces at me.
Just what in tarnation is going on here? Auntie Carol is saying.

Jermy! Grandma is yelling. Sissy! Grandma is yelling. Carol here is waiting for her omelet.

I make for the back corner of the kitchen, I make for the flat top, I make for the rack of pots and pans behind it. I'm not sure what my move is, but I'm looking for as many possible shields as I can.

2

It's thundering again, everything shaking, but no rain coming down. The radio back on the fritz. This might very well be the end times. The four horseman coming for me, but not the ones wearing wrestling tights.

The lights in the kitchen don't go off, don't flicker, but I do close my eyes for a moment. Imagine this is all just another work dream. One of those dreams where I'm twelve tickets deep and no one else there to help me but Grandma licking everything I put in the window.

Looking for something? Sissy's voice only inches away now. The stench of weed and that bottle of Febreeze Rog keeps back there for just such occasions.

Whoa, whoa, whoa, Wayne is saying from somewhere over my shoulder. Let's all just cool our jets a bit here, eh?

You done pissed off the wrong mama bear now, boy. It's Rog from a bit farther back. That mouth of yours, I done told you, he's saying, as he makes his way towards the kitchen.

Will someone please tell me what is going on here? Auntie Carol is saying.

What I feel first is that big sweaty mitt of hers palming my face. It's so warm, soft. For a moment I imagine taking a nap in it.

I'm thinking of all those times Dee-Ann'd engulfed me with those thighs of hers, that one time she'd nearly drowned me with that Loch Ness monster of a tongue.

I'm thinking about the Crippler. That poor little-dicked bastard. What kind of pep talk he must've had to've given himself to be able to throw on his finishing maneuver, what he must've been telling his wife and kid right up to the point they could no longer tap out. The moments after.

I'm up on my tip-toes and puckering up before I notice that it's Sissy that's doing the puckering for me, using me like a puppet.

Me and Jermy here's just having a little conversation here is all, she's saying. Ain't that right, there, Jermy-wormy?

She turns my head to face Auntie Carol. Tell ol Auntie, would'ya Jermy, she says, tell her we's just having a little talk. She nods my head for me. I nod my head along with her.

See, Jermy here, he was just telling me how bad he felt about telling all those lies about my baby, weren't you Jermy?

Sissy? I hear Grandma say.

Sissy, I hear Auntie Carol say. Maybe we should all sit down and have a talk. How's that—

What's a matter? Sissy's saying to me. Is pointing my face up at her face, making my eyes meet her eyes, backing me up until I'm leaning against the front of the flat top for balance.

Well, she says, cat got your tongue? Tell these fine folks. Tell everybody all about what you been saying about my baby.

Spawn of Satan, I think, but decide not to say.

She's got my head tilted back over the grill now, I can feel the nobs getting turned up as I bump back against the front panel. My toes barely touching the floor.

Tell ol' Auntie all about these vicious lies you been telling people about me smoking while pregnant.

Tell everyone what a miserable little shit you are.

I can feel the heat from the grill creep up my back, each drop of sweat sizzling as it drips down my spine.

Say somethin smart now, motherfucker, she's shouting.

I've heard somewhere that you always hear the thunder after the lighting hits. That the rumbling only comes after the actual destruction. That's how you can tell how far it is, the time it takes between seeing it hit and hearing the sound of the thunder roll.

But it's the rumble that I feel first, the shaking of the pots and pans above my head, the plates over by the window.

Everything seeming to vibrate for a moment before the darkness hits. For a second I almost convince myself it's the skin on my back starting to sizzle. Maybe I'm starting to black out from the pain, I wonder. Maybe she's slipped me into a sleeper and I just haven't noticed til now how tired I am.

How quickly it hits, that moment of darkness. Just a flicker.

But long enough for me to make move. To kick, or rather to knee. It's not as if I'm aiming for the baby, though it works just the same. Allows me my inch of freedom to squirm and wiggle, to eventually make my momentary escape.

1

By the time I've realized what it is I want to do next, I've already found what I've been looking for all along. Rog's newspaper folded up next the ticket machine, that headline: *POLICE SUSPECT PROFES-SIONAL WRESTLER IN DOUBLE MURDER-SUICIDE.* That eight-inch carving knife resting on top.

I am not a goddamned wrestler, I'm shouting, pointing the tip of that knife at each one of them. At Sissy bent over in front of the grill. At Wayne at the other end of the kitchen, Rog hiding behind him.

94

At Grandma standing there with her arms crossed in front of the double doors. Auntie Carol right next to her.

I'm just a stupid manager, I'm shouting, I wipe up the mats, do the dirty laundry. Get water, I'm shouting. I'm clutching the knife handle with both hands, waving it like my own personal flag: The United States of Jeremy.

Somehow the lights around the kitchen seem to be growing brighter and brighter with each swipe I take of the stale dingy air around me.

I get in their faces. You hear me?

Jeremy, one of them says.

Jeremy, someone else says.

I get in Sissy's face, I get in Wayne's face, I get in Rog's.

Jeremy, they all say. Jeremy. Giving me all my syllables for once.

Do you hear me? I shout. I'm bee-lining it straight for Grandma and Auntie Carol. When they step out of my way, the double-doors out to the restaurant. Heading for the light.

Jer-e-my... they're chanting. Jer-e-my.... It's getting louder as I push through the double-doors. I see now that the sun's finally come out. All that light spilling into the front of the restaurant, it's almost blinding.

The screams echoing all throughout the restaurant, deafening.

My national anthem.

Turn it up, I shout as I wave my flag high for all the people to see. Get up, I'm yelling. Put your hands over your hearts. Everybody. Show some respect.

Loco Mask II

My old-ass Chevy Cavalier began overheating as I pulled into the municipal fairgrounds. I knew it would. It was about as stoked to meet Mom's current boyfriend, Jack, as I was. She hadn't said much, and with her track record, that's exactly what I expected:

Not much.

There was Bucky, who drunkenly drove Mom's Pathfinder into a jewelry store window; Warren, I remember, ran off with a thirteen-year-old cousin of his; Charles died sitting up—he'd had a heart attack on Mom's sofa while reading *Soap Opera Digest*; as for Dad, well, he was neglectful and has spent the last decade or so in solitude, painting horses—he doesn't care for much else.

I sat and let the engine cool. I couldn't decide, like the Clash song says, whether to stay or go. Shakespeare shit. Enough to make a man existentially queasy.

I sat awhile.

Mom had on one of her silly straw hats. This meant she was happy. When she pulled me into her, I got a good whiff of the Dollar Tree perfume she nearly drowns herself with on special occasions. Then I kissed one of her jolly, beer-reddened cheeks, and suspected her of being reckless.

She said, "Ronald, my boy," stepping away to straighten the brim of her Happiness hat, "I can't wait for you to meet Jack."

Crack. Smack. Lack. Whack. Nothing good to rhyme with. A bad omen.

Jack-off.

"Well, where is he?" I asked. I didn't see him.

"Over there," she said, pointing to a bunch of screaming hicks. "He's performing!"

"Performing what," I said, "lobotomies?"

Saliva, or Drowning Pool, or something kicked me in the dick through a shitty PA system as a big son-of-a-bitch announced as Loco Mask II—wearing a sequined blue hood with crazy yellow dragons stitched onto the sides—charged through the curtain and down the aisle towards a shoddily built ring. On his way there, an old woman in the crowd lobbed a plastic cup of beer at him. It exploded against his greasy pectorals.

Mom said to me, "That's Jack. He's what you call a 'heel'—a bad guy."

Jack, the heel, stopped to get in the old woman's face. It looked like he was about to clock her one. The crowd booed.

Jack's opponent, already in the ring, dressed in fatigues and waving an American flag above his head, was named Corporal Crusher.

Mom said, "That's Bruce, Jack's best friend. He's a 'babyface'—a good-guy, G.I. Joe-type." She was a sudden expert.

The bell rang. Jack and his buddy Bruce tossed each other around awhile. Mom knew all the moves—everything from a "Cobra Clutch" to a "Flying Insiguri." No holds were barred; even ordinary household items were used as weapons: folding chairs, ladders, staplers, and even a cheese grater which Jack had introduced to the referee's skull.

Mom went bananas, loving every minute of the choreographed bloodshed that had the crowd of questionables on their fat feet; only when Jack was slammed through a fiberboard table did she show any real concern.

After the match Loco Mask II stood proudly in the center of the ring, arms raised, as trash thrown by rabid imbeciles accumulated. He wasn't the moral victor. Not by a long shot. He was Mom's new man.

One by one the cars drove off till only Jack's rusted Sanford and Son mobile remained. I knew it was his because Mom had pointed it out. Standing beside it was a guy who looked about my age, maybe a little older, but he was big, built like a stallion in one of Dad's paintings. His ratty blonde hair was tied into a ponytail, and he wore a pink tank top with baggy zebra-striped pants tucked into cowboy boots. His left arm was bandaged.

A specimen of inbreeding?

I wondered.

I said to Mom, "Is that Jack's son or something?"

She laughed nervously. "No, no, no," she said, "that's… well… that's Jack."

I shook Jack's hand. It sounded like a shit-ton of firecrackers had gone off; it was quite a grip. He said, "Please to meet you, Ronald," before spitting tobacco juice at my feet.

Instead of a championship belt, he wore a fanny pack around his waist. I shook my head. Then I noticed blood starting to seep through the bandages wrapping his arm. I pointed it out.

"Oh, it's nothin'," he said, dabbing it with an entire roll of paper towels.

I tried being cordial. "Quite a show out there," I said. "It looked like you were really about to hit that old woman."

"That was Miriam," he said, grinning. "She was my kindergarten teacher."

I had nothing.

"Listen," Mom said to me, "we're heading back to the house to get cleaned up. Then we'll grab some food, maybe go bowling. How 'bout it?"

I thought maybe I could take him. Without the hood-and-cheese-grater gag, Jack wasn't so threatening. Still.

"Ronald?"

"Oh. Sure, Mom. How 'bout it?"

The Chevy gave me some trouble on the way, but not much. Having to stare at Jack's license plate the whole time, that was the real trouble: LOCOMSK2

Christ.

I considered running Jack off the road but knew Mom would've probably had a breakdown. Her *and* my car. Both.

When we got to Mom's, Duker came running up to greet me, stopped to leak, and continued on. I shook him behind the ears. Old boy.

I snooped around while Jack showered and Mom got ready. Propped behind a folded-up Ping Pong table was a family portrait Dad had done before going horse-mad. In it my hair is combed, and I'm half-smiling; Duker, only a puppy, is in my arms, and his tongue is out; Mom has on one of her hats; Dad looks stoic, distant, almost gone.

I must have been eleven or twelve, then.

Dad didn't know about Jack or Bucky or Warren. He knew about Charles, though; no use keeping that one a secret. He said of Charles: "Serves him right. The same would have probably happened to me too, had I stuck around."

I saw Jack's wrestling boots resting against the bathroom door. I picked one of them up, looked it over. Then I smelled it. It smelled as you would expect: not like roses. I put it back.

Mom came out of her bedroom wearing some Roy Rogers/Joe Buck-looking shirt with white denim jeans. Classy as always. "Well," she said, brushing a towel through wet curls, "what do you think of Jack?"

"Well, I'm afraid to ask how old he is," I said.

"Oh, Ronald, you know age doesn't matter much. But if you must know," she said, "he's twenty-eight."

"Jesus," I said. "He's only got three years on me! That doesn't bother you any?"

"Nope," she said. "I'm past all that. I love Jack."

"Yeah, well, at least he has a really great job," I said. "How much those gorillas get paid, anyway?"

"More than painting roomfuls of horses, that's for damn sure…" Mom let the bitterness fade as quickly as it had surfaced. "Oh, Ronald, can't you just give it a chance? I promise you, Jack's really great."

"Well, I suppose," I said. I lied.

Mom got me in her arms and squeezed. "We're all gonna have so much fun tonight, just you wait!"

"So your mom tells me you're in school?"

"That's right," I said, picking senselessly at a basket of soggy fries. "Communications. Not as exciting as what you're doing, I'm sure."

"Eh, probably hurts less," said Jack. "But hey, if communicating doesn't work out, and it's okay with your mom, I can teach you to be a wrassler like me."

Mom said, "Oh, Jack, don't…"

"Why the hell not? I could always use a tag partner. The Loco Mask Connection. Nice ring to it, huh?" Jack nudged me while sipping his beer.

"What happened to Loco Mask I?" I asked.

"Retired." From his pocket Jack pulled out the sequined blue hood. He was damn proud of it. He said, "It's an honor to carry on the legacy," and then paused to reminisce. "A big draw in the Southeast territories, that Loco." Then he turned to Mom, who was glowing, and winked.

I pictured a seedy motel room. Shades drawn. Ratt playing in the background. Loco Mask II lowering his muscular frame upon my dear old mother, ready to put her in his infamous "Love" hold.

I gripped the table. I nearly fainted.

Mom said, "Ronald, what's wrong? You look like a ghost done gotcha." She laughed.

"I'm fine," I told her, "just dehydrated."

Just mortified.

Jack nailed his sixth strike of our last game. Another Turkey. He went up to Mom, gave her some tongue, and then slapped her on the ass. The fucker.

I started to grow balls. I said to him, "I see you're not as lousy a bowler as you are a wrestler."

Jack flashed his tobacco-speckled teeth. "Only one way to find out," he said.

A challenge.

Mom looked on, smiling. "Oh, you boys, I swear…"

I didn't respond. I drank my beer. I drank like it tasted bad.

While Mom was at the jukebox, no doubt searching Kenny Chesney, I asked Jack if he wanted to take a shot. A peace offering. He shrugged, nodded, and then followed me to the bar.

I said to the old man behind the bar, "Two shots of Kentucky Gentlemen." He poured them, and I raised my glass for a toast. "To mothers!" I said, smugly.

Jack didn't like it. He looked straight through me while downing his shot, and then calmly walked off without saying "Thanks" or "Fuck you" or anything.

It was like the irresistible force meeting the immovable object. I couldn't get through. So I got drunk, gloriously drunk, and watched from the bar as Mom slow-danced with Jack to a Gretchen Wilson ballad.

Mom was happy; she had the hat to prove it. Still, I knew in my heart that Jack was a brute. I could picture him getting belligerent and knocking Mom around the way he did his opponents. I didn't like him.

Clutching chairs and tables for balance, I tottered onto the dance floor. From there I got Jack in a rear chokehold and nearly took him down. His legs were kicking, and I could feel his head growing hot with anger as tobacco juice ran down my arm. Mom screamed for help, but nobody did anything. Not that they needed to. Jack simply reached behind and flipped me onto a table which, unlike the one he'd gone through earlier, did not break. So I lay sprawled on top of it, watching the ceiling spin as pain shook my spine, thinking I would soon end up like Charles.

Mom got me in her arms again. Her hat was off, and she was sobbing. "Ronald, my boy, what's gotten into you? Jack's sorry. I swear he is. He didn't mean nothin'. Oh God!"

I felt bad. I should have let the two of them alone. Mom was a grown-ass woman, and she could do whatever the hell she wanted, which she usually did. I was just her son, and I was shitfaced, and everyone in the bar watched as I carefully got up off the table and onto my feet. I bet they all thought I couldn't do it. A few of them clapped.

First thing I did was apologize to Jack. I said, "Sorry, dude. You won," and I raised his arm. Then I turned and kissed Mom's tear-soaked face. I said, "Put your damn hat back on," and she did, and I staggered off.

"Ronald, come back!"

I looked around the parking lot. I couldn't remember driving there myself. Mom was shouting. *"Ronald, honey, please come back!"* It wouldn't stop. Relieved, I got into my Cavalier and sped off, leaving smoke and crap rubber. Mom's voice kept on.

It didn't take long for my shit to burn up, and when it did I pulled the car to the side of the road and waited awhile. When I tried restarting it, the damn thing wouldn't turn over, so I got out and walked.

I walked a long time. I didn't know where I was going, what direction. Cars whizzed by, blinding me. They didn't stop. They had places to be. They didn't overheat.

Delirious, I imagined Dad coming to rescue me on one of those horses he'd spent so much time capturing on canvas. He'd say, "Hop on, son," and I would, and the horse would be a Tri-Star Pictures horse—a magical white thing sprouting wings—and it would kick its legs up and make horse sounds, and we'd be off.

I saw a set of lights up ahead, brighter than any before it, and it was then that I decided I would quit school. To hell with communications, I thought. I would quit school to become a professional wrestler. I would train hard. And I would say my prayers. And I would eat my vitamins. And I would challenge Jack to a steel cage grudge match. I'd pile-drive him on his thick head. And I, too, would wear a hood. I'd be known as Loco Mask Assassin. I would be the first.

It's All Fake

The title above speaks for itself. I love when people say that to me; "It's all fake, isn't it man?" Or they will have beer muscles and call me a phony, an actor, even a pussy. What they don't know is I have three black belts, I am a former Marine, and I was All-State as a high school wrestler. Not to mention, I am 6"4 and 265 pounds of mostly muscle. But these guys look past all that. Because I'm just a pussy, an actor, a phony. I'm just a pro wrestler.

In the old days, if a wrestler was confronted in a bar, especially if the drunk confronting you accused the business of being fake, you had to fight them. Actually, let me clarify; you had to HURT them. When pro wrestlers begin training at a school (yes we go to school, just like nearly every other profession,) before you are taught the proper way to fall, and before you are taught how to cut a pro wrestling interview, you are taught what are known as "shoot" techniques or "shoot" holds.

In the pro wrestling world, the word "work" means it's phony or it's predetermined. So we "work" our matches, or we "work" the fans. A "shoot" however means it's 100% real. There have been "shoots" right there live on TV, without the fans knowing what they were seeing. Usually it's two guys who really have "heat" (intense dislike) and they bring it into the office. One guy will take a cheap shot, the other guy will respond with a "receipt," and usually it's over just as quickly as it started.

Another "shoot" can be when a wrestler says something he isn't supposed to say, either on the microphone, or on TV, that either gives away a part of the business, or it refers to "real life." But let me get back to "shoot holds." I know a way to break a guy's thumb before he's even blinked. I know exactly where to hit someone in their solar plexus to send them to their knees, and I know exactly where to hit someone in the skull that will guarantee their lights go out.

I know exactly how to put a choke on someone that will render them unconscious within ten seconds, and I know exactly how to pluck out a guy's eye with minimal effort. Have I done some of those things to stupid, macho, bar fighters who were looking to make a reputation on my name? Yes, I have. But those days are long gone. Too many fucking camera phones, cameras on corners, cameras in the traffic lights. You can't get away with anything anymore. It always winds up on TMZ.

Ah ha, that leads me to my TMZ story. So, around two years ago when I was still with the big wrestling federation, we were on a tour (we never stop touring actually) and our stop for a show that Saturday afternoon was New Orleans. That means the show started at two o'clock, and ended around five o'clock. That means with nothing to do, and no flights until the following morning, twenty wrestlers were turned loose on Bourbon Street.

Let me tell you something about how wrestlers party; I worked for another big company in the late nineties. I was in my mid-twenties then, one of the youngest guys on the roster actually. In those days, there was literally NO policing of the locker rooms and the backstage areas. Guys drank out in the open, guys took and traded pills out in the open (Somas, Percocet, OxyContin, Valium, you name it,) guys smoked weed anywhere they pleased, and guys snorted lines of cocaine right out of their bags. One guy, who actually has a very famous name and is a buddy of mine, had a thing for doing three thick lines of cocaine off of his championship belt, before doing any interviews. So when you hear people describe "coked up wrestling interviews," now you know that for a period of time, that was pretty accurate.

Anyways, back to New Orleans. So you have twenty wrestlers roaming the biggest party area in the US. They are all alpha male types, they've all been drinking, some are on steroids or HGH, so they are walking hard-ons. If you were on Bourbon Street that night, and you had your girlfriend or wife with you, firstly I ask "why did you bring sand to the beach?!" and secondly, I apologize. I've never seen so many beautiful women in my life, who were both scantily clad, and willing to do nearly anything you wanted them to do, all for a string of beads. Most of them did it right in front of some poor sap who they were dating, or was stupid enough to marry them.

So I was at a bar with a balcony (yes I know, that could be one of a dozen,) when I saw across the street, on a balcony directly across me, there was a row straight across, of six of the most beautiful women you've ever seen, all flashing the masses below…except one. They was one extremely beautiful girl, dressed rather conservative in a black long sleeve shirt, and jeans, with the longest most beautiful brown hair I had ever seen. She was surrounded by supple, naked breasts and more, but she was the only one not giving into temptation or pressure. I couldn't stand it, and I yelled over to get her attention.

"HEY!" I said, full of class. What an opening line, huh? She responded with a smile, and cupped her ear, like she couldn't hear me. I made the "pulling up your shirt to flash me" motion, and she giggled adorably, and shook her head rapidly. But I was not to be denied. I waved my hand up and down her line of friends who were all making their fathers proud, by most likely ending up on a Joe Francis video. She shrugged and shook her head again.

I tried to yell over to her again, but I was completely drowned out by incredibly loud jazz coming from inside the bar. So I went with a plan B. I went inside the bar to find something to write on, and I noticed a dry erase board on the wall over by the dart boards and pool table. I went over to lift it off its pegs or whatever nail it was resting on, and found it had been drilled into the wall. So I did what common sense told me had to be done at the time. I summoned my asshole roided up wrestler strength, and I pulled the thing right off the wall, drawing blood in the middle finger of my right hand, due to a wicked splinter.

I brought it back out to the balcony, where across the street, my lady desire was still watching her friends in amusement, and refusing to join in. When she looked over, I mimed that I was going to write her a message. She pointed to her watchless wrist, as in, "Hurry up, I'm getting out of here!" I knew a few of the guys had markers they always carried, in case an autograph opportunity came up. Also some of them would try to pay for drinks with their autographs. You'd be surprised how often that worked.

So I went over to a friend of mine, who was currently wrestling under a pirate gimmick. A little old timey and corny, yes, but it really worked for him. His eye patches and t shirts sold like hot cakes at shows all over the country. I went over to him and asked him for his marker. He looked at me, red eyed and confused, but he handed it over while telling me "Make sure I get that back. That's my lucky marker. I've had it with me on every flight I've ever taken." I nodded my head in sincere understanding.

Lucky for me, the creepy bastard had a glow in the dark marker, so it would easily be spotted from across the street, as long as this broad had good eyesight. I wrote on the dry erase board (which now had permanent marker on it,) "SHOW ME YOUR TITS! I WILL GIVE YOU $2,000!" Ok, so it was a jackass move, but I had the money at the time, and her refusal to join in on the debauchery with everyone else drove me insane for some reason.

I held up the sign and watched as her eyes squinted and she read it. Every other girl on the balcony with her flashed immediately, screaming and laughing. I yelled "NO!" and made a cutting the throat motion. I pointed at my sweet little innocent princess and loudly annunciated "HER! NOW!" Pretty suave, huh?

She was laughing uncontrollably, and continued to shake her head, but she was blushing, and I could tell the idea turned her on. Plus, who couldn't use two grand to pay bills, or catch up on student loans, or buy enough coke to last you almost a week?! I could tell right then and there that she was going to do it, but she still remained hesitant. She was going to play hard to get, but it was going to happen.

I screamed over, "C'MON BABY, LET THOSE GIRLS FREE!" She shook her head defiantly again, and I yelled "I JUST GOT DIVORCED AND YOU ARE THE SEXIEST WOMAN I HAVE EVER SEEN! I GOTTA SEE THOSE TITS! I'LL MAKE IT $2500!" Her friends had surrounded her, some grabbing at her shirt, the rest trying to convince her. I am sure they heard $2500, and had drinks all night and Molly in their bloodstream on their minds, if their friend earned that kind of cash.

She stepped forward, and my dick got so hard I could've done chin ups with it. As she came to the edge of the balcony, I could tell she wasn't wearing a bra. This was going to be good, I thought. I called some of the other wrestlers over, and we all braced ourselves for a few seconds of boobies. It didn't matter that we'd seen them all night. This girl was special, and we all knew it.

So she lifted her shirt, jiggled for a full 4.5 seconds, and then pulled it back down, continuing with her beautiful laugh. She made the universal sign for money, rubbing her fingers together. I pointed down to the street, indicating that I'd meet her down there. She turned to reenter the bar, go down the steps, and collect her winnings.

I was hoping to collect another notch on my bedpost myself (or in this case, the hotel's bedpost.) As I walked back in I noticed the wall I had partially destroyed by pulling the dry erase board off. Then I noticed the four large angry bouncers surveying the damage, and then looking at me. "Hey motherfucker; we got you on camera doing this! We already called the cops, so why don't you just come with us?"

I was about to respond with something witty. You know, "suck my dick," or "your mother's a whore," something that befit my large IQ properly. But before I could get a word out, my pirate amigo stepped forward and said "He's not fucking going anywhere!" ran forward, and punched the closest bouncer directly in the temple. He went down instantly. Before I knew it, I had six more fellow wrestlers with me. The bouncers were down to three now, but the boys in blue were beginning to file in.

I knew I was in deep shit, not only because I was getting arrested, but because my promoter was probably going to find out, which would lead to a fine at best, rehab in the middle, and a firing at worst. I didn't want to get any of my brothers in trouble, so I stepped forward and said "It's my fault officers. I caused the damage and I hit that guy. Just take me in, nobody around me did anything." The other bouncers started to argue and point at Jack Sparrow, but I spoke over them as I approached. "I am happy to go in and just get this the fuck over with."

So they cuffed me, and led me downstairs. Two of the guys actually asked me if I would give them autographs for their kids, once we arrived at the station. As I was being led out, I didn't see my dream girl anywhere. Perhaps she had waited, and finally left, full of disappointment. Damn it, I didn't even get her name, so I couldn't look her up, Facebook her, anything. I fully intended to pay her, too.

I was shoved into the back seat of the police car, cursing my bad luck. In reality, it wasn't a matter of luck at all, it was a matter of an arrogant prick (me) doing whatever he felt like without worrying about the consequences (which was my go to move for almost a decade.) But I had no idea how much worse it would get. By 7 AM the next day, my arrest was on TMZ. That's not all though. Someone had recorded the entire exchange on their phone, including my brilliant line about being divorced, my offer to pay over two grand to see a nineteen year old's breasts, and me saying she was the sexiest woman I had ever seen. Of course, I wasn't really divorced. But I was about to be.

The Last Word Luchadore

The poet is who I am, who we are,
the last of the word luchadores
Our minds, rarely understood,
are sent running to hurdle hate and mispresentation
springing off words woven together
into ropes that tear like razor blades into the flesh
of both the underestimated poetic face
and legend killing viperous heel.

The luchadore fights for true freedom
before it becomes a piledriven island of rubble
pieced together into society's tombstone
with the only words on its face simply reading:
REST IN PEACE.

The luchadore armored in ink fights with
fists of letters born of heart, soul and perseverance
and used to make words, to make lines,
to make this poem, my wall of Jericho
and it will never be brought down.

The shadows try bringing us to our knees
try making us submit, give up, tap out
all for nothing....
because they fail to remember

The poet is who I am, who we are.
the last of the word luchadores.

Amherst, Massachusetts

Emily Dickinson calls me up at midnight to
ask if I want to get really stoned and
watch old wrestling videos.

"Just let me
put some pants on, Emily. I'll be
right over."

My car is a yellow Camaro.

There are French fries all over
the floor.

I turn on the headlights.

And zoom on over

to see the only girl in town
who still knows what poetry

is all about.

Life is Okay

getting wasted
watching wrestling on TV
life is okay
life is okay

WrestleMania Sonnet

They muffed up the pay per view in my town.
None saw men bent in shapes polyhedral.
So to make up for letting the fans down,
gathered at the Scottish Rite Cathedral,

a week later, on the local tv,
they apologized to the angry fans
and showed WrestleMania 1 for free.
By chance, I saw it, but now I make plans

to watch WrestleMania 31.
Nobody will be as good as Piper
ever, and it may not be as much fun,
but, near my end, in an adult diaper,

watching WrestleMania 86,
I will still need that boyhood wrestling fix.

Excerpts from *Blog Love Omega Glee*

The Bodyslam Poet (25 February 2012)

This week's episode of <u>Grapple Groove</u> opens not in an arena, but in what appears to be a small, dark coffeehouse. The camera pans the interior to show beatniks dressed in black turtlenecks and berets. Everyone in the coffeehouse wears glasses. Steaming hot cups of coffee are served, and people nosh on French pastries. The walls are covered with abstract expressionist art as if decorated with the unsold remains of Jackson Pollock's garage sale. After panning the interior in general, the camera zooms in on a stage outfitted with bongos, acoustic guitars, and a single microphone on a stand. The camera cuts to a sign next to the stage, which reads, "Tonite: Open Mic Poetry Slam."

Jake, watching this on television, can hear a large arena crowd start to boo and knows this is no real coffeehouse, but what a wrestling writer and set builder think is shorthand for a coffeehouse in the minds of a wrestling crowd in the television audience and the live audience watching the skit on giant video screens in the arena. The camera focuses on the stage; a young beatnik with a goatee and a bad ponytail approaches the stage and starts to recite poetry into the microphone, "War. Bore. Endless tour. Stop loss. Gotta stop stop-loss or we'll all be lost. Society tries to compel me to serve in the military. Ferry me off to war. Oh, lord. Swing a sword. Fire a gun. Ain't killing fun? I explode some guy I don't even know. Yo! Oh, no. People got to know. Wake up to the military industrial complex. Technology likes to flex. We got to spend less. It's straight up senseless. We got to go 'Om, om' instead of 'Bomb, bomb'. Create enemies for you and me and all the money. Tax tax tax. Get the facts. It's all an illusion. You're under a delusion. If you want peace, work for justice, cause it's just us in this here piece. My private is private. I ain't going be no buck private for the public. This hubbub sick. I want to go to the pub and have a beer with no fear. Military is silly scary . . ."

At this point, a large sweaty man wearing black trunks, a dark blue and white striped shirt, and a Mexican wrestling mask that vaguely resembles the head of Mickey Mouse with its big, floppy ears steps onto the stage and puts the poet into a headlock. The man says, "All right, I don't think your three minutes are up, but my patience is. I won't have anyone badmouthing the military. If it weren't for them protecting you, you'd be dead by now. Too bad for you they're not here to protect you now, but I won't hurt you. Much."

The man in the mask punches the beatnik in the face, then releases him, and pushes him offstage. "I'm next," the masked man says, "My name's The Bodyslam Poet and I'd like to read you some better poetry than that."

The masked man digs into the front of his trunks, pulls out a wet piece of paper, and says, "I wrote this one this afternoon and it's called, let's see, 'Love Is An Abdominal Stretch'."

The beatnik has returned with a woman who looks to be the open mic organizer, and they point and shout at The Bodyslam Poet to get off-stage. "Shut up!" he says, pointing at them menacingly, "I listened to your crap, now listen to mine!"

The beatnik takes out a clipboard and threatens to pass around a petition condemning The Bodyslam Poet. He waves it in The Bodyslam Poet's face, who grabs the clipboard and hits the beatnik over the head with it, then The Bodyslam Poet casually throws the clipboard behind him. The Bodyslam Poet then spins the dazed beatnik around in a circle by pulling on his ponytail, lets go of the ponytail, picks up the beatnik when he slows down from spinning, and bodily throws him off-camera. "Okay," The Bodyslam Poet says, smoothing out the piece of paper in his hand, "I hope you don't count that in my three minutes. As I said, this is 'Love Is An Abdominal Stretch'."

The Bodyslam Poet clears his throat and reads, "Love is an abdominal stretch / It makes my insides want to wretch / When I see you I cannot think / You make my stomach start to sink / Like a steel chair shot to my head / I see stars and my face goes red . . ."

At this point, the coffeehouse crowd has risen en masse and surrounds The Bodyslam Poet booing him and pelting him with the remains of croissants. After one woman splashes a doppio latte macchiato in The Bodyslam Poet's face, he throws down his poem, and starts scooping up audience members and body slamming them to the ground. Most flee, but the last remaining audience member, the beatnik who read before The Bodyslam Poet, gets slammed on top of a table. The Bodyslam Poet looks around at all the carnage--spilled drinks, stepped-on pastry, bent poetry chapbooks, broken chairs and tables, and sprawled bodies of beatniks--and says, "I'm going somewhere where I'll be better appreciated."

The camera cuts to a sports arena in Dubuque, Iowa USA filled with wrestling fans, and on the screen flashes, "Next week: The Bodyslam Poet debuts in ring on <u>Grapple Groove</u>."

The arena crowd cheers. The television cuts to a commercial for the U.S. Army. The army pays to advertise; beatnik peaceniks don't. Wrestling always butters those who give it bread.

Rest In Peace Ed "The Bedwetter" Driphoski (16 March 2012)

He went in his sleep, peacefully wetting the bed one last time, according to the news reports. Jake's a little sad, feeling a little older, upon hearing the news that Ed "The Bedwetter" Driphoski has died. Driphoski was one of the first wrestlers Jake ever saw, and Jake took to him and maybe even wrestling in general because as a kid he wet the bed too. He always felt slightly ashamed of it since it took him a long time to grow out of it, but here was a grown man on television who didn't seem to care if people knew that he wet the bed, and that made Jake feel better. The Bedwetter wore trunks that looked like diapers, and he'd often wet himself if his opponent was about to pin him and, then disgusted, the opponent would jump off him before the referee could finish the three-count. Then Driphoski'd come back with his finishing move, "The Clean Sheets", where he'd pick up the opponent over his head and then just drop the opponent to the mat, following up with a dropped elbow for the pin.

Sometimes though he used the "Wet Dream" submission, but they wouldn't let him do that on television, so Jake didn't see that until years later on bootleg videos of old matches.

Driphoski was usually a heel, but Jake still liked him instantly. The reasoning behind his gimmick and character was that he was seeking revenge on the kids who made fun of him for wetting the bed when he was a child. When he turned face occasionally, the pathos of the character being trapped by his childhood and unable to overcome it was milked for all the milk of human kindness that could be gotten out of his soggy diapers. Since a great deal of the wrestling audience were kids, they could relate to Driphoski's problems and imagine themselves in his place fighting against all the bullies and mean kids of the world.

Since Driphoski predated the steroid era, he had a long career in the ring. He didn't take unnecessary physical risks in matches, preferring ring psychology, and low impact mat wrestling, saving his showmanship for his promos and ring entrances. He retired from ringwork shortly after Jake started watching wrestling, transitioning to being a manager of other wrestlers, usually tag teams, many of whom he guided to the championship. His gimmick was kept intact though, and he'd occasionally win matches for his wrestlers by distracting their opponents with a well-timed leak. In the past few years, he quit the road but would still occasionally show up on <u>Grapple Groove</u> when they filmed in his hometown of Chicago, or at big events like the yearly Grapplelution, always to Jake's delight. Even when he couldn't wrestle at the end, they'd let him win hall of fame battle royales because he couldn't go over the top rope to lose because of his hip replacement, and the fans still loved him.

Jake writes up a eulogy for his blog: "I'm glad they're dedicating tomorrow's <u>Grapple Groove</u> to The Bedwetter. One of my all-time favorites, he made the lives of wrestling fans damp with enjoyment, moist with excitement, and soaked through with passion for the business."

The Bedwetter's tradition carries on through his son, Jack "The Dripper" Driphoski, who adopted his father's gimmick, but made it more extreme, taking it in a fetish direction, to match the direction of contemporary wrestling. Today, The Bedwetter's gimmick, once controversial, looks tame, reminiscent of a more innocent time in wrestling and society.

Sleep on sweet bedwetter, soak that coffin good.

You Don't Want Your Bladder to Explode (5 April 2012)

At a run-down warehouse on the west side of Cleveland, Jake and North show up at their first evening of wrestling training. There's a half-collapsed ring and about fifty cats roaming around. "Hello!" Jake says, looking for their instructor, retired wrestler Lew "Life of the Party" Zsyrjba, whose gimmick used to be wearing a lampshade to the ring.

"Yeah, what you making such a racket for?" the bentover old man shuffles out of a far corner's shadows, taking a swig out of a bottle in a brown paper bag.

North whispers to Jake, "Dude, I told you we should have gone with the school run by the younger guys!"

"But he's a legend!" Jake whispers, "Those other guys never wrestled outside of Ohio."

"He's a drunk," North hisses.

Lew stumbles towards them, and points at the ring, "Get in, Boys. Time for your first lesson."

As North climbs in the ring, he says to Jake, "It smells like cat piss in here, and it's freezing too."

Jake just sighs and slides beneath the ropes into the ring.

Lew has set down his bottle and dragged himself into the ring, "OK, first lesson: how to land on your feet from the top rope."

North raises his hand, "Um, this is our first lesson. Shouldn't we learn how to do a headlock or take a bump or something?"

"Boys!" Lew shouts, "This one time, I was about your age, and I was wrestling in Malden, Massachusetts, and it was one of my very first shows in this business, and I was lacing up my boots and Jack 'Hot Stuff' Pepper, old Jack was in the locker room, and he said, 'You better use the toilet before we wrestle', and 'I said, 'Ah, we got plenty of time. I want to wait until it's closer to when we go on', and Jack said, 'You better go', and I ignored him and started combing my hair. I wanted to look good for the girls, and the promoter . . . oh, what was his name? He was a mean old son of a blender. Oh, what was his name? . . . Chuck! Chuck Kerouac! That mean old son of a button Chuck Kerouac came back and said you guys are on now, and I said, 'But I'm not ready. I still have to use the toilet.' And he said, 'I don't care what you have to use. You get in that ring or I'll find somebody else.' So I went in the ring, but I really had to piss, and I wasn't concentrating on my wrestling. I was just trying not to piss myself, and Jack put me in a suplex and, when we landed, my bladder exploded. Boys, let me tell you something. You don't want your bladder to explode! It does not feel good! So I had to go to the hospital and I was almost out of the business, but I came back and I learned my lesson to listen to those veterans. They know what they're talking about, so I want you to listen to me, and when I tell you the first thing we're going to do is learn how to land on our feet from the top rope, then the proper response is for you to jump up on the top rope."

Jake and North look at one another and shrug. Jake climbs up on the top rope in one of the corners. It's hard to stay balanced. With a grace surprising for his age, Lew jumps up on the middle rope and grabs Jake's right arm, tugs, and sends Jake to the mat with a loud thud.

"Ow!" Jake says, lying on the mat, his back spasming in pain.

"That," Lew says, pointing at Jake, "Is not how you want to fall from the top rope. Here is how you want to land."

Lew scoops up an orange cat lying down on the edge of the ring near the apron and sets it up on the top turnbuckle. The cat meows. "OK, Killer, show 'em how it's done," Lew says, then he picks the cat up by its belly and chucks him into the air where he tumbles tail over head.

Jake and North shoot out their hands in horror and almost look away--Jake notices in the midst of the tumble that the cat appears to have a very clean butthole and he wonders why his cats never have buttholes that clean--but somehow the cat lands on his feet on the mat, and appears to take a bow before running to Lew, who takes a treat out of his pocket and feeds it to the cat, while petting him. "Good Boy!" Lew says.

"OK, your turn," Lew points at North. North gulps.

When Jake and North leave later that evening, they now know the human body can experience such pain and still live. They shuffle out bentover to the car, and North says, "Dude, that is one crazy old man. How can he wrestle so well drunk?"

"I don't know, but when he started beating you with the lampshade, I thought we both were going to die. Are you going to come back?"

"Let's see if I can get out of bed tomorrow."

"Ha! I just hope I can get into bed tonight!"

"I'm just glad my bladder didn't explode."

"I think everything else did though. Why did we want to be wrestlers?"

"We're idiots."

"No, we're idiots covered in bruises and cat hair."

The Angry Housewife Finds A New Use For The Blender (14 April 2012)

A bit of easy listening orchestral music plays on <u>Grapple Groove</u>. The pleasant but mediocre sounds soon become laced with screams, which occasionally ungarble themselves into recognizable snatches of American English such as "I slaved over this dinner all day and you come home drunk!" and "Why don't you try staying home with the children, and see how 'easy' it is?"

Jake, watching on television, perks up his ears because the music means one of his favorite wrestlers, The Angry Housewife, is about to be in da house. Or, actually, out of the house and in the wrestling arena.

Wearing a blue apron and a scowl over her wrestling singlet, a woman with frazzled hair like a perm gone horribly, horribly wrong approaches the ring, pushing a vacuum cleaner and carrying a blender. On the way, she stops and scolds fans, who yell back at her. One young man gets his baseball hat turned on his head from back to front, "as it should be" according to The Angry Housewife. A young woman is told to tuck in her shirt and to next time wear a dress like "a proper young lady".

When The Housewife reaches the ring, her opponent, The Right Wing Blonde, who as of late has been on a libertarian slant, complains that The Housewife should let fans dress the way they want since that's freedom. The housewife stares blankly at her like she's just taken some tranquilizers to get through the afternoon.

The bell rings, and The Housewife snaps out of it, and fans are treated to some impressive distaff technical wrestling on the mat rather than the cheesecake portion of the program that they were perhaps expecting.

The anticipated dessert arrives however when The Housewife starts to choke The Right Wing Blonde with The Blonde's Barbara Bushesque pearl necklace, and tears off her blue Monica Lewinskyesque dress, complaining in the process that The Blonde wears her hemlines too high. The Blonde wears S&M leather underwear and is quite embarrassed at this turn of events, covering herself with her arms as best she can.

The referee, trying to be chivalrous, gets out of the ring to get her dress back which The Housewife has thrown out of the ring. While the ref's back is turned, The Housewife grabs the pitcher from her blender and whacks The Blonde over the back of the head with it. The cheap plastic shatters (if she had used glass she would have killed The Blonde so pardon her appliance faux pas), and The Blonde folds over like laundry fresh out of the dryer. The referee returns with the blue dress, but finding The Housewife pinning The Blonde, drops it and himself to the mat where he slaps his hand, counting 1-2-3.

As the ref raises The Angry Housewife's hand in victory, she points at her prone opponent and asks the ref to please take out the trash since her husband isn't here to do it. When he, confused, looks at her, she gets her vacuum cleaner and starts to vacuum her opponent until security makes her stop.

The Top Of The Bottom And The Bottom Of The Top (19 May 2012)

The tag team tournament for the vacant championship continues this week on Grapple Groove. The Pettifoggers have succeeded in getting entered into the tournament and wait in the ring for their surprise opponents: another last minute addition necessary for the orderly reconfiguration of the tournament. The entrance music starts in the arena, ushering in sounds of whipping, flogging, paddling, scratching, smacking, and other painful ings and things.

The crowd stands and cheers. It's the long-awaited return of Top And Bottom, everyone's favorite pair of bondage freaks. Out for a month after a serious nipple clamp injury occurred to Bottom during an erotic asphyxiation incident, the team likes to wear black leather, chains, clamps, and other things that would seem to make everyday activities such as walking difficult, let alone wrestling. They come down the entrance ramp with Bottom in front on all fours being walked with a leash around his neck by Top, who occasionally smacks Bottom on his bottom with a paddle when he stops too long to get affectionately slapped by a fan on the side of the ramp.

In the ring, The Pettifoggers put their hands on their heads in disgust. No one likes to wrestle an opponent who enjoys pain. Victor Verdict picks up a microphone and points at Bottom, "Objection! Is that man medically cleared to return to the ring? I don't want to have any liability issues later on."

Bottom pulls the ball gag out of his mouth as he stands up and gives the referee a piece of paper he had been holding in his mouth. The referee unfolds it with disgust.

Felix Fatality, the television announcer, says to his partner Steve Dore, "Steve, I prefer to keep my medical documents in a file folder myself."

"Well, Felix, Top And Bottom are a different breed," Steve says.

"Speaking of different breed, do you remember that tag team from the eighties called The New Breed?"

"I don't, Felix, that was a bit before my time."

"I just was wondering what happened to them because if they were still around, they'd be The Old Breed now."

"A punch drunk moment, eh? Well, nothing new stays new forever, Felix. Speaking of which, the action in the ring has begun. Stuart Subpoena is punching Bottom, and Bottom appears to be enjoying it."

"Well, only so much. Now, Bottom wants to tag out, but Top is refusing to tag him."

"Those two have an odd working relationship. They are an unorthodox tag team to say the least."

"Didn't they use to wrestle in pornographic movies?"

"Yes, that's indeed how they started."

"I watched one the other night in my hotel room."

"Really, Felix?"

"Well, you know, there's not a lot else to do in Omaha on a Thursday. That's a fine town though, no disrespect intended. But, also, I had heard Top And Bottom were coming back and wanted a look at their earlier work."

"How was their performance?"

"It was fine, but . . . well, let's put it this way, Steve, there were unusual stipulations in the match of the nature that you won't even see in a hardcore match here."

"It's a different kind of hardcore. Speaking of hardcore tag team wrestling. Vic Verdict had just put Bottom in a submission maneuver, and Top made a blind tag."

"Well, Bottom's a submissive, right? Top was probably afraid he would tap out."

"Well, that and he had left the poor guy in there for the entire match. That's not your usual strategy in tag team wrestling. That's more like a handicap match."

"Speaking of handicaps, what is Top wearing into the ring? Is that what I think it is?"

"That is what you think it is. Vic Verdict is running away. The referee's spotted it too, and he's calling for the bell."

"It looks like Top And Bottom are being disqualified. Can I even say what for?"

"If they're showing it, then you can say it. I didn't know this either folks because . . ." Steve coughs, ". . . it's never come up as an issue before tonight, but apparently you can't wear a strap-on dildo into the ring because it qualifies as an illegal foreign object."

Watching at home, Jake realizes that the ratings must be down because when the ratings dip for Grapple Groove, the raunch goes up.

On Seeing a Particularly Wacky Bumper Sticker

Driving home on La Canada Drive
I saw a bumper sticker that said
"Just Say No to Barry O,"
and I thought, well, that's mean.
Barry O was the stage name of
pro wrestler Barry Orton, brother
of "Cowboy" Bob Orton, and
uncle of Randy Orton.
Barry was a preliminary wrestler,
what my father used to call "dog meat,"
unlike his brother, perhaps because
he refused to perform sexual favors
on World Wrestling Federation
higher-ups, ergo the wrestling
sex scandals of the early 90s.
Then I thought, well, Bob Orton
wasn't a prelim guy, he had
success in the WWF, did he
play ball with these guys?
Then I thought, hey, you wanna
get yourself sued? But how can
I be sued for my thoughts?

So this sticker was pretty mean
because "no" was what the higher-ups
said to Barry O when he wouldn't
do nasty things for them.
The next morning I Googled
"Just Say No to Barry O"
and found that Barry O is actually
Barack Obama.
So, of course this was a
conservative bumper sticker.

They love rhymes, those conservatives.
If Bush had been a Democrat,
I could have seen
"Say 'Kiss My Tush' to GW Bush"
stickers and T-shirts everywhere.
Then, I thought, well,
I did kind of say no to Barry O
because I didn't vote for him,
which doesn't make me a racist,
does it? You'll say it makes me
a racist if you're a liberal because
liberals love calling people racist
even more than conservatives
love political rhymes and more

than Barry O probably hates WWE
even though his nephew has been
one of their top stars for years.

Man Wearing Zubaz

I saw a man wearing Zubaz in Vegas.
They were green and gold, like a leprechaun
protecting his treasure or a box of Lucky Charms.
He didn't look like a weightlifter or a wrestler,
who are the only people I've ever seen in Zubaz,
but even then it was twenty years ago.

He was holding a bunch of those hooker baseball cards
the Mexicans give out on the Strip with a slap of their hand,
which he probably picked up off the ground,
because littering is twice as bad when it's smut like that
and the Mexicans won't give you but one or two cards.

I saw a woman wearing an Ultimate Warrior jacket
at a Hannaford supermarket in Leominster, Massachusetts.
She was buying Drumsticks and Diet Dr. Pepper,
and sporting blue sweatpants and white Converse sneakers.

She was standing behind me and I kept looking back at her
because I wanted that jacket, and how cool would it be
to wear the jacket of the guy who beat the Honky Tonk Man
for the Intercontinental Title in thirty seconds back in '88,
and then beat Hulk Hogan cleanly two years later?
It would go great with my Jake "the Snake" Roberts boots
that don't fit me anymore and that I wore just four times in high school.

I thought Warrior Jacket Lady should meet Zubaz Guy somewhere
for coffee or maybe a hot dog at a high school gymnasium
where local wrestlers and 80s legends can entertain them,
but I didn't know where Mr. Zubaz was from or if there's a Mrs. Zubaz.
Perhaps they live in Oakland, where the baseball team's colors are
green and gold like his pants, and their kids probably wear
silver and black ones to show their love of the Raiders.

And maybe Warrior Jacket Lady has a Warrior Jacket Man
who was watching old Coliseum Video wrestling tapes and
gave her twenty bucks to go to the store and get him some
ice cream and soda because he's on the wagon, and he would
go but he's depressed because wrestling isn't what it used to be
and so many of them have died and that's why they wear the jackets.

A Haiku for all the Russian Wrestlers of the 80s

Half the Russian wrestlers
I booed as a child
were from Minnesota.

BOBBY MAC ISN'T GONNA GO OVER by Kelly Froh

The Promoter

It happened July 2008. I did something I had set out to do and had worked on for just about a year. I put on the first ever *Rock n Roll/Pro-Wrestling/Poetry* reading event...and nobody came.

Well not nobody, most of my friends are quick to remind me if they were there or not whenever the subject is brought up. It's a painful lesson made all the more painful because it was done completely out of love. Isn't that strange? I just loved the idea of something so...wacky happening in my city. It was, in my mind, the sort of thing that could only happen in Milwaukee. And only in Milwaukee, my friends are quick to say, would nobody show up. That's not fair of course. I was a poor promoter and not a bright one either. I ran the show against one of the city's 350 Gallery nights, a Trusty Knife show, and (someone told me) a hipster wedding. I ran it in a college area during the middle of summer during a recession. I am not smart. I obviously watch pro-wrestling.

All bitterness and masochism aside the event still makes for a great story, one I thought I'd share in addition to the DVD of the event and the *American Movie* style documentary my friend Gabe Spangler is responsible for (both these efforts).

I slept a light sleep. All week I had been having nightmares of an empty Miramar with me standing in the middle of the ring looking at empty seats. To say that these kept me up does no justice to my frequent bouts of insomnia, still they were worrisome. I had managed to get enough sleep but woke up that Friday trying to figure out if I was still dreaming. I was putting on *my show!* I had spent the last few days posting a handful of flyers in what I later deemed to be unmemorable places and folding and stapling by hand two hundred copies of *The Dead Wrestler Sonnets*. The plan for months had been to print out Karl Saffran's poems about dead wrestlers that Karl liked when he was a kid and a handful of my poems about wrestling. In the end I chickened out on mine because they were so obviously written by a hack mark there wasn't any chance anyone could read them without cringing. Karl's on the other hand were exactly what they needed to be: funny, slightly critical, and a little bit gay. They also had a touching side where the melancholy of discovering some figure from your childhood that you hadn't thought about lately but made you smile to do so winds up overdosing in their 40's. Mine weren't like that. They didn't even mention death. So I gave myself the axe. It wasn't the first time. I didn't include myself in the Burdock issue for Jim Hazard because nothing I had to say seemed to make a dent when I reread it.

My hands were still recovering from the folding action; such is the life of a book-maker. I stuffed all the copies into my sharp looking gym bag and dressed for action. I threw on my Lakefront Brewery T-Shirt that I had received after they agreed to donate a barrel to help pay for the show. It wasn't much and everyone who was involved in wrestling that I had talked to kept repeating that I should get sponsors. I figured it must be easier to do when you are a straight up wrestling promoter but as soon as you mention Poetry to a beer vendor they look at your pants to see if you remembered to zip up. Music, like Heavy Metal, that makes sense, even the noise band gets a walk but the poetry angle, that's a bit too weird for anyone to respond to an email or take a phone call on. Walking over to Lakefront in person worked though, even though I showed up looking the way I do with a patchy blonde beard and snarly matted down hair. Did I mention I have a leather jacket? That didn't have the effect I had hoped for at first, but it did get me referred to Orlando by Russ the president. These are good people I decided. They make good beer and are going to sponsor me. I asked if they had any shirts I could wear to return the favor. Orlando gave me a white T and a black polo work shirt. "The blood will show up on the white one better." I agreed with him but it didn't register that it might be my blood.

Walking from the house on Kane Place towards the Miramar got me thinking on everything that lead up to this.

The show had been called off until further notice. I just didn't have the money in 2007 mostly because I was never able to keep a steady job. Note: English Majors are not in demand, ever. Oh sure, we may rule the world secretly with our effective use of language and subtle plot devices but it doesn't pay. Toward the end of the year I managed to get work as a stage hand at the Bradley Center. It was as one of the black shirted peons I had my biggest mark out moment as a fan: setting up the ring and stage for the WWE. I stood next to Triple H like before and after photos, ate lunch with Bob Holly and Beth Phoenix gave me a glance as if to say "I could eat you." All this mind you was done in silence, stagehands are absolutely forbidden to speak to talent. The Beth Phoenix thing was real though damn it!

I worked a few more shows before the first big tragedy of 2008. I was on the lighting crew piecing together giant light cubes for the Hannah Montana concert of all things when I felt a twinge in my back. Nothing serious, I reported it, but played it off. I went home to lie down but when I tried to get up for the load out I could barely stand. Over the next few days the pain became unbearable in my back and down my leg. After some minor drama I managed to get on worker's comp and get an MRI done. I learned that I had slipped a few discs and had an extrusion in one with an annular tear. That tear was leaking the fluid that makes the disc nice and cushy for my spine. The fluid leaked onto my sciatic nerve sending searing constant pain down my leg. It felt as if someone struck a match to my bones.

I lay in bed for weeks on end in between visits to a fetching physical therapist named Gretchen. I wasn't even really able to limp right until just after mid February. I had stopped in the Cathedral after a therapy session looking to be absolved but unable to find my way in the darkness of St. John's. I sat in a pew near the door. I didn't pray for my show. It was far from my mind at the time.

I didn't work again until April. I have the purple Van Halen local crew T-shirt to prove I did make it back to fully functional status. But I was always a little scared after that. You don't forget that kind of pain. Not working but getting a workman's comp check and not eating much I managed to squirrel away a neat little nest egg. Now, with that money, I could have done a few things. I could have used it to pay for applications to graduate schools or I could have paid off my old Columbia house debt (yeah right) or could have cooked dinner for all my friends. Could have been drunk for weeks. All those things I could have done but instead in March I called up the Miramar and reserved the date of July 25th, 2008. Are you able to offer a down payment? Why, yes I am. And so, come July, as I hot-stepped up Oakland I had my mind on my money and my money on my mind. But every third step I thought about my Grandpa.

David Anthony DeMars was born on June 13th 1921. As a boy he used to make moonshine with his mother until one day there was a gas leak in the house from the still which was hooked up to the stove. He had to drag his mom out of the house to the porch where he said to her it's time to stop. A few days later the cops showed up to raid the house but found everything dry. His father died when he was young and so he became the man of the house with his brother and sister. He married his cousin related by adoption, or so I'm told, this way we're off the hook but just in case I must remind the court he has a French last name. He was drafted in WWII and was on the boat over to Japan when the bombs were dropped. He was a mechanic and would not have been directly under fire but you never know what could happen in war, I tell people, it just might be I'm here because of a Fat Man and a Little Boy. His wife, my Grandma, Irene, passed away just after I graduated High School. He had been living alone for 9 years. When I had a car I used to drive to visit my family in Slinger and always tried to include a stop on Buchanan Street, the street of my childhood.

When he was by himself he would often just sit and watch TV or read one of his western paperbacks, the Park Falls Herald or maybe a biography on Eisenhower. These things we brought to him in the nursing home, I baked him a dacci or Dougen (*doe-jen*) and told him about the great day I had at the ballpark, Ryan Braun bobble head day and Dairy board day with free milk, ice cream and cheese curds. He smiled at the thought of cheese curds. That was the last memory I have of him.

These things I thought of as I marched off to lose my ass in an ill-conceived merger of Poetry and Wrestling.

Finally there, I met Bill, the man in charge at the Miramar. A professional promoter who immediately told me about a great way to make extra money that involved clicking on ads for hours at a time online. I explained that I didn't have a computer at home that could handle the internet, just a glorified typewriter. And since as of the show I was once again unemployed I had to spend my time at the Library looking for jobs. Jobs I wouldn't get and wouldn't even hear back from after applying.

But I figured out pretty quick that Bill was a nice guy, he did after all think my show was a great idea, weird, but a great idea. It was just the sort of far out stuff nobody tried anymore. After he said this I recalled how a few nights prior I went with my friends Chris and Shane to a show at Vnuck's lounge: The Luchagores, a band fronted by former WWE wrestler, Lita, a pretty looking woman who reminded me in person of a grown up, tightly constructed, version of Punky Brewster. Her band didn't draw many people at ten dollars a head but it did draw a few guys who were putting on a show in September called Mondo Lucha. Their show did all the things mine did and more: they were gonna have women there, burlesque and roller-derby flavors. They were giving all the wrestlers masks and lucha gimmicks. They only had one band though and they didn't have a poet. They were doomed to success.

Lance Stansky owns a wrestling ring. One night a few years ago I went to an AWA-BCW show alone and with only 5 bucks. It was $15 at the door. I offered to help tear down the ring, maybe I'd even train to be a wrestler (this was before my back died, obviously) if they'd just please let me sit there and watch the fat guys pretend to punch each other. I was introduced to Lance, a barrel-chested guy with glasses and Harley Race facial hair, that's mutton chops into a moustache for you non-marks. At that time I had short hair and no beard, I looked like a big soft college kid who didn't make the team. He looked at me and asked if I was in college, yes.

"What do you study?"

"I settled on English, finally."

"You gonna be writer?"

"I think so, I write, but writers get paid. I'm told that's the difference."

"You should write a book about me. Man, I got so many stories."

And just like that we hit it off. On occasion, back when I had a car (what a life that was!) I'd drive out to Waukesha to help tear down the ring. If I had ever been able to get out for set up there was a chance I could learn a thing or two from one of the wrestlers. Jose El Vato Guerrero had once offered to train me but I dragged my feet on it after I had to give up Judo due to injury. I'm not made of glass or anything but I have found out over time exactly why it is I'm not an athlete. The list is long and starts with asthma and ends with X-rays.

Lance even let me into shows as a member of the ring crew making me his charge rather than any of the promoters. I didn't get a ring crew shirt though so when I worked the biggest Indy show in Milwaukee, Blizzard Brawl, I made sure to stick close to him and the rest of the crew. At one of these shows is how I first met the best local ref, named Billy Oates, a great stage name for a ref. Through these various connections I managed to get a respectable looking roster for my little show along with some help from Frank DeFalco at BCW whose name lent either an air of credibility or whatever the opposite of that is depending upon who I spoke to. It's tough being a promoter. Thankfully, I thought, I'm just doing one show.

We started setting up the ring at three and were wrapping it up by five in the afternoon when the bands and wrestlers started showing up. I ran around like a chicken with my head cut off trying to get things in order. One of the wrestlers had contacted me earlier saying he was sick and that I should get a replacement. He said he had a 100 degrees plus fever and couldn't make it. The same shit happened about a week before with the bands. I had a band then I had no bands, save IfIhadaHiFi. Through them and the drummer from the cancellation I was able to get two more bands to commit to the show. The opener would be Put Her in the Trunk, a metal band, then Leopold & Loeb, a loud Pop band sounding like b-sides from The Who. HiFi would close the show by playing during the battle royal.

The Wrestlers were shifting though. First Bobby Valentino had cancelled do to illness and Playboy Troy just wasn't going to come on his own since he booked through Dysfunction at ICW. So I had Jason Parxxx, or J.P., coming instead. JP had called me earlier to say if I needed any alternates he had them. JP was enthusiastic about the show and so when I called to say Bobby couldn't make it he immediately called Brandon Haze and basically booked his own match since, I later found out, none of the ICW boys wanted to work with him at the time. Oh shit, I'm in deep with a bunch of wrestlers whose drama, whose real drama, I know nothing of! I shrugged it off and plowed ahead.

What do you think happened then? Bobby shows up with Troy! Troy, in my opinion and in the opinion of other local fans, is a really good young hand. How about that, I called him a hand, I can do that because I'm a promoter, duh. SO I have Bobby and Troy, JP and Jason Hades, El Vato, Jason Dukes, The McCoys, and Chris Black and T.C. Washington (the Urban Horsemen at my show, Keepin' It Gangsta at most others).

Gabe, my filmmaker, was freaking out about lighting and sound, a true director. Meanwhile I realized it was 6 of the clock and I had not eaten at all yet that day, nervousness and lack of time had gotten in the way. My buddy Nick was there with a pizza from across the street and he let me have a few slices and a Mickey's to wash it down. I took it figuring I needed to calm down with some malt liquor. It didn't do anything except make we want another. No time for that shit though I gotta book the matches!

JP and his man Haze was the first match. That was easy. But what to do with Troy? I liked the kid a lot and thought he could do some great shit here, I'd seen him do great shit at ICW but who would be his opponent? Nearly everyone else asked to work him and it racked my brain, but I knew that since at the time of the show The McCoys were tag champs at ICW and The Urban Horsemen were champs at BCW it was only natural to have them work each other. I had already planned to do it with a DQ finish so as not to create any animosity toward me from either promoter. I knew I was treading thin ice when I posted a thread on a local message board about Champion vs. Champion and one of the promoters response was simply "uhhhh...."

But he can relax, I told myself, I'm no dummy. I know how to book a champions vs. champions match between two baby face teams. I knew how, but nobody else did.

If you were walking past Atomic Records (RIP) and went down the alley off Locust at about 6 pm Friday July 25th you would have seen me in a heated discussion with several wrestlers, some in tights, debating the appropriateness of a DQ finish between two face teams. "End with a run in from the other teams," I said.

Nobody heard me. Nobody was hearing me. I towered over most of them so perhaps I needed to talk down to them? No, I wasn't going to go that route. After all I hired these guys, I respect them, and they will listen eventually. Not to me but to one of the other wrestlers.

Jason Dukes looks like a shorter Playboy Buddy Rose. Judging by his Myspace he does this on purpose. When I first went to shows I gave him so much shit. He was heel and he looked out of shape. Like an asshole I continued to give him shit, even booked as a babyface, it wasn't until I saw him work against Tiger Mask that I understood the effort he put in. I didn't think the match was the best thing I'd ever seen Tiger Mask in, I mean the guy's wrestled Jushin Thunder Fucking Liger! Yet, here was this guy in the Midwest putting on a solid match and keeping up with him. I became a fan of his then. I became a bigger fan of his when he quieted everyone down by saying to the wrestlers:

"Who's your promoter? He is. He's paying you; you do what he wants you to do. That's what being a *professional* means."

Thoroughly professional. We all calmed down after a little while, even laughing at Bobby Valentino's chest. To make his gimmick work he had a habit of shaving his chest but he had neglected to do so for a while and the hair was beginning to sprout again. It looked like someone had sprinkled pepper on him during a tanning session as if to add flavor to the boy.

Everyone seemed to relax a bit but I didn't do myself any favors by saying it's not important how these matches end, I just want everyone to have fun. Fun is not professional, I guess. Still they agreed that it should be DQ but the Urban Horsemen insisted on working as heels with the heel team of Troy and Bobby doing the run in. They in turn would run in on the other tag match, which would lead me to come out and declare a battle royal.

Okay, got that?

Good.

Meanwhile it's seven and the joint is empty. Where are my lines around the block? I didn't really think I'd pack the place, I make a point of selling myself short in all matters so not selling out wasn't going to offend me, but empty? Really? Nobody wants to see Music, Wrestling, and Poetry converge? No dumbass, it was a bad idea. How am I gonna pay for everything? Idiot, they said get sponsors. Oh yeah, that's right. Shit.

So we waited till 8. Everyone hated me for not starting, the bands were antsy, the wrestlers wanted free drinks, and the poet, Karl, was getting nervously drunk. Then my favorite moment happened. One of the wrestlers found me and pulled me aside.

"Look, I'm not telling you this like a threat but the house looks bad tonight."

"Yeah, I know, wait. What?"

"It's just I've seen some shit. If the boys don't get paid, I'm not saying me, but some of the boys, they'll fuck you up."

"Everyone's getting paid, don't worry." I said calmly.

"Yeah, with what?" I heard antagonism. Maybe it was the heat of July, the Miramar starting to become an oven, but I heard a challenge being issued in the alley behind the venue.

"Who's gonna beat me up?" I said arrogantly.

"I'm just saying it's not going to be me, but some of the other guys."

"Nobody's gonna beat me up! You'll get your money."

"80 right?"

What? No. I had distinctly remembered him offering to work for 75.

"No, 75."

"What the FUCK! Everyone else is getting more and we're going to work two matches for less money!"

A tag and a battle royal, no hardcore shit, I thought, no iron man contests. But I didn't care, at this point.

"Alright, fine! Five bucks isn't gonna break me anymore than I'm already being broke. But listen, you said 75."

"No I didn't."

"Yes you did. Calm down and hear me. You're getting 80 but just so you know you said 75 to me back at ICW when I first approached you."

"Alright." He smiled. Was it out of victory or was I actually getting through?

"And as far as that other shit goes don't threaten me—"

"I'm not! I'm just tellin' ya!"

"Don't threaten me. And if anyone really wants to throw down for fun I'll do it and if anyone tries to jump me —"

"I'm *not!* I'm just letting you know, I've seen some shit!"

"But you still want that five bucks." It occurred to me that he may just be trying to tell me but it's not something I needed to be told: Pay your employees.

Finally the first band went on and the show went on. I barely remember what all happened but thankfully there is a DVD of it somewhere to help me recall how I participated on stage. Backstage, however, was where the story was.

I was told, not threatened, by at least two other guys about what happens if you don't pay the wrestlers. My response was "get in line." The bands and the poet weren't getting paid either. This was fun for them, but then the money is what makes you a professional, even if it's a couple of twenties, the point is you have the dignity of getting paid for your work. Poets don't often get that privilege (makes me appreciate poet's Monday at Linneman's all the more) and bands are lucky to get gas money back from tours, unless of course they are Hannah Montana. People have broken their backs for that underage floozy!

At intermission I went to get the little bit of gate money that we had, it was all going to the wrestlers but it wasn't enough. I told Nick we'd have to drive to my bank a few blocks away to make a withdrawal. I pulled out 200 bucks, overdrawing by 37 dollars, fucking myself over. What stupid fucking shit! Dumb motherfucker, why didn't you get sponsors? Why didn't you put out more posters? Did you think people would actually read the Onion and come to your show based on that? Okay, common sense, you are in control now, you have no money and people want to kick your ass. I had already voted for Obama in the primaries but I knew how he was going to feel should he win. Hawaiian babies with single Midwest mothers, we are so cool!

Getting back in time to shove Karl into the ring for a great reading, if controversial, I felt not so much safe as potentially respectable. I was going to pay all these wrestlers the money they wanted. Not the bands, except HiFi, I had to give back the twenty I borrowed to start the bank. Oh Shit. Lance.

What makes him drive from Shawno the five hours to Milwaukee to sweat it out in a theatre on the East Side? I don't know but I bet he'll never do it again!

What made Karl's poems controversial was all after the fact. Some local wrestlers felt the whole thing as disrespectful to their business. Most of the criticism came from wrestlers who were not on the card. In fact the mood backstage among the guys working the show was positive. Many sat there laughing at the poems they had picked up in advance. Mickey McCoy at one point turned to his tag partner Chase and pointed out that the wrestler referenced in the poem about Dino Bravo, the one he beat by count out, was Bret Hart, Mickey's favorite wrestler. T.C. was laughing at the Dino Bravo poem, even reciting the line to the locker room. "Nobody gave a shit about Dino Bravo," he said chuckling. It may have been the most *over* Dino had been in a long time.

T.C. Washington may be short on stature, the phrase might start out in a real pro-wrestling article, I'd finish with: but he still wrestles for shit pay with a broken thumb! El Vato and Dukes formed the impromptu tag team of the East West Texas Connection to face Playboy Troy and Bobby V AKA: The Tough Customers. When T.C. and Chris interfered payback for their match being messed up it lead to yet another DQ and me calling for a battle royal. If you look on the DVD you can see an un-amused Ed Schumann scoping out the place. I can't imagine what made him decide against running there.

Okay, battle royal time. Hifi, You ready? No? You had like an hour to get ready. Oh well, fuck it, let's go. Shane "Hot Dog" Heyward, you wanted to be in a wrestling match. So in we jumped and as soon as we get in the ring Shane decks me, hard. He doesn't just deck me he follows me down, mounts me, and rains down punches. Thud! Thud! Thud! My head is being dribbled off the canvass like a basketball. Get off me fucker! I try to push him off but he's over 200 pounds and suddenly I think, that pizza didn't last very long.

Finally somehow he gets off me. I'm sick and dizzy from the blows. Shane admitted later to safely punching the back of his hand while it was on my head.

"I didn't hit you once."

"No, but have you ever played croquet?" I then delivered one of his patented perfectly safe punches to his head.

"OW! Oh, I'm sorry dude." It's okay, Shane, it looks good on the DVD.

Back in the ring I get my revenge by tossing him out. I then lean on the top rope waiting for someone to clothesline me over. All my hair is in my face and I'm worn out from heat, setting up, head banging, and overdrawing at the bank — somebody please clothesline me!

Nothing. I stumble and collapse in the middle of the ring where Chris Black sees me, picks me up, and tries to toss me over the ropes. But I'm too tired and I can't see my feet through all my hair. I don't know where I am in the ring so I try to jump. Too early, I smack my face into the ropes. OW! Did I break my nose? Did I remember to take my glasses off? I don't know. Oh God. What a dumb asshole. Stupid shithead. Get up! I can't get up though. I put my hands under my chest to push up, nothing. My strength is gone. Now I'm scared.

Suddenly I'm being rolled over, someone's cradling my head. A paramedic? Why is he punching me? "Ya gotta bleed! Ya gotta bleed!" All I can see is a brown chest and fists. My nose isn't broken because it seems to be holding up under the punches. I had told El Vato that I had thought about blading for the camera. He discouraged me in the dressing room. "Don't worry," I told him, "I don't even know how and I don't have a blade." But I had a ring rope. And now I had a crimson trickle down the right side of my nose. The cameras never picked it up and nobody noticed it later either until I told them. I think nobody wanted to look me in the face that night.

Somebody tossed me out, one of the McCoys, I think. I didn't know what happened but, as HiFi played on I paid off the boys. I can say that because I'm the promoter. I even made a loud comment that anyone who wants to meet me in the alley can expect me in an hour or two. Luckily, I found my glasses on a table behind the stage curtain. I left them there when I went to make the battle royal announcement. I was as depressed as could be. I still owed the Miramar hall rental. Kenny the head security had been cool all night. When word got to him about wrestlers wanting to beat me up he said he had my back, "Don't even worry about it, man, I think you'd kick all they asses."

"Yeah but are *you* gonna kick my ass?"

"Man, don't even worry about it, talk to Bill you can work something out."

Sure enough I talked to Bill and offered my services. Luckily being 6'4" I at least look the part and I know I can take a beating. Dishing it out and getting people to respect my authority is another thing. I was able to work off that debt. I don't think it's the sort of thing that happens very often but Bill and his wife Pam are good people. Pam felt so bad for me the first night I stopped by to help and I couldn't shake the sulk of my face she gave me a hug.

Lance and his crew started tearing down the ring, he wouldn't get home until 4 or 5 in the morning, and luckily he had his son Shane and his pal Tommy along. I gave them Lakefront Brewery shirts and apologized to Lance. And just like in the dream he gave me a walrus hug and said it would be alright. I helped as best I could with the ring but most of my strength was gone. I carried the boards and some of the frame but I left the posts for Lance's son. "Watch this," I told Karl as the 14 year old kid walked in and casually grabbed a ring post and walked out. "That's a Northwoods boy," I said to Karl to whom that sort of thing is meaningless.

"Lance, I'm just so sorry you drove all this way for nothing."

"Don't worry about it." If he was pissed he was the best actor of the year, "You'll pay me back someday. Hey, let's write that book, huh?"

"Sure, Lance. Just let me know."

I got to the after party. Which was only slightly less well attended than the actual show.

"You did it!" Everyone said.

Did what? I thought, and sometimes said, in between gulps out of a pitcher of water. I deposited my sweaty exhausted fat body onto a couch and took to warding off the early stages of dehydration. My head was pounding and I was nauseous. My arms felt like they'd float away. I was broke, no, in debt, not that fake ass credit card debt either: I owed real people money.

"This footage is gonna rule." I hear Gabe saying to the rest of the posse as they toast High Lifes. I could be anywhere else. I could have spent that money on a plane ticket to anywhere. Nope. I tried to have my show. Not even a real stroke of the ego either, all I did in public was get beat up and tossed around. They (the movie industry) just released *The Wrestler*. I haven't seen it yet, don't have the cash. The Onion says it's "The Passion of the Christ" for wrestling fans. I assume that means nobody will read my book then either.

MICHAEL D. GOSCINSKI

the "song and dance man"

a trailblazer
long before
hogan was hollywood
or the rock
was cookin'
the inter-gender champion
of the world
manhandled
a 327 pound woman
took on the king
in the redneck capitol
showed all of memphis
how to use a bar of soap
he didn't need
to juice up
shave his body hair
or sport the ball-kini
while showing
his lack of vocabulary
on the microphone
he was a true performer
a "song and dance man"
sadly
unknown by this generation
the greatest wrassler of all time
andy kaufman
the man who brought the show
to the business

after the lights burn out

the letters have all stopped
along with the parties
and the pussy
no longer do they chant my name
or boo me
no longer do they ask for autographs
or even recognize me
i am now approached with indifference
the limos escort others
others who still have firm skin
and bulging pecs
others whose joints aren't swollen
and have pretty faces for the camera
others who put asses in seats
and sell shirts and caps
i'm spent
used
forgotten
thrown away
with nothing left
nothing left but scars
no money
no fame
no voice
no more bright lights
they have all burned out

a true champion

21 weeks
together in a house
legends of the squared circle
warriors of the ring
some "has beens"
some "never weres"
careers over
they reminisced on the good ol' days
honked at geese with busey
argued like children
danced as chippendales
and on the last night
opened up
shared dark secrets
of drugs
alcohol
and homelessness
then
one of the legends spoke
54 years he survived the industry
secretly gay
for once
there was no bravado
arrogance
or show
it was all real
and i
was looking
at a true champion

Florida Championship Wrastlin'

My friend & I used to wrestle in the front yard
Mimicking wrestlers we would see Saturday mornings
Or read about in Pro Wrestling Illustrated

My father noticing this interest
Would load up his old Volkswagen van
With the neighborhood kids
& drive us to the West Palm Beach Auditorium
To Florida Championship Wrastlin'
Before the show the fans would be
Hanging over the railings
Cheering or booing as the wrastlers
Walked in through a tunnel below

Inside the air was electric
There was The Magnificent Muraco
That would spit out into the crowd
Every time he got punched
& he got punched a lot
The crowd hated him
They would scream and spit back
There were the redneck villains
Dick Murdock, Dick Slater,
Worse of all The Funk Brothers
Terry & Dory Jr.
Then there was the hero
The main event
The American Dream Dusty Rhodes
Dusty would take a beating
He was a bleeder, he would bleed just about every match
Not like today's PG entertainment

I remember once at the auditorium
Dusty was getting beat down

By his arch rivals The Funk Brothers
They had a bullrope & Dusty was bleeding bad
The redneck villain always brought a bullrope
One old man in the front row
Got so pissed off
That he picked up the metal folding chair
That he was sitting on
& threw it in the ring to help Dusty
He was escorted out of the building by security

Then one day things changed
No more Funks, No more Dusty
Magnificent Muraco was there
But he didn't spit out into the crowd anymore
New heroes like Hulk Hogan
New villains like Andre The Giant
No Saturday morning Florida Championship Wrastlin'
Replaced by WWF
Wrastlin' died a little

The Black Eagle of Harlem

First there is Henry James
Literary man
Who wrote a stack of thick books
Deep thoughts
Buried inside them

Then there is Hank James
Professional wrestler
AKA "Hoodoo Hank James"
"Hurricane Hank James"
"The Black Eagle of Harlem"
And in another incarnation
"The Money Man"
Under whose guise
He would wave
A flag of $100 bills
Into the exasperated face
Of Lord Athol Layton
Host of Big Time Wrestling
While trumpeting the mayhem
He would inflict upon
His next opponent

To impress you
I long to say
That Henry James
Literary man
Taught me
More about the ways
Of the world
Than Hank James
Professional wrestler
But that would not be true

I never understood
Most of what Henry James
Was trying to get at
While Hank James
Big money tight in his talons
As off the top rope he flew
Taught me simple truths
About this world
Of blood, sweat and melodrama
That Henry James
Couldn't seem to get
A grip on

Lord Layton, the Slave Girl and Dr. Jerry Graham

"Being bad pays off big!"

That's what the wise Doctor of Philosophy
Jerry Graham said to Lord Athol Layton
On the TV show Big Time Wrestling

When I was a kid I lived to watch
Dr. Jerry, Dick the Bruiser and The Sheik
Beat the crap out of just about everybody

The Sheik, in that epoch accompanied
By The Slave Girl who handed him
His prayer rug and handled his headpiece
With reverential care, would holler
At The Slave Girl in some unintelligible language
While she cowered in trepidation

Lord Layton, gentleman scholar and protector
Of all women and children
Especially beautiful slave girls
Would take The Slave Girl aside
And try to talk sense into her
Telling her that if she left
The terrible clutches of The Sheik
He would do whatever he could
To nurture and sustain her

The Slave Girl never seemed to understand
What Lord Layton was talking about

But Dr. Jerry Graham always knew the score

When his turn to wrestle finally came
Just after a troop of Boy Scouts

Paid a visit to the show
And were saluted by Lord Layton
For their good citizenship, modesty and sobriety
Dr. Jerry smiled at the Lord
And pointed a stubby finger
At the troop of Boy Scouts

"Okay kiddies, if you want a body like mine
Here is an exercise you must do
Every single day"

Dr. Jerry thrust out his huge belly
And sneering at the camera
Extended his big arms and proceeded to do curls
With the baby fingers of both his hands

Lord Layton was outraged

But later
When Dr. Jerry would not stop battering
His helpless opponent
Lord Layton felt compelled
Despite his suit and tie
To enter the ring and attempt to pull
The maniacal doctor away

Dr. Jerry turned from the opponent
And gripped Lord Layton's throat
Digging his strong thumbs deep into the Lord
And throwing all his weight
Into forcing Layton back into the corner turnbuckle
To choke him relentlessly

It looked like all hope was lost
For the valiant Lord Layton

Until six wrestlers
Some of them in street clothes
Suddenly emerged from the dressing room
And with great effort pulled Dr. Jerry
Off Lord Layton
Slowly dragging him down off the apron

Dr. Jerry Graham grimaced like a beast
Straight into the camera
Until the very last moment
Of television exposure
After which I suppose he took a shower
Put on his suit and tie
Drove to his quaint suburban home
Repaired to the knotty pine den
And, sipping a martini, resumed
Scribbling notes for a monograph
About the life and times
Of Jean-Jacques Rousseau
Immanuel Kant
Or perhaps Friedrich Nietzsche

Mr. Wonderful Teaches the Capstone Seminar at Wrestling School

We can't always know for certain whether we are heel or face.
We are not all born with a nickname on the ass of our tights.
Not all of us had a father so eager to toughen us up.

Today's prompt is to write about the night I battled Hogan in the cage.
Appeal to the senses. Make your reader believe. Call it "The Unbearable
_____ of _____."

> *When you lose, it's scripted.*
> *When you win, it's something else.*
> *It's a feud when both sides deal from the bottom of the same deck.*

By this point you should know what you want to achieve.
By this point you should have fallen in love
with someone you do not deserve.

This is not an elegy. I am not dead. Change your name if you want
but be sure to choose something you will remember.

The Squared Circle Shoots on Over the Edge '99

Humans, under their flesh
and fat, are only bone.
In that way, I am
plywood and steel.

There never could have
been enough padding beneath
my canvas or inside
my turnbuckle covers or wrapped
around my ropes for me
to catch brother Owen

even if his harness didn't drop him
where my skin was thinnest,
where I had so little to cushion.

150

153

154

The Manly Arts (or What I've Learned About Being a Man Watching Professional Wrestling)

They say adversity introduces a man to himself.[1] Hard times are when the auto workers are out of work and they tell them go home…when a man has worked at a job thirty years: they give him a watch, kick him in the butt and say a computer took your place, daddy—that's hard times.[2] I have endured a lot—abusive fathers, prison time, psychiatric treatment, and even a little bit of shock therapy.[3] I've been abused, I've been misunderstood by everybody in the United States.[4] Nobody knows what it's like, nobody but me, to go out there and stand in front of 22,000 people and feel the hate, feel everything come down right on top of me.[5] It seems like everybody wants to cripple me somehow; it seems like they want to treat me like some kind of animal.[6] You see all these old nasty cuts on my head, all these old big scars on my head?[7] I had eighteen stitches put in my head.[8] I've seen my ear thrown away in Munich, Germany, I've seen my skin hanging off of barbed wire in Japan and I've been bludgeoned in Nigeria.[9] We all know a universal truth—our differences lie in how we distort it.[10] Evil is just that: evil—and sometimes we mistake it for happiness.[11] Sometimes we suffer in silence, sometimes we seek redemption.[12] I may go down, but I'm going down in a blaze of glory, and I am going to take absolutely everybody I can with me.[13]

I don't shoot a lot of bull.[14] This has been my dream since I was nine years old and I think it totally

---

[1] Arn Anderson, *WCW Saturday Night* (1992).

[2] "The American Dream" Dusty Rhodes, NWA Mid-Atlantic Wrestling (1985).

[3] The Monster Abyss, *TNA Impact Wrestling* (2009).

[4] Adrian Adonis, "Piper's Pit" interview, *World Wrestling Federation* (1985).

[5] Magnificent Don Muraco, WWF Madison Square Garden Promo (1983).

[6] Jimmy "Superfly" Snuka, WWF Madison Square Garden Promo (1983).

[7] Bruiser Brody, *NWA World Championship Wrestling* (1983).

[8] Moondog Lonnie Mayne, *NWA Hollywood Wrestling* (1978).

[9] Mick Foley, *WWE Raw* (2004).

[10] Jeff Hardy, *TNA Turning Point* (2010).

[11] Sycho Sid, *WWF Raw* (1997).

[12] Raven, *WCW Monday Nitro* (1987).

[13] "The Heartbreak Kid" Shawn Michaels, *WWE Raw* (2007).

[14] Arn Anderson, *NWA World Championship Wrestling* (1987).

proves that if you have passion for what you do, you can make it anywhere.[15] What I am is what I am—I'm a real American, I love my family, I love my God, and I love all my people who believe in me.[16] I always take my vitamins, say my prayers, and drink my milk.[17] I'm not the strongest guy, I'm not the fastest guy, but if you've got a lot of heart and a lot of desire and if you've got conditioning, you can win against anybody.[18] I worked my ass off in a gym for seventeen years.[19] I train six days a week, three to three and a half hours every time.[20] I've trained like a champion, I've lived like a champion…I'm ready, more ready than I've ever been in my life.[21] It's time for me to be numero uno, number one.[22] I'm ready, I'm 100%.[23] I guarantee I'll give you 110%.[24] I'm going to be the superstar that I always knew I could be.[25] I'm going to be there 210% to make that successful for me.[26] Dreams do come true.[27]

My whole life, people have been telling me I can't.[28] The difference between them and me is that I know that I'm the best.[29] There are a lot of great athletes, but you're looking at the greatest.[30] You are talking to the all time best right now—you got the Cadillac of the line.[31] I've proved over and over and over again that I'm the best there is, the best there was and the best that ever will be.[32] Everything I've ever done in my

---

15 Tommy Dreamer, *WWE ECW* (2010).

16 Hulk Hogan, *The Arsenio Hall Show* (1991).

17 Owen Hart, *WWF Over the Edge* (1999).

18 Bob Backlund, *AWA Championship Wrestling* (1985).

19 Lance Storm, *ECW Wrestling* (1999).

20 Bruno Sammartino, World Wide Wrestling Federation Promo (1975).

21 Kerry Von Erich, *AWA Championship Wrestling* (1988).

22 Eddie Guerrero, *WWE Smackdown!* (2003).

23 Ricky "the Dragon" Steamboat, *WWF Saturday Night's Main Event* (1986).

24 Hacksaw Jim Duggan, *WWF Royal Rumble Promo* (1993).

25 Steve Austin, *ECW Wrestling* (1995).

26 Nick Bockwinkel, *AWA Championship Wrestling* (1981).

27 Rey Mysterio, *WWE Smackdown!* (2006).

28 Diamond Dallas Page, *WCW Nitro* (2000).

29 Triple H, *WWE Friday Night Smackdown* (2008).

30 "Dr. Death" Steve Williams, *Herb Abrams UWF Wrestling* (1990).

31 Harley Race, *Pro Wrestling USA* (1984).

32 Bret "the Hitman" Hart, *WWF Friday Night Main Event* (1997).

life has been absolutely perfect.[33] I've always been nothing but a winner.[34] I'm the cream of the crop.[35] I'm the cock of the walk, ain't nobody gonna try and mess with me.[36] It's hard to explain how you get this great, it's not from eating your Wheaties, it's not from going to bed at nine o'clock and getting up at five, it's from being a man.[37] When you walk around this world and you tell everyone you're number one, the only way you get to stay number one is to be number one.[38] Every single one of you knows right now that you are looking at greatness.[39] Around here, there are a lot of players, there's one champ.[40] All I ask you to do is open your eyes and it will hit you in the head like a shot—for you are looking at the man who is superior to all.[41]

You know what cool is? You're looking at him.[42] It's not what you do, but how you look doing it.[43] If I want to grow my hair long, then I'm going to grow my hair long; if I want to put tattoos on my body, I'm going to put tattoos on my body; if I want to pierce my belly button, I'm going to pierce my belly button.[44] Do you know how difficult it is to maintain this delicately baby smooth skin?[45] I'm well groomed, brother: PEG Principle—Politeness, Grooming, and Etiquette.[46] It's not my fault that I have beautiful hair or a beautiful face or a sensuous body.[47] I do not weigh 271 pounds, I weigh a slim trim 217.[48] I am the most mesomorphically magnificent physical specimen beyond perfection.[49] I can walk down the street looking

---

[33] Mr. Perfect, *WWF Wrestling Challenge* (1988).

[34] Terry Taylor, *UWF Wrestling* (1987).

[35] Macho Man Randy Savage, *WWF Primetime Wrestling* (1987).

[36] Gorgeous Jimmy Garvin, *NWA Great American Bash Promo* (1986).

[37] Adrian Adonis, *Greater St. Louis Wrestling* (1983).

[38] "The Nature Boy" Ric Flair, *WWF Royal Rumble* (1992).

[39] "The Franchise" Shane Douglas, *ECW Barely Legal* (1997).

[40] John Cena, *WWE Raw* (2007).

[41] Sid Justice, *WWF Royal Rumble* (1992).

[42] Carlito, *WWE Raw* (2003).

[43] "The Model" Rick Martel, *WWF Royal Rumble* (1991).

[44] "The Heartbreak Kid" Shawn Michaels, *WWF Superstars* (1997).

[45] Dashing Cody Rhodes, *WWE Raw* (2010).

[46] Captain Lou Albano, *World Wrestling Federation* (1984).

[47] Michael "P.S." Hayes, *NWA Georgia Championship Wrestling* (1980).

[48] Playboy Buddy Rose, *AWA Championship Wrestling* (1986).

[49] "The Narcissist" Lex Luger, *WWF Royal Rumble* (1993).

pretty every day.[50] I understand you're a little bit overwhelmed by my ravishing body.[51] I'm going to show you the body that women love and that men love to fear.[52] I've got a gorgeous figure when I make my chest expand.[53] My belly's a little big, my hiney's a little big, but brother I'm bad and they know I'm bad.[54] That ain't no beer belly, it's a fuel tank for a whoop-ass machine.[55] I'm bigger, I'm taller, I'm stronger—I'm the rooster and I'm going to prove it.[56] If you wake up and zoom in on the largest arm in the world, brother, you can see the 24-inch python with the main vein that's full of ice cold water is ready for the challenge.[57] I am not only the arm wrestling champion of the world, I am the arm wrestling champion of the entire universe.[58] I want you to take out your cell phones, text your friends, take a picture, shoot a video, send an email, call them all and tell them that the sexy beast is back, baby.[59]

Power, strength, invincibility—if it sounds like I'm talking about myself, I am.[60] What kind of a guy are you?[61] I don't have to come out here and call people names but I will, you slime, you greaseball—I get a kick out of calling people names, you know why I can do it? Because I'm man enough to do it.[62] Listen, you pencil-necked geek.[63] I want to tell you something, you back-jumping polecat...I want to tell you something you yellow-bellied rat.[64] I'm gonna let you in on a secret, you ugly old goat.[65] You're a joke of a man.[66] You

[50] Tommy "Wildfire" Rich, *Continental Wrestling Association Promo* (1987).

[51] Ravishing Rick Rude, *WWF Primetime Wrestling* (1989).

[52] Mr. Wonderful Paul Orndorff, *WWF Championship Wrestling* (c. 1984).

[53] Exotic Adrian Street, "Imagine What I Could Do To You." Song from *Memphis Wrestling* (1983).

[54] "The American Dream" Dusty Rhodes, *NWA Mid-Atlantic Wrestling* (1985).

[55] Stone Cold Steve Austin, *WWF Raw* (2001).

[56] Colonel Robert Parker, *WCW Uncensored* (1996).

[57] Hulk Hogan, *WWF King of the Ring* (1993).

[58] Superstar Billy Graham, *AWA Championship Wrestling* (c. 1973).

[59] Chris Jericho, *WWE Raw* (2007).

[60] "The World's Strongest Man" Mark Henry, *WWE Smackdown!* (2011).

[61] Jerry "The King" Lawler, *Late Night with David Letterman* (1982).

[62] Sgt. Slaughter, *WWF Championship Wrestling* (1983).

[63] Classy Freddie Blassie, *WWF All Star Wrestling* (1984).

[64] Blackjack Mulligan, *World Class Championship Wrestling* (1986).

[65] Rowdy Roddy Piper, *NWA Hollywood Wrestling* (1978).

[66] Alberto Del Rio, *WWE Smackdown!* (2010).

are a disrespectful, snotty-nosed punk.[67] You are a whining, egotistical, backstabbing pussy.[68] You're a con artist, you're a thief, you're a liar, you're a lowlife, you're a loser, you're the scum of the earth, you're a dirtbag.[69] You're a jerk and you're stupid.[70] You're a stupid, stupid man.[71] You have been the personification of stupidity since 1997.[72] You're nothing, you're nobody.[73] You're nothing but a sissy.[74] You're gonna suck eggs like an egg sucking dog, thundermouth.[75] You are lazy, complacent, and take jobs you don't like because you don't have the guts to speak up.[76] Shut up, you beer bellied sharecroppers.[77] One more word out of you, I will drop you where you stand.[78] Know your role and shut your mouth.[79] We may be in the Great White North, but you can bite my white south.[80] You keep on kissing babies and hugging fat girls.[81] They are just like you: weak, shallow, insecure human beings, hypocrites and liars who need to be shut down and shut up for their own good.[82] You're not human—you come from a test tube.[83] Come from under your mother's bed; come out here and meet a real man.[84]

As a man, sometimes you've got to know when to talk, sometimes you've got to know when to walk

---

[67] "The American Dream" Dusty Rhodes, *WWE Raw* (2007).

[68] Raven, *TNA Impact Wrestling* (2003).

[69] Sting, *TNA Impact Wrestling* (2011).

[70] Rowdy Roddy Piper, *WrestleMania VI* Promo (1990).

[71] Chris Jericho, *WWE Summerslam* (2010).

[72] Edge, *WWE Raw* (2010).

[73] Demolition's Ax, World Wrestling Federation Promo (1988).

[74] Dirty Dick Slater, *NWA World Championship Wrestling* (1984).

[75] "Big Cat" Ernie Ladd, *Georgia Championship Wrestling* (1979).

[76] John Bradshaw Layfield, *WWE Smackdown!* (2004).

[77] Bad News Brown, *The Arsenio Hall Show* (1990).

[78] Randy Orton, *WWE Raw* (2005).

[79] The Rock, *WWE Raw* (1997).

[80] John Cena, *WWE Smackdown!* (2003).

[81] Batista, *WWE Raw* (2010).

[82] Chris Jericho, *WWE Raw* (2009).

[83] The Dynamite Kid, *Stampede Wrestling* (c. 1982).

[84] Bad News Brown, *WWF Superstars* (1988).

away, sometimes you've got to know when to fight.[85] I do love to drink, but tonight you're gonna find out how much I really like to fight.[86] I would rather hurt a man than love a woman.[87] When I'm on this side right here looking over there at you all, I don't have butterflies because we all know for sure exactly what's going to happen.[88] I'm gonna kick your teeth so far down your throat, you'll be able to chew your own ass out for pissing me off.[89] I'm going to stomp a mudhole in you and then I'm going to stomp it dry.[90] I'm gonna kick you where the good lord split you, if you know what I'm talking about—it's on like neckbone.[91] All the king's horses and all the king's men won't be able to put your humpty dumpty ass back together again.[92] I've got balls the size of grapefruits and come Sunday, you're gonna be picking the seeds out of your teeth.[93] I'll take that gold tooth, knock it out of your head and I'll make a bracelet, a necklace, a ring or whatever I want to make out of it.[94] You claim to be the man of 1000 holds…I know 1004, and I wrote them all down.[95] I clown around and I can still kick your ass.[96] Every dog needs a bone to chew on and you are my bone.[97] It's a dog eat dog world…I'm a dog eat dog man.[98] I'm going to keep clawing and I'm going to keep biting.[99] I have more teeth than you.[100]

I'm a monster—don't you see that?[101] I remember the very first time I heard a bone snap, and I

---

[85] "The Heartbreak Kid" Shawn Michaels, *WWE Raw* (2002).

[86] The Sandman, *WWE ECW* (2007).

[87] Cactus Jack, *Herb Abrams' UWF Wrestling* (1990).

[88] Barry Windham, *NWA War Games Promo* (1988).

[89] The Undertaker, *WWE Raw* (2000).

[90] "Captain Redneck" Dick Murdoch, *NWA World Championship Wrestling* (1989).

[91] Booker T, *WCW Monday Nitro* (1998).

[92] "The World's Strongest Man" Mark Henry, *WWF Heat* (1999).

[93] Vince McMahon, *WWF Raw* (1998).

[94] Stone Cold Steve Austin, *WWE Raw* (1998).

[95] Chris Jericho, *WCW Monday Nitro* (1998).

[96] Matt Borne, *ECW Wrestling* (1994).

[97] Junkyard Dog, *WWF Main Event* (1990).

[98] Mad Dog Vachon, *AWA Championship Wrestling* (1985).

[99] Mad Dog Buzz Sawyer, *NWA Georgia Championship Wrestling* (1983).

[100] Kurt Angle, *WWE Smackdown!* (2002).

[101] Kane, *WWE Raw* (2003).

thought to myself, what a fundamentally perfect sound.[102] We live in the age of specialization…I specialize in various forms of pain.[103] Can you take pain like a man?[104] You know nothing about pain.[105] I live with pain every day.[106] I'm coming to inflict pain.[107] You want to know why I do the things that I do? The only way that you can know is by experiencing them yourself—you need to feel my pain.[108] I have become the best by becoming the worst, untouchable and untouched, a perfect killing machine.[109] I might as well be the poster boy for ruthless aggression.[110] I enjoy wrecking lives, it turns me on.[111] You say I'm insane—I say thank you very much.[112] It's violence for the sake of violence, and now I will turn it around to my violence, my lightning bolts, my fire, my thunder.[113] I am a killer and a warrior and a slaughterer of so many souls that God, Allah and Buddha working overtime are having trouble keeping score.[114] I'm the only judge, I'm the only jury, and if need be, I'm the only executioner.[115] I am the new millennium…all hail the Ayatollah of rock and rollah.[116]

I may not be the most sensitive guy in the world, but I'm a businessman.[117] Sometimes, you have to set an example in business; this is not about my personal ego or about me having to win all the time—it's about business.[118] I may at times be a dirty rotten scoundrel, I may at times do things that you peasants don't

---

102 Road Warrior Hawk, *AWF Warriors of Wrestling* (1996).

103 The Masked Assassin, *Championship Wrestling from Georgia* (1984).

104 Jake the Snake Roberts, *WWF Saturday Night Main Event* (1988).

105 Vampiro, *WCW Monday Nitro* (2000).

106 Kurt Angle, *WWE Smackdown!* (2006).

107 Vader, *WCW Pro Wrestling* (1995).

108 Kane, *WWE Raw* (2003).

109 Raven, *TNA Impact Wrestling* (2003).

110 Kurt Angle, *WWE Smackdown!* (2002).

111 Vince McMahon, *WWF Royal Rumble* (2002).

112 Rowdy Roddy Piper, *WWF Saturday Night's Main Event* (1986).

113 "The American Dream" Dusty Rhodes, *NWA World Championship Wrestling* (1988).

114 Raven, *TNA Impact Wrestling* (2005).

115 The Big Boss Man, World Wrestling Federation Promo (1988).

116 Chris Jericho, *WWF Raw* (1999).

117 Eric Bischoff, *WWE Vengeance* (2002).

118 Vince McMahon, *WWE Raw* (2011)

like.[119] A good businessman makes money like I do—and I got it all.[120] I got a big house on the big side of town, I got life pretty much the way I want it.[121] I am now CEO of a company that bears my name, a self-made millionaire.[122] I'm a national hero, I'm a millionaire, I'm man admired in my country…my bloodline comes from kings.[123] Do you know the meaning of the word genuflect?[124] I have my own busboys, my own waitresses waiting on me.[125] I have ten nickels on this belt buckle, which adds up to 50 cents.[126] Don't you dare judge me because I live a privileged lifestyle and all of you wake up every morning and wish you could be just like me.[127] You're talking to the Rolex wearing, diamond ring wearing, kiss stealing, wheeling dealing, limousine riding, jet flying, son of a gun.[128] I'm handsome, I'm rich, I'm powerful.[129] Money isn't everything, it's the only thing.[130]

Friendship is friendship, business is business.[131] What is friendship? In this business, it's nothing more than an illusion.[132] I don't have to pretend to be your friend because I never was and I never will be.[133] I don't have any friends. I'm not looking for any friends.[134] I don't need friends…I go in there and take care of business, business for me and me only and that's the way I want it to stay.[135] I don't know who my friends

[119] Lord Steven Regal, *WCW Saturday Night* (1996).

[120] "The Million Dollar Man" Ted Dibiase, World Wrestling Federation Promo (1988).

[121] "The Nature Boy" Ric Flair, *National Wrestling Alliance* Promo (1988).

[122] John Bradshaw Layfield, *WWE Night of Champions* Promo (2008).

[123] Alberto Del Rio, *WWE Smackdown!* (2010).

[124] Jerry "The King" Lawler, *WWF Prime Time Wrestling* (1992).

[125] Mr. Wonderful Paul Orndorff, WWF *Championship Wrestling* (c. 1984).

[126] Freebird Buddy Roberts, *World Class Championship Wrestling* (1984).

[127] Ted DiBiase Jr, *WWE Superstars* (2010).

[128] "The Nature Boy" Ric Flair, *NWA World Championship Wrestling* (1985).

[129] Alberto Del Rio, *WWE Superstars* (2010).

[130] "The Million Dollar Man" Ted DiBiase, *WWF Superstars* (1988).

[131] Macho Man Randy Savage, *WCW Halloween Havok* (1995).

[132] Jeff Hardy, *TNA Impact Wrestling* (2010).

[133] Ole Anderson, *NWA Georgia Championship Wrestling* (1980).

[134] Mr. Perfect, *WWF Royal Rumble* (1989).

[135] Bruiser Brody, *Wrestling at the Chase* (c. 1979).

are and I don't know who my enemies are.[136] I don't need anybody.[137] I came into this world alone, I will leave alone—I don't need a damn soul with me.[138] I can take care of myself.[139] The only person I trust is myself.[140] I don't care who my partner is.[141] I've had a lot of partners in the past and I know that for a fact I cannot trust anybody but myself...all I need is my two fists.[142] I got the only tools I need right here—these two fists is all I need.[143] I'm nobody's workhorse—I'm my own man.[144]

Women...I play with them and then I cast them aside and break their hearts.[145] I've left thousands and thousands and thousands of women in distress.[146] I'm just a sexy boy.[147] I'm the shaman of sexy, the Tuesday night delight, the honcho of hotness, the Shao-lin master of manliness, the Chuck Norris of Nookie.[148] I'm a good kisser.[149] I'm the real deal, au naturale...the gift that I have, no other male on the face of this planet has ever ever been blessed with.[150] Everything about me is larger than life—everything I have is big.[151] I love my testicles.[152] How about that girl who was calling me Secretariat as I was walking out the door?[153] Size does matter and they know they don't have to wait for the earth to rotate on a forty-seven degree axis so the stars can stop the sky and create an equinox so they can see the big dipper.[154] The

[136] Big John Studd. *WWF Royal Rumble* (1989)

[137] Triple H, *WWF Heat* (1999).

[138] John Bradshaw Layfield, *WWE Smackdown!* (2004).

[139] Blackjack Mulligan Jr., *Mid-Atlantic Championship Wrestling* (1982).

[140] Chris Benoit, *WWE Raw* (2003).

[141] Stone Cold Steve Austin, *WWE Raw* (1997).

[142] Greg "The Hammer" Valentine, *WWF Royal Rumble* (1989).

[143] Brutus "The Barber" Beefcake. *WWF Royal Rumble* (1989).

[144] Larry Zbyszko, *AWA Championship Wrestling* (1985).

[145] Macho Man Randy Savage, *WWF Tuesday Night Titans* (1996).

[146] "The Universal Heartthrob" Austin Idol, *NWA Georgia Championship Wrestling* (1979).

[147] "The Heartbreak Kid" Shawn Michaels, "Sexy Boy," WWF Theme Song by Jim Johnston.

[148] John Morrison, Survivor Series Promo, *WWE ECW* (2007).

[149] Mankind, *WWF Raw* (1997).

[150] Val Venis, *WWF Raw* (1998).

[151] The Ultimate Warrior, *The Arsenio Hall Show* (1990).

[152] Test, *WWE Raw* (2002).

[153] "The Nature Boy" Ric Flair, *NWA World Championship Wrestling* (1986).

[154] Scott Steiner, *WCW Monday Nitro* (2000).

real giant is right here.[155] You don't have to go to Florida—you can be right here and you can ride Space Mountain.[156] Whether the girls are home or here in Dayton, they're watching me and masturbatin'.[157] If it's a woman I want, I want her to stand up and be what I want.[158] Even as a baby, I grabbed the nurse instead of the bottle.[159] I like them better with their clothes off.[160] When I die, it'll either be here or on top of a wild woman.[161]

Women are weak and men are the dominant species.[162] When a woman challenges you to give her a spanking, you lay her ass over this couch and you lay into her.[163] You leave your broad at home, I got my successful marriages, I don't need another one.[164] They say a man doesn't know true happiness until he gets married, and then it's too late.[165] It's bad enough you gotta take orders from a dog, but you gotta take orders from a bitch.[166] My second wife, I used to practice strangleholds on her all the time.[167] Then there's my sweet darling honey, but when she beats me at home I kinda like it.[168] I believe in equal rights—she wants to jump in, I'll slap her, pull her by the hair just as fast as I'll pop a man.[169] I didn't see a woman yet I couldn't whip.[170] Just when they think they got the answers, I change the questions.[171] I'm gonna walk by and hit

[155] Andre the Giant, *Herb Abrams's UWF* (1991).

[156] "The Nature Boy" Ric Flair, *NWA World Championship Wrestling* (1985).

[157] Joel Gertner, *ECW Heatwave* (1999).

[158] Rowdy Roddy Piper, *WWF Saturday Night Main Event* (1986).

[159] Precious Paul Ellering, *NWA Georgia Championship Wrestling* (c. 1980).

[160] John Cena, *WWE Raw* (2004).

[161] "The Nature Boy" Ric Flair, *TNA Impact Wrestling* (2010).

[162] Jeff Jarrett, *WWF Unforgiven* (1999).

[163] Ravishing Rick Rude, *The Arsenio Hall Show* (1990).

[164] Rowdy Roddy Piper, *WWF Superstars of Wrestling* (1987).

[165] Jerry "the King" Lawler, *WWE Raw* (2012).

[166] Bret "the Hitman" Hart, *WWF Prime Time* (1986).

[167] Classy Freddie Blassie, *WWF Tuesday Night Titans* (1984).

[168] Chris Candido, *ECW Living Dangerously* (1998).

[169] Rowdy Roddy Piper, WWF Madison Square Garden Promo (1984).

[170] Tony Atlas, *NWA Georgia Championship Wrestling* (1983).

[171] Rowdy Roddy Piper, *WWF Championship Wrestling* (1984).

some women.[172] I don't care if every women's organization in the country writes me—it's gonna happen.[173] Pimpin' ain't easy.[174]

When I was brought into this world, I could not rob, I could not steal, I could not lie, I couldn't even cheat, but boy did I have help learning.[175] What's mine is mine and what's yours is mine too.[176] I ain't got no damn integrity—how do you think I got so far?[177] You don't want to play cards with me because I cheat.[178] You say I don't play with a full deck—no, I play with a stacked deck.[179] You gamble with the Devil, the Devil always wins.[180] I'll do what ever it takes to win: I lie, I cheat and I steal.[181] Win if you can, lose if you must, but always cheat.[182] Behind you, there may be one, or there may be many waiting to stick a knife in your back, but you don't have to worry about me, because I'll shoot you right between the eyes.[183] I have no remorse, I have no conscience, and I will stop at nothing.[184] I'm so tired of people like you calling me a thief.[185] I'm a predator, an opportunist.[186] I'm the dirtiest player in the game.[187] I've always been the snake you should have been worried about.[188] I ain't no goody two-shoes—when I see Donny Osmond on my TV, I shoot the TV.[189] I get hit in the head with a steel chair for a living, and I drink beer, and I flip people

[172] The Honky Tonk Man, *WWF Superstars of Wrestling* (1986).

[173] "The American Dream" Dusty Rhodes, *NWA World Championship Wrestling* (1985).

[174] The Godfather, *WWF Raw* (1999).

[175] Jake the Snake Roberts, World Wrestling Federation Promo (1989).

[176] Repo Man, *WWF Royal Rumble* (1992).

[177] Rowdy Roddy Piper, *WWF Royal Rumble* (1992).

[178] Jake the Snake Roberts, *Heroes of Wrestling* (1999).

[179] Michael "P.S." Hayes, *NWA Georgia Championship Wrestling* (1980).

[180] William Regal, *WWE Raw* (2002).

[181] Eddie Guerrero, *WWE Summerslam* (2004).

[182] Jesse "The Body" Ventura, *WWF Saturday Night's Main Event* (1990).

[183] Kevin Nash, *WCW Monday Nitro* (1998).

[184] Triple H, *WWE Bad Blood* (2004).

[185] "Hot Stuff" Eddie Gilbert, *USWA Memphis Wrestling* (1994).

[186] Edge, *WWE Raw* (2010).

[187] "The Nature Boy" Ric Flair, *NWA World Championship Wrestling* (1987).

[188] Jake the Snake Roberts, *WWF Survivor Series* (1991).

[189] Rowdy Roddy Piper, *NWA World Championship Wrestling* (1982).

off—what do you expect out of me?[190]

There's not a man on the face of this earth that I'm afraid of except one, and he lives in Glen Falls, New York, and I call him Dad.[191] We're the tightest family I've ever seen in my life.[192] My father used to use a four-letter word that was very shocking to people…the word is spelled f-e-a-r.[193] When I was a kid, I used to have to watch my Dad come home from being on the road all black and blue, bruised up, hurt, in pain, arm in a cast.[194] I didn't know any better when I was a little kid, when my dad came home smelling like beer.[195] I guess it's true what they say—like father like son.[196] I followed in my father's footsteps and I ended up being better than he ever was.[197] My dad hit me and he said take a look at yourself son, take a look at the scars, take a look at the burns, take a look at the missing body parts.[198] I ain't never had my ass whipped so fast in my life.[199] My dad taught me when I was real young…we got to move on and be strong.[200] I wanted to prove to prove to my father that I could do it; well, it doesn't matter man—he's gone.[201] I love you, Pop, and I'm sorry.[202]

The difference between me and a robot is I have emotions.[203] It's okay for macho men to show every emotion available because I've cried a thousand times and I'm gonna cry some more—but I've soared with the eagles and I've slithered with the snakes, and I've been everywhere in between.[204] I've lost a lot of

---

[190] Stone Cold Steve Austin, *The Tonight Show with Jay Leno* (2001).

[191] Hacksaw Jim Duggan, *WWF Prime Time Wrestling* (1991).

[192] David Von Erich, *World Class Championship Wrestling* (1983).

[193] Terry Funk, *NWA Georgia Championship Wrestling* (1980).

[194] Randy Orton, *WWE Raw* (2005).

[195] CM Punk, *ROH WrestleRave* (2003).

[196] Kane, *WWE Smackdown* (2012).

[197] Randy Orton, *WWE Raw* (2007).

[198] Cactus Jack, *ECW Wrestling* (1993).

[199] The Rock, *WWE Backlash* (2003).

[200] Jeff Hardy, *WWE Vengeance, After the Bell* (2008).

[201] Jake the Snake Roberts, *2CW Live and Let Die* (2010).

[202] Triple H, *WWE Raw* (2011).

[203] Chris Benoit, WWF Backlash (2000).

[204] Macho Man Randy Savage, *The Arsenio Hall Show* (1992).

things, and one of them has been my smile.[205] What hurts most are my feelings.[206] You feel the burn when you cry.[207] I'm naked and I don't like it.[208] If you're a man, you don't cry about it, you take life, the ups and downs—if you're a real man, you never go down, you just stay up.[209] I can handle defeat because defeat makes one stronger, it makes the soul stronger.[210] My daughter Kimberly said my daddy falls down a lot, and my daughter Brianna says my daddy always gets up.[211] I tell my kids: you learn all about history so you don't repeat the same mistakes.[212]

Don't you ever forget it, or forget who I am.[213] I have done my best to be an open book in front of all of you; it's just easier for me to be who I am.[214] Just in case you've forgotten, let me tell you just who the hell I am.[215] I'm the man of the hour, the man with the power, the man that's too sweet to be sour is talking to you.[216] I'm not fake, nothing about me's fake.[217] I'm not a baby.[218] I am not a little boy sitting in front of the TV watching my idol.[219] I am the highlight of the night.[220] I am the true meaning of Macho and that cannot be denied.[221] I'm somebody important, man—I'm like Adam in the Garden of Eden—I'm the only real man.[222] I'm the best there is, and that's the bottom line.[223]

---

205 "The Heartbreak Kid" Shawn Michaels, *WWF Raw* (1997).

206 Sting, *TNA Impact Wrestling* (2011).

207 Mark Henry, *WWF Raw* (1999).

208 Arn Anderson, *NWA World Championship Wrestling* (1986).

209 Ric Flair, *NWA Georgia Championship Wrestling* (1985).

210 The Undertaker, *WWF Fab 4* (1996).

211 Tommy Dreamer, *WWE ECW* (2010).

212 Shane Douglas, *ECW Wrestling* (c. 1996).

213 Sting, World Championship Wrestling Promo (1994).

214 "The Heartbreak Kid" Shawn Michaels, *WWE Raw* (2010).

215 Triple H, *WWE Raw* (2002)

216 Superstar Billy Graham, *WWF All Star Wrestling* (1975).

217 "Dr. D" David Schultz, *The Morton Downey Jr. Show* (ca 1984).

218 Mikey Whipwreck, *ECW Wrestling* (2000)

219 "The Heartbreak Kid" Shawn Michaels, *WWE Bad Blood* (2003).

220 Chris Jericho, *WWE Judgement Day* (2003).

221 Macho Man Randy Savage, *WWF Tuesday Night Titans* (1996).

222 Razor Ramon, *WWF Raw* (1996)

223 Stone Cold Steve Austin, *WWF Superstars* (1996).

THE
CAN-OPENER !!

© Janne
Karlsson

THE
TOOTH-SHAKER !!

© Janne
Karlsson

THE
HOLE-FILLER !!

© JANNE KARLSSON

Wrestling with Wrestling

I guess I don't really believe in guilty pleasures. At least not when it comes to entertainment choices. So maybe you're into some sick shit. None of my business. But don't compartmentalize your pleasures. Own them. You can dig Ibsen and *The Simpsons* without feeling guilty about either. I mean, I write "serious" stuff and consume "serious" books and movies. But I also love professional wrestling or "sports entertainment" or whatever bullshit they're calling it these days. I follow the Iron Sheik on Facebook, but I also follow an Allen Ginsberg tribute page. No, those interests aren't anywhere near intellectually equal, but I refuse to feel guilty about either.

However much I tried not to feel guilty about my love for professional wrestling, there was a time when people loved trying to make me feel bad about it. When I was eight, nine, ten years old, there were a host of people, both kids and adults, who enjoyed the living hell out of pointing out that wrestling was "fake." And it made them pretty full of themselves, too, as if they'd just discovered Fermi's paradox on their own. But alas! We are alone in this vast universe!

There were a lot of these people, but some voices were louder than others. For instance, this goddamn nuisance babysitter of mine. It was early 1991. I was ten years old. The babysitter couldn't have been much more than two or three years older than I was, yet he certainly had a superiority complex, as most pricks usually do. Goddamn, this guy was just the worst. He's probably middle-management at a car dealership now.

Early 1991 was a great time in my wrestling-watching life. I mean, there was a daily wrestling show on ESPN. It aired every weekday after I got home from school. I used to make a beeline to the basement to make sure I didn't miss anything. I was just enjoying myself, but my babysitter loved waving a finger in the air and shouting "Fake! Fake!" at every opportunity.

"Faaaaaaaaake!"

Oh, just shut the fuck up.

Of course, I knew in the back of my mind that he had to be right. Not too long before, the World Wrestling Federation had a storyline where a voodoo guy named Papa Shango placed a curse on various wrestlers, including the Ultimate Warrior, that made them ooze a green puss out of their wrists...because... magic? It was a bit too over the top, even for a ten year old. Still, this babysitter was an ass, so I had no choice but to argue with him. No, I insisted, wrestling was indeed a real sport. How could it not be? It aired daily on ESPN, for God's sake.

One day, my babysitter decided to put the matter to rest for good. He proposed a solution: We videotape a match and then play it back in slow motion. We'd see if the wrestlers' moves held up under scrutiny. I was nervous, but I accepted his bet.

So he taped a match and then rewound the video. Then he fast forwarded until he came to a place that he thought would best prove his point. The bad guy wrestler had the good guy wrestler on his back, and was supposed to have been stomping on the good guy's face.

Well, in slow motion you could clearly see that the bad guy pulled his boot up just before it made any contact with the good guy. Sure as shit, my babysitter had won the argument. But, being ten years old and therefore more than a bit of a prick myself, I argued the point. No, no, the bad guy's boot had clearly grazed the good guy's nose. After all, if the bad guy had made full contact, he would have broken the other guy's nose. These were, after all, professionals. The heel wanted to hurt the babyface, not kill him. He knew what he was doing.

Goddamn, I sure was an ass.

My babysitter was apoplectic. He started pacing about the basement, his arms up in exasperation. Was there nothing he could say that would convince me? Was I completely insane?

Maybe ... but he never brought the subject up again, which was victory enough for me.

Anyway, that incident left my faith in wrestling on very shaky ground. Sure, I was going to abandon my belief in its legitimacy sooner or later, but the incident with my babysitter had almost totally removed the facade. It wouldn't take a person to shatter my beliefs. Instead, it was a wrestling pay-per-view.

Later that year, just days after I had turned eleven, a friend and I were in another friend's basement watching SummerSlam. We were bouncing-off-the-walls excited for the event. My friend Doug and I were too poor to have seen a pay-per-view event except when it was released on VHS a few months later. My friend Andrew, whose house we were gathered at, couldn't afford it either. But his dad worked for the cable company, so he had all the pay-per-view channels turned on permanently. This officially made Andrew the most awesome kid in the neighborhood.

Needless to say, I was hyped as hell.

The event started out great. After two forgettable matches, we saw one of the greatest single wrestling matches of all time: Bret Hart (our hero) taking on Mr. Perfect (the arrogant villain) for the Intercontinental championship. These guys put everything they had into their match. It was fast-paced, with neither man gaining a clear advantage. Every time it seemed as if one of them had the other pinned, a shoulder would come up at the last second, stopping the count. Bret Hart even kicked out of Mr. Perfect's signature finishing move, the Perfectplex. And no one had ever kicked out of the Perfectplex! Finally, after an action-filled and exhausting match, Bret Hart beat Mr. Perfect and held the Intercontinental title above his head as the crowd roared and my friends and I bounced around the basement in our pajamas, screaming like the sugared-up maniacs we were.

Tell me, how could one of the most exhilarating entertainment experiences I'd ever had be fake? I mean, how the hell wasn't that match real? I found myself wishing my babysitter had been there. Surely he would have eaten his words. Right?

Right.

Well, just a few matches later, I learned a hard lesson: that nothing quite disappoints a wrestling fan like wrestling itself.

How else to explain this stupid fucking match between the Big Boss Man and the Mountie?

In case you've never heard of these jokers...well, you can probably guess their gimmicks. The Big Boss Man was okay, I guess. He was supposed to be a former cop from Cobb County, Georgia. I guess he liked his uniform, because even after he became a   professional wrestler, he kept wearing it. Same for the Mountie, supposedly a member of the Royal Canadian Mounted Police, except his uniform was missing the sleeves. I mean, who needs sleeves in Canada? And for some reason, the Mountie carried a cattle prod with which he tortured his opponents after they had been pinned. And whenever he was angry (which was all the time), he was given to shouting, "I am the Mountie!" for no goddamn reason at all.

So these two idiots are going at it, exchanging punches and such, and they're wearing their respective cop outfits, when the Mountie is finally pinned and beaten. They haul him off to jail. Yup, there was a match stipulation that said the loser had to spend a night behind bars. Something to do with...justice being served or whatnot?

Looking back, I consider this kind of a brilliant match. It was so over the top and stupid and made such little sense that there was a kind of naive surrealism about the thing. It was just about everything that, nowadays, I actually love about wrestling. But, Jesus, at the time I was crushed. I knew it was time to give up the ghost.

That sucked for a while, but I was right back over to Andrew's house for the Royal Rumble early the next year. I had to admit that, now that I was in on the joke, wrestling was still fun, maybe even more so, because there wasn't any pressure to watch it with a straight face.

But however in on the joke I might have been, I knew I would never give away the punchline. Believing that wrestling was real made the world just a little more colorful. It meant that superheroes were real. Why the hell would anyone try to make a kid feel guilty about that?

Mars in Virgo

Cougar called in sick. Fucking Wal-Mart. He worked in the gun section, though, so that was somewhat cool. Sally got to be sick all the time. She received disability because it was easy enough for her to convince a psychologist appointed by the state of Texas that she was too bat shit crazy to hold down a job for any reasonable length of time. So Cougar called in sick and Sally got her toenails painted by Kim Wu at Lucky You salon then Cougar and Sally hit the fucking road to Dallas in Cougar's jacked up Ford Ranger.

"San Antonio is such bullshit," Sally said. She was smoking Marlboro reds while Cougar hauled ass down I-35.

"Baby, shut the fuck up. Nothin' wrong with San Antonio. You know you like the tacos. I need some George up in this bitch before you drive my ass to drink," Cougar said. He turned up the stereo and George Strait sang about Fort Worth.

They checked into the Best Western and got their fuck on pretty goddamn quick. Up against the wall. On the bed with the ugly ass floral print bedspread. Doggy style, Cougar's favorite. Reverse cowgirl, Sally's favorite. Then Sally sucked Cougar's dick with tears in her eyes.

"What the fuck, babe? You're cryin'? What the hell?"

"I just love you so much."

"Shit."

At the convention center Sally decided she would die unless she spent thirty dollars on a Stone Cold Steve Austin t-shirt. Cougar let Sally stand in line while he grabbed a beer and headed to the seats. Cougar loved his common law wife but she confused him on a regular basis. She fucked like a twenty dollar hooker and talked like a teenager who still had unicorn posters on the wall and Sweet Valley High books on the bedside table. Sally's theory was that Stone Cold Steve Austin would kick the living shit out of The Rock because Stone Cold Steve Austin was born on a more advantageous day.

"Uh. Hello. News fucking flash. Stone Cold is Sagittarius with Mars in Virgo? Uh. The Rock is Taurus with Mars in Gemini? Ain't no fuckin' way The Rock is gonna win that fight," Sally said with Chee-tos dust all over her mouth and fingers. She was sexy in a retarded/mentally challenged kind of way that really got Cougar's dick in the air.

"Them stars are too far away in outer space to give two shits about who wins a wrestling match that's probably engineered by gay dudes in Miami, anyway. But I'll make ya a ten dollar bet. The Rock is gonna serve Stone Cold his own ass for supper. I guarandamntee it."

"You are on like Donkey Kong, baby darlin'. Shit. With ten dollars I can buy a new lace bra."

There had been other women but none like Sally. "I guess she's my damn soul mate," Cougar told Pablo once during smoke break at Wal-Mart. Pablo looked off into the smoky distance with a wistful look in his eyes. "Soul mate. Yeah. Had me one of those in junior high," he said.

Two Wrestlers on the Road to yet another High School Gym in the Middle of Nowhere

"Hey, kid, you want a beer?"

"Ummm … no, sir. I'm driving, you see."

"That's right, I forgot. Kids today are pussies. Harley Race? There's a guy who could drive drunk. Truth is I don't know if he ever drove sober. That's just how we did it back then."

"'We'? How old are you if you don't mind me asking?"

"47 years old. How old are you exactly?"

"23."

"You're a kid. That's why I let you drive me from show to show. You've got potential, but you need someone like me to guide you along the way. You need to do more shutting up and less asking stupid questions."

"Yes, sir, but it's just that you're too young to have ever travelled with Harley Race. I don't think he's wrestled in over 25 years."

"You kids today with all your facts and all that crap you read on the internet and in the dirtsheets. Ruined the business…no, ruined the sport. They ruined my sport. See, when I say that's how 'we' did it back then I don't mean it literally. It's the myths that make wrestling so great. Maybe I never traveled with Harley Race, but the stories they tell me make me feel like I did. When I was a kid, before I got into wresting… let me ask you, did you know what words like 'kayfabe' meant?"

"Yes, I did."

"Because of the internet, right?"

"Yeah."

"See? In my day that was all a mystery. You had to learn it. Now they just hand it to you. I was four months into my training before I even knew it was a work."

"But, sir, with all due respect… I know it was different back then, but that seems pretty ridiculous. Clearly you knew it was not a legitimate athletic competition before you decided to become a wrestler, right?"

"Did I know? I didn't not know, but I didn't know. The world was different back then. We weren't so cynical."

"But… this was the mid-eighties. There's not being cynical and then there's being stupid."

"Stupid? Fuck you."

"Sorry, I…"

"No, no, no, you listen to me now. Did I know when I started training at age 18 that pro wrestling was most likely not a legitimate sport? Of course I did. Would I have ever disrespected my trainer by letting him know that before he told me? No. Because back then to have someone involved in wrestling tell you that it was a work… that was an honor. You couldn't go on Google and look up inside wrestling terms. Each and every nugget of knowledge someone entrusted you with was a great honor and you wouldn't disrespect your trainers by saying 'yeah, I know.' You get what I'm saying?"

"Yeah, I think so I really am sorry."

"Shit, that's OK. That's kind of why I enjoy travelling with you young guys. You don't know shit so I have to tell you everything. Hey, want a hit off my joint?"

"No, sir. I'm still driving."

"Fuck. You kids today. Can't drive drunk, can't drive stoned. You kids ain't no fun, no more. You still fuck the rats, right? Tell me that you at least get some pussy."

"Yeah, I guess…yeah. But I have a girlfriend so…"

"A girlfriend? Oh, for fuck's sake. I've been married for 20 years and I still get some side action. Shit, where we're wrestling tonight, there's this broad I've been banging for about 15 years every time we come to this town. I think she has a daughter if you're interested."

"No, thanks. Wait, how old is she?"

"Mother's around 30, daughter is 16 or so. Around there."

"But… wait."

"Kid, we don't do the math when it comes to the rats."

"But when you first met her…"

"We don't do the math, OK? Listen, kid, a whole Hell of a lot of wrestlers you grew up watching, a whole Hell of a lot of wrestlers you love have done a lot of horrible shit. Underage girls is just the tip of the iceberg. I've been on this circuit for a long time and the things I've seen…"

"I've kind of been meaning to ask you about that, but wasn't sure how. You've been doing this for a long time, but you never did make it big. You did short stints in the WWF and WCW, but you spent most of your career just working the indy circuit. Did you ever just want to quit?"

"Quit? No. I…I know it's a little sad to pushing 50 and still working high school gyms for a hundred bucks a show, but I love it. I can't do what I used to do, but I can still take a bump. I can still cut a promo. I'm still known enough that I can set up a table at comic book conventions and what not and still make a few bucks. Not a lot, but all it takes is a few fans out of a thousand to pay you $20 for an autographed picture to make it worth your while. And my stints in the big time were short, but they were profitable and

I'm not stupid. Look, a lot of guys my age would rent their own car just for the appearance of it, but I'm not ashamed to share a ride. And I'll tell you something else, my stints in the big leagues were not long, but they were profitable. I treated those paychecks as the anomalies, not as anything I expected to last. I wish they had lasted longer than they had, but I was prepared for them not to. I might be a complete fucking idiot about everything in this life, but when it comes to money I know what I'm doing. And that's what you've gotta do. If you're not making money by age 30 you've gotta pack it in. Give it up and get a real job."

"Would you have done that? Would you have packed it all in to get a real job?"

"No. No, I wouldn't have. But I was different because I knew I was going to make it. No doubt in my mind whatsoever. But you're different. You don't have my natural gifts. I think you're good, but you're hardly a sure thing. Hey, you sure you don't want a beer or some weed or anything? I feel bad having all this fun while you're stuck driving."

"I appreciate it sir, but no."

"Suit yourself, buddy."

Gimmicks

Twenty years in the ring and you wonder what brought you to this point. Was it the first time you put on The Mask? When you took it off? No. It goes deeper than that. You are twelve years-old, you and your mother are living in a flat above the taxidermist's shop. That's when it begins, the first time you risk body for money. For being brave you win fifty cents. The bet, proposed by Jack Juarez, your best friend, is to stick a hand inside the mouth of the raccoon for ten seconds. The raccoon more than any of the other more imposing beasts in the taxidermist's is by far the most frightening. Everyone knows there's still some life left in it. You can almost see it twitch from the corner of your eye, hissing its purple tongue through yellow teeth bared in a perpetual snarl.

You close your eyes and stick your hand into the raccoon's mouth. Knuckles brush against the roof. You feel the ridges, you think you can feel its breath. Jack Juarez counts out the seconds—one Mississippi, two Mississippi—slower than the referees count when matches spill outside the ring. Ten seconds to get back in the ring, ten seconds to keep your hand in the raccoon's mouth. Both seem a lifetime. Jack Juarez holds his count on nine. Nine and a quarter, nine and a half, nine and three-quarters. Ten. You pull your hand out as fast as you can and drag it across buzz-saw teeth. Show Jack your bloody hand. Proof that you've earned your half dollar. There is a fang imbedded in the soft meat of your palm. You dig the tooth out and hide it in your shoe. Wipe the blood off on your jeans.

You've accrued scores of other injuries risking body for money. Twenty years in the ring and there are stitches: 525. Six herniated discs, two missing teeth, three ribs cracked—all of them bruised at some point, concussions too numerous to count. There's the separated right shoulder that occasionally pops out of place during matches. Bone chips float in both elbows. The fluid in your knees is drained more frequently than your hair is cut. A broken right wrist, a broken left thumb. Bruised kidneys make you piss blood for three months. Broken nose. Shattered cheekbone. Torn meniscus. Cartilage has worn away; bones and joints are free to grind together, to cannibalize themselves. But you work through the pain as best you can because the show must go on. You eat pills and inject serums not to cure, only to patch. Duct tape for your insides. There is no off season in wrestling. No time to rehab. You become your own practitioner.

Twenty years in the squared circle and you're a walking pharmacy. You eat Vicodin, Lorcet, Percodan, and Percocet like they're M&Ms. Demerols remind you of Pezz. You spike up Cortisone injections with the same indifference as a diabetic pumps insulin. You take all this knowing the best you can hope for is to numb the pain. What you need is a body transplant. Sometimes, even your hair seems to hurt.

Pain requires medication, but so does success. You're a hotrod and your body is the cherry paint job.

It's your armor and your billboard. It's your life. It's the difference between midcard and main event. To tare down and rebuild your muscles faster, to get bigger, to get monster big, you stack Dianabol, Anavar, Halotestin. Deca and Depo. You mix and match, whip up testosterone cocktails. You get legitimate prescriptions when you've got the cash, but you'll take what you can. You buy some Teslac from a guy at the gym, trade one of the Cannonball Crew a few grams of coke for Maxibolin. You start dating a ringrat even though she's balled more wrestlers than you've pinned. You date her, you fuck her, because during the day this ring rat works at a veterinary clinic and she can score you horse steroids.

After a show you're still rolling on the rush of the match. The adrenaline helps you make it to your motel. At three a.m. you're still amped because the Dexedrine and Dianabol keep punching away at you. You grind your teeth loud enough to wake the other guys you're rooming with. They call you an asshole, hophead, juicer, speedfreak. You laugh because they're all of these things as well. Someone tosses you a baggie of pills, says sweet dreams. You wake up in another town; they're all different, but the rooms are the same.

In the beginning you wake up in places like the parking lot of the Boys and Girls Club in Dubuque. You wake up at a Howard Johnson's on your way to a match in Joliet. You wake up in front of the YWCA in Kenosha. At an armory in Muncie. In the gravel parking lot of a VFW hall in St. Cloud. You wake up in Kalamazoo.

You start to make a name for yourself and graduate to working civic centers in Rock Island and Gary and Muskegon. You're booked at state colleges in Minnesota, Missouri, the Dakotas. You can almost live on your share of the take. You can afford things like meat and eggs graded higher than D, an occasional trip to the ER to set a broken bone, matching boots and trunks, to sleep in a motel room rather than your car. Fans begin to recognize you. Some chant your name before you're announced, some know your moves and call for your patented finisher when you've got your opponent on the ropes.

You wake up to a packed house in a real city, maybe The Joe in Detroit or The Kiel in St. Louis. You get lucky and there's a guy from the Global Wrestling Federation or the Continental Wrestling Alliance sitting ringside, probably an Upper Midwest talent scout. If you've built up a following, created enough of a buzz, an actual V.P. catches your show and takes you out for a steak dinner. Hands you papers. He wants you to come work for Mike O'Malley Jr. or Smilin Joe Spiceland. You wake up in the GWF. You wake up in the CWA. Instead of living out of your beater car, sleepwalking and bodyslamming your way through the Rust Belt, you bounce from region to region. You're in the big time now. National wrestling's the new thing, cable television and pay-per-views. No more fiefdoms run by cheap carnies. Now it's CEO's. You wake up in VIP lounges of hub airports instead of interstate rest stops. You wake up in O'Hare and do a show, a *Friday Night Free For All* or a Tuesday Night Demolition for 20,000 live and millions more watching on TV. Then you rent your Continental or Deville and drive to Grand Rapids, to Milwaukee, to Indianapolis, Peoria, the Twin Cities; every night a packed house. After the last show in the last city of this leg you catch a redeye for New York, San Francisco, Denver, LA, even Atlanta, now that the southern territories have finally opened up to the promotion you work for. And you do it all over again. Three hundred days a year you wake up someplace else. For most of your career you wake up *someone* else. And you wonder if it was your talent or your gimmick that got you here.

In twenty years there have been nearly as many personas. You begin as yourself: Earl Atlas. The man who trained you, Art Stigma, said it best. "Son, you've got one ass kicker of a wrestling name, but you got the charisma of a donkey turd." Of course he's right, but you're nineteen and want to prove the old man wrong, so you wrestle as Earl Atlas. Your career goes nowhere. You lose to midgets and women; little kids and old ladies give you the finger, chuck batteries and frozen hardboiled eggs at you. They aim for your head. You become Rockabilly Elvis Atlas, the heel Elvis impersonator who bashes guitars over unsuspecting opponents' skulls. Fans don't completely hate this version of you, but you can't afford to keep buying guitars so you become someone else. Now you're Atlas Vespa, the snobby European artist who smokes in the ring and wears sunglasses and a black beret. This gimmick, you think, is shit. It wasn't even your idea; some promoter handed you the glasses and beret and told you to talk like Frenchman. Maybe it isn't a bad gimmick, but once you begin to think it's stupid the fans can tell. Self doubt kills careers in the squared circle. You wonder if you should try for a babyface gimmick so you change your name to Atlas God of Thunder, a good guy with the official superpower to use thunderclaps as a weapon and the unofficial power to empty out the bleachers. Somebody suggests you do what Pete "The Polish Falcon" Rakowski did. You remember how Pete had struggled to get over with the crowds until one day he announced to everyone that he had legally changed his name to Polish Falcon. He showed you the documents to prove this. Months later he showed you the contract he'd just signed with GWF. But you want to keep some part of yourself in your character. Earl Atlas is your name. It's all your father left you with. It's who you are. The problem is, no one wants to see Earl Atlas.

You're twenty-four, you've been wrestling for five years now. At some point you give up on keeping your name. You call yourself The Paper Boy, The Plumber, The Garbage Man, Major Tom Strange Love, The Space Cowboy, and The Space Coyote. You've experimented with countless adjectives to enhance these names: super, grand, magnificent, remarkable, abominable, friendly, gorgeous. You've considered insignificant, ineffectual, invisible.

And you wake up in a motel room sardine packed with nine sweaty, snoring wrestlers. Since you were the last to leave that evening's show, bed space is nonexistent and floor space is scarce. You walk to the lobby, find a soft chair, and try to get a couple hour's rest before you're on the road again. The night clerk knows you're a wrestler and that you're cramming nine guys into a room that's been charged to one person—that you're stealing space—but he doesn't care. He's sixteen or seventeen and only cares about the midnight movie he's watching. It's a black and white film. A Zorro movie. And the movie reminds you of something. There was a show that you watched as a boy. It was a low budget Western, even as a kid you noticed how cheap the sets seemed, how the pistol shots sounded like cap guns, how the horses looked sickly, almost dead; the animals in the taxidermist's shop you lived above had more life in them. But you liked this show. There was something about the hero. He was like Zorro, like the Lone Ranger, a masked man. What was his name? What was the name of the program? *Deathmask* something. *The Gaucho's Deathmask.* Like the Lone Ranger, Gaucho carried two ivory handled pistols and had an Indian friend. No, the sidekick was a fat Mexican, like Pancho from *The Cisco Kid.* Instead of a sword like Zorro, Gaucho swung bolas, helicoptered them over the tumbleweed and sagebrush to ensnare fleeing villains.

The memory of this show does not transform you. You don't magically become a superstar. You don't even become El Gaucho then. Instead you toil on, gimmick after gimmick.

Tonight your name is The Zodiac Thriller. You're getting ready for your match, the main event at a Knights of Columbus hall in Peoria. You're fighting "Samson" Greg Samsa in a "Peoria Street Fight." The name changes depending on the city. Last week it was an "Omaha Street Fight." Tomorrow it will be "Springfield." You open the white canvas duffel that's filled with gimmicks to find a suitable weapon. You're allowed to bring one to the ring for these "Street Fights." You sort through brass knuckles, lengths of chain link, piano wire, clubs, a cattle prod. You're considering a sledge hammer, checking the balance of the weapon in your hand, when you see something stuffed inside a football helmet. A black mask. You hold it to your face, take in the musky smell, feel the sheer black satin, the laces zipping up the back, the leather patchwork around the eyes and mouth. You put your hand through the mouth hole and think of Father Kinski giving you First Communion. You remember the raccoon in the taxidermist's.

You pull your hand from the mask's mouth and the leather scrapes your palm, tries to bite you. This time there is no blood. You roll the mask down over your head, the satin is cool and sheer against your face. You tighten the laces in the back so that it fits true. You enter your "Street Fight" without any other weapons.

You wake up and you're a masked wrestler. But The Mask isn't a bag of beans that sprouts a stalk for you to climb to the top. It's only a stepping stone. You call yourself El Gaucho, but you're still Earl Atlas. Change is gradual. You keep working, dogging yourself, night after night. If there is any magic in The Mask, it's the wall it throws up between you and the crowds. It frees you from the weight of their stares. You stop worrying about them and concentrate on your matches. The Mask frees the crowd as well. They can see you as who or whatever they need you to be.

Slowly Earl Atlas becomes El Gaucho. You begin to make a name for yourself. With The Mask on you win titles. On the independent circuits the recognition comes in belts that are smaller than most cowboys' rodeo buckles and titles with grandiose names to make up for their small stature. You win the CCMAW Super Mega Wattage Championship, Dream Team Wrestling's Trans-Galactic Championship, and the Interspecies title at Friar Tuck's Wrestling Road Show. Independent Wrestling North crowns you King of the Lumberjacks on three separate occasions. You raise the Last Man Standing trophy over your head after winning the Tournament of Tough Guys.

All that hardware means nothing though. It's not what keeps you going, pushing through the pain of the endless injuries, the horrible food of the road, of wrestling in shithole nightclubs in Flint, Michigan and Rockford, Illinois. You want real gold. You want CWA or GWF titles. You want to be the best of the best. So you do time in a semi-national promotion, a blood and guts act like the Rinaldi Brothers' Action Alliance Wrestling, just so you can get to the next level; if they don't kill themselves, the top talent for the Rinaldis often make their way to the big show. A referee almost bites your ear off in your first match with the promotion. You juice, bleed, blade. One night, during a ladder match in Pittsburgh, a drunken fan rushes the ring and tackles the ladder you're climbing. You're standing on the top rung, twenty feet in the air, reaching for the belt when he topples you. Nothing's broken but now there's a hole in your tongue you can pass cigarettes through. And then that scout, that V.P., Bodacious Bill Boscoe in your case, shows up after an AAW show where you've lost ten pounds in one match, not sure how much in blood and how much in sweat. He's wearing a fake beard and a baseball cap, incognito because the Rinaldi Brothers don't take kindly to the CWA and GWF raiding their talent. He takes you for prime rib and shoves contracts in your face. Tells you that Smilin Joe's seen you in action. Thinks you're gonna be huge. You're the future for the CWA. The Future, he whispers in your ear.

You sign on the dotted line.

A Never Ending Day in the Shadow of the Garden

It had just been a few months since I attended my first professional wrestling show: A WWF event headlined by Hulk Hogan against The Canadian Earthquake. My parents had taken me and a friend, likely after much cajoling on my behalf. Our seats were at the top of the arena ("the blue seats"). The wrestlers looked so small all that way down but it was a special evening for me. My next event would be very different.

My father had a friend who he worked with in his public school, who happened to be a huge pro wrestling fan. This man, a librarian in the school, had granted me access to a world of wrestling beyond the WWF through the magazines of the day, especially Pro Wrestling Eye. He had told my father that there was a small wrestling show coming up on a Sunday at the Penta Hotel, across the street from Madison Square Garden. My dad knew how much I enjoyed the last show, so he said that we could all go together.

What a world of difference this was. We made our way to the hotel and noticed a long line snaking around the block. Everyone would have to wait outside until tickets were checked and then take an elevator up to the ballroom for the show. It seemed like it took forever but when we got in the elevator my eyes opened wide. The other occupants were Cactus Jack, Steve Williams and Paul Orndorff. I was dumbfounded. These were the guys from the wrestling magazines! I didn't have anything to say and the ride was over in just a moment.

When we made our way to the seats, I was surprised how close we were to the action. We were on bleachers a few rows from the ring. Match after match occurred with many names I was familiar with, such as the Samoan Swat Team, The Killer Bees, Don Muraco, Bob Orton Jr. and some guy named Sunny Beach. Many of the familiar names seemed to be wrestling a rogue's gallery of masked guys. My father's friend speculated that it was the same guy that kept coming out.

After what seemed like several hours, there was an intermission. I was able to go over to the wrestlers and get autographs. The most special one for me was Bruno Sammartino. I found that the well known guys had better attitudes than the lesser known ones, such as the Power Twins.

It had been a draining day and we weren't sure how much more time was left. My father went over to the ring announcer and asked how many more matches were left. The response? "I ain't gonna count them." Well that did it. My father said he couldn't take much more of this. We stayed for a few more matches and then left. I didn't want to go but I wasn't sure how much more I could take myself.

In the year that followed, I saw the matches played (and replayed) on Sports Channel America. It didn't have the same feel as being there live but it was a special reminder. Once the promotion was off Sports Channel, I thought it was done. It wasn't until years later I heard about how Herb Abrams' UWF limped along with a terrible pay per view in Las Vegas and Herb meeting his own untimely demise, apparently from a drug overdose. None of that changed the special day for me. Thanks Herb (and dad).

CATFISH MCDARIS

El Milagro

During the depression my grandfather
wrestled when weather didn't cooperate
to make a good harvest, he was a big strong
man and feared nothing but his family
going hungry or without necessities

The WPA came along and put farmers
to work building roads and bridges, my
grandfather moved to New Mexico and
started a bricklaying company

On Fridays we'd go pay the laborers
and go to the wrestling matches at a
huge Quonset hut with bleachers up to
the rounded ceiling, it was crowded

It smelled of sweat and excitement,
drunks staggered around selling green
tomatoes to throw at the wrestlers you
didn't like, it was a wild adventure I
shared with my grandfather.

Most of the good men were from Texas
and Mexico, the great Lou Thesz with ears
the size of tortillas because of all the head
locks he'd been in, the three Funks

From Borger, Texas noted for their spinning
toe hold submission move, my favorite was
Ricky Romero, he would dance into the ring
and throw tiny sombreros to the crowd

He'd put a choke sleeper hold on his opponent

and they would be out and flopping around like a fish, then he'd cover them with a Mexican blanket and bring them back to life.

The North Pole Blues

My cousin married a coal mining hillbilly from West Virginia. His hick accent was thicker than chunky peanut butter. His brother, Quick could do a perfect English accent, he'd score chicks with it. Quick was a top shelf bullshit machine, I figured one day somebody would stick his nuts in a vise. He was always talking about Davy Crockett and wrestling bears. I'd thrown down with him a few times and he was a salty son of a bitch. When he'd try to put a hold on me, I'd open up a can of whoop ass, I trained for Vietnam in Ft. Polk, Louisiana. Also with a Puerto Rican guy that beat Bruce Lee in Madison Square Garden. Maybe Quick could handle a bear, but fighting to me was like knowing how to swim or ride a bike, it came natural.

Out of the blue, Quick invited me to a concert at the North Pole. He said he'd won some free tickets with transportation included.

The Reston, VA, based Molson Brewing Co. planned to send about 250 people for a four-day trip that included cruising the Arctic Sea from Resolute Bay aboard an icebreaker. The Red Hot Chili Peppers would entertain the group while aboard the icebreaker. A dude in the band named Flea raised sheer hell on bass guitar.

The temperature was warm for the concert featuring Metallica, Hole, Moist, Cake, and Veruca Salt. We saw huge bears eating seals, Polar and Kodiak. The concert was in Tuktoyaktuk, a village on the Beaufort Sea. The winners along with about 400 townspeople gathered in a heated tent for the show.

Quick and I partied with some funky ladies from Hole and some Eskimo babes. The stars were pulsing hypnotic blue diamonds. The wind was moaning on the tundra. Quick decided to wrestle a bear, I guess he just got tired of living. The Polar bear hit him once with his massive claws and his head went flying, the bear picked up his body and strolled away. I went over and looked at Quick's head, he was still smiling.

The Muscle

Legend had it
he was born
with only one muscle

his gut.

His head
His arms
they merely sprouted from it
like tendrils
their sole purpose
to move The Muscle around
to toss it against ropes
and fling it off ring posts
to wave, taunt and crassly gesticulate
at the palpitating audience
until popcorn spilled from lips and into the aisles
until crime retreated from the streets for a TV break
until every grandmother in Mexico
was as close to their beloved *Nino Terrible*
their *el Dimonio Dorado*
the Musculo Antipatico
as their failing eyesight would allow

He was *el Dimonio Dorado*
The Golden Demon
and no one could best
his solid mass
as round and resilient
as Mayan rubber
Unmovable
Ungraspable
it rebounded

off of everything put in its path
and the only weakness
Nino Terrible offered up
to his sweaty, masked adversaries
was the opportunity for a grab at the hair
which grew more plentifully
on his chest and back
than on his head

The Muscle
was fed only the finest liquid nutrients
Mestizo cerveza had to offer
Cooked to a golden brown by the sun
Oiled to glistening perfection
by the finest oil from the fattest coconuts
el Musculo Antipatico
was well taken care of
and from behind the golden mask
came a voice of undying self-assurance
the voice of a champion
and the voice of one who knew it

He was the reigning champ
from the Summer of 1966
to the Fall of '69
and the secret darling
of every grandmother in Mexico
who cherished him
as if her own grandson
Too old to care for his faults
and drinking themselves silly
on everything he had to offer
good or bad.

For it was as hard to tell

if he was bad or good
as it was to keep count
of all his nicknames
but in the ring
it didn't matter
and what else did grandmothers
secretly have to wish for
but the lingering lusty feelings
his oiled up frame
flying about the ring
conjured up in near dry wells
as he grappled
with the all-time greats
the *King of Saints*
Mr. Whiskers
Wred Fright
Eduardo Thomas del Honduras

On Sundays
after broadcasts
all of Mexico was said
to eat the best meals in all the world
thanks to abuelita
None of them even remotely aware
as they smacked lips
licked chops
and recapped just-finished matches
with open-mouthed foodfuls
that grandma hadn't made those meals for them
    ...and she hadn't made them for Mexico either
He'd never know it
and that was ok
but the entire country dined so finely
on a thousand meals made
just for The Muscle

All of Mexico was in love with him
as if he were a giant metaphor
for something else
and nobody was sure what that was
and nobody cared
but they were sure that it was something good
and that was good enough.

He was the president of Mexico
He was the saint
the father, the sun, the holy ghost
and Judas of Iscariot and the devil
Mexico and tequila
and lemons and tortillas
and everything
everything!
on Sundays

...until the things that made him strong
ate away at him
The beers that fed The Muscle
weighed him down
The screaming fans
made him deaf
And the meaningless sexual conquests
stole his charm...
In just three short years
his fame became so big
that even The Muscle could not lift it
and even abuelitas grew tired
of giving their best
for someone who never showed up
to even burp or smack their fingers in appreciation
when there was nothing but bones left

They weren't going to live forever
and they didn't want to spend what little time remained
with just one man
when there were so many to pick from
on TV these days

Underneath the mask
behind the muscle and oil and hair
the glamour and bravado and acrobatic flights
he was just another slob
who drank too much
like most of us
and beat his wife
when he was angry
at things that couldn't be touched
let alone hit
who let his dreams
run through his fingers
like sand
until all that was left
was a heap of unsorted promises
that would never
draw a crowd.

He had been the champion
of all Mexico
the nation united
under him
Once the streets had emptied
and plaster walls had bulged
until all that could be heard
from coast to coast
was the tinny sound of televised cheers
leaking out into the streets.

Like everything
he was now nothing
but for a brief moment
on Sundays
from the Summer of 1966
to the Fall of '69
every grandmother in Mexico
had been in love with him.

The venue, generally reserved for rodeos and stock shows, stunk like sweaty cow balls. Our seats were extra-awesome though.

That night "Sugar" Shane Helms, with WCW Cruiserweight Title still in tow, fought Colorado indie mainstay Psycho Sarge.

The two had a hell of a match. Helms even broke out his rarely-used Vertebreaker.

Jimmy Hart, who was engaged in a nation-wide publicity stunt, wrestled local radio personality "Boobzilla." Mercifully I can't remember a moment of their "match."

The move of the night was performed by an unnamed performer dressed like a Chinese stereotype. He old-schooled his opponet halfway around the ring before flattening him with a flying headscissors.

The show was entertaining as hell, and scoring me mad points with Jen. I'd hoped the match between Madusa and Nikita would put me over the top.

A plucky local grappler against a bonafide wrestling legend? For a young feminist that's gotta be like wrestling Spanish Fly, right?

Former WCW manager Sonny Onoo was in Nikita's corner for some reason. He would spend a good portion of the match jawing shamelessly with Rod and Paco.

About thirty seconds into their contest, Madusa mooned Sonny, and by proxy us.

Jen was not amused.

Their proceeding bout contained spankings-a-plenty.

198

Around the ten minute mark Madusa turned her attentions to Sonny, who was casually conversing with the rest of my party.

She broached the edge of the ring, inhaled deeply, and sent a hot white flurry of spit sailing towards him.

With cat-like speed, Sonny sidestepped her flying phlegm.

Some of Madusa's speutum hit the ground, some of it hit the rails...

... and some of it hit me.

THAT IS SO DISGUSTING!

It was then that I knew I wouldn't be getting any.

C-Blockk's match followed. He retained his title. Honestly, I was too busy mourning my newly-squashed love life to catch much of it.

Afterwards I brought everyone to meet C-Blockk. Secretly I'd hoped the champ might wingman me some points with Jen.

Instead he snubbed me for some big-breasted groupies.

Jen never went out with me again, but y'know what? I got spat on by a WWE Hall-of-Famer. What has she ever done?

I never bought tickets from C-Blockk again.

To this day Rod still gives me shit about that night.

Wrestling Is...

In 2011, mental illness killed Larry Sweeney.

That's a fact. It's a thing that was and it ate him up and it stole his genius and his brilliance from us.

I was supposed to go to King of Trios that year; a now ex-friend of mine had tickets and I had a training and couldn't attend. I missed a lot of great wrestling but I also missed the experience of a group of people coming together to mourn a lost family member, and I guess if I had gone I would have understood the way I feel now a little bit better.

See, in 2013 I was diagnosed with depression, which has since had the bonus stat of anxiety added onto it over the last year. I knew from the time I was a little kid that there was something "wrong" with me – inside my head was always a black, tangled mess; it felt like I was always crying in there even if I was smiling at everyone, showing my teeth to the world because sharks do that and they aren't afraid of nothin'.

However in 2013 I hit a rapid succession of low points and the one thing that kept me alive (and I say this to you with all seriousness) was wrestling.

I was lucky enough to be picked up to work on a wrestling site called Drop Toehold and I was able to talk about wrestling with all kinds of people. Sometimes they didn't like to hear what I had to say, because who wants to hear what a girl on the internet has to say to them about the manliest sport in existence? More often than not, though, I was listened to. And I started attending more shows. And I started talking to more people. More fans. More wrestlers.

I've never felt included in many things, partially because of the way I grew up being told I wasn't gonna amount to anything, and partially because having depression is a real bitch because you feel worthless and start questioning people all the time. "Why would anyone want to hang out with me?" "Why do you like me?" "Why do you care?" Friendships get fractured and you just hide in yourself for days.

You can't attend a wrestling show and hide. You can't go to a CHIKARA show without someone there understanding that you might be a little shy and taking the time to quietly seek you out and talk to you, REALLY talk to you, about how you like the show. Bryce Remsburg will do it; UltraMantis is forever behind the merch table talking music and ethics; Ashley Remington will finger-gun you and shoot a smile and you're ok. These folks know how hard it is to wake up and do things, but they're out there every weekend, just about, doing it.

They know what it's like to have a friend who has to fight sometimes. And they still wrestle their hearts out for the kids who make shirts of them and for the kids like me who became adults like me and who are so glad they go out of their way to share their art with us.

201

Wrestling is everything I want in life: Color, movement, the feeling of being united in our hate for the heels and our love of the faces. Wrestling is the one thing I've had consistently to hold onto since I was 7. Wrestling is a giant, sprawling, glorious extended family.

Wrestling is the one thing I can't ever stop loving and it's the one thing I can't thank enough.

On Dressing Up As Goldust for Halloween

He applies the makeup himself: a video of him drawing the outlines of where the black foundation shall go shows the long sweeps he makes—up and over the contours of his cheekbones, over the tops of tightly shut eyelids. The patterns have gotten more elaborate as he has gotten older: earlier days included a squirt of gold face paint into cracked palms, a washing over of sparkle over splotched skin chaffed red from too many drinks, or too many headlocks. Now, there are angles that you've never seen: the flaring of nostrils, the erasing of eyebrows, the caking of necks until beard stubble cannot push through the gold like an unwanted dandelion.

I cannot do this on my own. My hands do not turn the right way: they grow tired from their own mechanics; they cannot hold anything worth holding. Every finger I have is broken except for the thumbs: only spared by my clumsiness—a misjudged football, a slip on the ice braced for every way but correctly.

As you sit on the coffee table in a blonde wig, you paint circles around my eyes—we start with the gold first, my head shaved for the artifice: of the makeup being soaked up by the dryness in my cheeks. You are concerned that this will be inauthentic: that the colors will smudge together—that there will be no way to tell the difference between the gold and the black, that it will combine to a sparkly mud of nothing—a bronze instead of a gold, a dullness less bizarre, a second-loser instead of something victorious.

The man beneath the makeup spoke only in quotes—of famous starlets and dashing leads, of always being ready for one's close-up. You are the only one that I allow to look me in the eye—the rest of the time I keep my nose to the ground, I look toward the sky as if I have forgotten everything I've ever wanted to say & I am active in the mystique of remembering. That all I can remember is my name & even then I am uncertain in how it sprawls out from underneath my tongue—that I used to speak with perfect diction, that I would never stutter, or stumble, or fear that a syllable would get caught and echo back down my throat and into my lungs. I too, speak in quotations: of things I have said before, of forgetting to tell you about fears, about deaths and marriages. Instead, I tell you about my day over and over again—of things I once said, of overheard nothings, of things you have told me that I have already told.

You know nothing about wrestling—about how men much larger than me fly through the air, how it is all choreographed, how you know that no one actually gets hurt, but you do not know about how every-thing hurts. You ask me who I am being, again—of gold paint and leotards, of being someone so grandiose yet so inconsequential: we are playing pretend, we are make-believing. You ask who you are supposed to be: the lovely accompaniment, the director, the producer, the woman in lamé, the name you forget because it means nothing; another character, a small bit-role in a story that has no end—a constant revolution of characters coming and going; of losing one's way, of giving up the gold ghost, of acknowledging that all of this is false. We all know how the story ends: of redemption, of putting the makeup back on, of slithering over feathers, of remembering that some things are worth remembering and other things are worth repeating.

You go back over the parts of my face that wish to remain uncovered—the dark concealer fading as it absorbs into my skin, as if I am trying to fight the cover up. I tell you to mind my lips, to make sure my jaw is covered, that I look as real as possible. We buy a cigar from the corner store to complete your outfit. You buy a dress that you will never wear again. You do this because you know this is important to me: to be mistaken for someone that wakes up in hotel rooms states away, who has brothers, daughters, who pretends to be hurt when he is not hurt. We will play the parts that neither of us are born to play. We will never break character: we will pose with strangers; we will drink gin through straws so we do not ruin the lipstick. We will return home, smoky and exhausted, a black smudge on your cheek. You will help me wash the paint off from behind my ears—I will spit black and gold when your head is turned. We will go to bed with our hair wet. We will wake up the next morning, and the next morning, and the next morning. I will remember your name each and every time. I will not forget my lines.

The Wrestler

I could have been a contender ...

Because the program didn't offer an affordable comprehensive insurance plan, my step-dad pulled me from wrestling the third week of practice, locking my fantasy in a sleeperhold.

But in my dreams, I conditioned my body and mastered signature moves: the crippling reverse suplex, the bowel-shattering powerslam, the fatal DDT.

I greased up and slid on my luchadore mask, spent my lean years wrestling the county fair circuit, dropped flying elbows into unconscious opponents, entertained herds of screaming spectators massed around illegal backyard free-for-alls and tractor pull side stages.

I made it into the pros, and nearly lost my knee to an illegal leglock, but in an amphitheater-pleasing turn of events, I regained footing and executed a 360 degree piledriver, stealing the gold belt from the reigning heavyweight champ, "El Padre Gordo," in a 60 minute, hardcore, ladder, casket, razor-wire, cage match, after which I dedicated the victory to my mom.

Capt. Lou

I bought some sweet new zombie comics, drank a 32 oz. Mt. Dew, watched a costume contest, and rifled through dirty cardboard boxes marked *Underground and Adult*, hoping to find a Crumb/Bukowski collaboration. Eddie Haskell was there. Lt. Worf from *Star Trek: Next Generation* was signing autographs, too. But no Capt. Lou Albano.

For weeks, I bragged to my friend Craig that I was going to meet Capt. Lou at the Motor City ComiCon – that I was going to shake his hand, take his picture, have him sign an 8x10 black and white glossy.

I was going to ask what the rubberbands meant and how they stayed on in the squared-circle. I was going to tell him about how I was going to be him for Halloween last year, but couldn't find an effective adhesive to keep the rubberbands glued to my face.

CANCELLATIONS, read the white sheet of lined paper taped to the door. Capt. Lou Albano was the first name on the list, followed by Former Tag Team Champions the Wild Samoans and television's own Corin "Parker Lewis" Nemic.

Craig got word of Mr. Albano's absence and left a message on my cell phone. "Hey, buddy," he said. "This is Cap'n Lou! Just calling to apologize for not showing yesterday. To make it up to ya', I'm sending you one of my very own favorite rubberbands … autographed. I write very, very small."

"Didja hear … ?"

"Didja hear the Ultimate Warrior died?" That's the question I'd been asking all week. "Didja hear the Ultimate Warrior died?" My wife couldn't have cared less. The tweaker who worked in the Holiday station pretended that she had no idea what I was talking about. "Didja hear the Ultimate Warrior died?" I asked my son, Jack, while we flipped through our local library's selection of new release DVDs. "Oh," he said with a pause, "I thought he was already dead."

Jack may only be ten years-old, far too young to have ever actually seen the Ultimate Warrior in action, all grease paint and veins and tassels, but he knew him from the various *YouTube* clips I'd shown him and the video games we played together, video games full of the likenesses of dead men. Andre the Giant, Mr. Perfect, "Ravishing" Rick Rude, the Big Boss Man, "Macho Man" Randy Savage, et cetera, et cetera, et cetera …

In the mind of my son, it must've been a safe assumption that all professional wrestlers are either dead or on their way to a premature grave, but at the same time, their lives must feel about as real as a cartoon character's. My question must have felt about as real as if I had asked, "Didja hear that Bugs Bunny died?" And when I think about it that way, there was no bigger cartoon character than the Ultimate Warrior.

This should be the part where I expound upon the idea that the Ultimate Warrior was bigger than life, that his legacy will never truly die, but all of that is about as obvious and, well, as cliché as the discussion of dead professional wrestlers, so let's avoid going down that road, altogether.

"Didja hear the Ultimate Warrior died?" I can't say why I keep asking that question, and I can't say for how long I'll keep asking it, but I'm sure it has something to do with it not quite feeling real to me, either, like it *was* a cartoon character who died, like it was Captain Caveman or the Tasmanian Devil, not James Hellwig (aka the Dingo Warrior aka the Ultimate Warrior). But when it comes down to it, as cliché as it may be, the Ultimate Warrior *was* bigger than life and his legacy *will* live on … Then again, you already knew that, didn't you?

So, I guess the only thing left to say is, Rest in Parts Unknown, brother.

Jorge, El Ratón Volador

Dedicated in loving memory to William Relling, Jr.
See you when I get there, pal.

1.

I'm not the best fight coordinator in professional wrestling, but I know the goddamn difference between a Spinning Sleeper Hold and a Spinning Sleeper Hold with a Cobra Clutch, for example, and a Reverse Neck Snap and an Inverted Neck Breaker, which is more than you can say for some.

I also know most professional wrestlers name themselves after something tough, something strong, or something that strikes fear in a man, but that said the most fearsome wrestler I ever met during twenty plus years in the business was from Tijuana and named himself after a flying mouse.

Who was The Flying Mouse? How old was he? Was there a Mrs. Mouse? I have no goddamn idea so don't even ask. I'll just call it like I saw it, and you can take that for what it's worth.

But before you can understand how I got involved with Mexican wrestling and The Flying Mouse, you have to understand how I screwed up my life previously. See, I used to be a fight coordinator for a hugely popular New York wrestling league. I don't want to get too specific about what I did, so let's just say I thought it'd be a good idea at the time to hump my General Manager's young wife in his office at Madison Square Garden.

I know what you must be thinking about my judgment right now, but you had to see this office. Lush red carpet, paintings that cost more than a college education and a mahogany desk as big as an aircraft carrier, not to mention panoramic windows with a view of the arena and its 20,000 seats. On fight nights, you could sit up there and watch wrestlers like The Empire State Building and The Brooklyn Bridge pound on each other with moves planned by yours truly as two huge video screens played highlights and pyrotechnics lit up the crowd.

The wife was no slouch either. She was half my age, a twenty-four year old featherweight wrestler named Maiden America who had the lean build and disproportionate boob job that made her a star with fans despite her complete lack of skill in the ring. Again, I don't want to get into detail, but I had Maiden America on that aircraft carrier desk with her star-spangled skirt pushed up to her star-spangled corset. As the crowd below roared to the bullshit brutality of an under-card bout, we engaged in our own pinning and submission moves, if you know what I mean. And that's when the GM walked in and caught us.

Maiden America was bucking against me and just about to reach the pinnacle of her patriotic fervor when I heard the office door click open and felt a draft on my exposed, sweaty cheeks. I turned my head, careful not to break time, and saw the GM standing there, his wrinkled old face a mask of rage, his glare hitting me like a Haymaker.

"Coward!" he screeched.

We had plenty of issues, the GM and me, and humping his wife wasn't exactly the most straight-forward way of dealing with them, I admit. But after he walked in, there wasn't much I could do except the thing that came naturally; I ran.

I only humped his wife that one time, but that didn't stop the old bastard from holding a grudge. He used his clout to freeze my bank accounts, plus he sent his goddamn wrestler goons after me as I fled cross-country. I had close calls with The Capone Brothers in Chicago, The Arch Fiend in St. Louis, and the Mile High Rocky Mountain Wrecking Machine in Denver. I finally fled to Mexico after a particularly hairy encounter with a wrestler named Third Degree Sunburn in San Diego who tried to drown me in two feet of water at Coronado Beach. He would've succeeded, too, if a jellyfish hadn't taken a liking to his leg.

Anyway, two hours later, I made it to Tijuana with only twenty-five bucks to my name.

2.

At the time, I considered Tijuana a city of goddamn smog and squalor—though, to be fair, I thought the same of any city that wasn't New York—but it wasn't like I had the means to move on. So Tijuana with its goddamn stray dogs and peeling storefronts and goddamn empty bottles that goddamn blinded you when the sun hit them and goddamn concrete steps that led goddamn nowhere was pretty much it for me.

The plan was to recruit my own wrestling team down there, build a little fame and fortune, and get my life back on track. I used a few bucks to rent a room at the Tijuana YMCA, and put the rest into turning the janitorial closet of a dilapidated downtown gym into an office.

The gym used to be a storage warehouse for tobacco, and the faint smell of cigars mingled with the smell of sweat between those corrugated metal walls. An old wrestling ring lay sprawled in the center like some K.O.'d goon, and around it were racks of black-iron dumbbells and heavy punching bags that hung by chains from dusty rafters.

An old man who stooped like a comma and smelled like cooked cabbage owned the place. He said I could use the closet only if I let his grandson help out with whatever I planned to do for a living. After I agreed to his senile extortion, he told me to stay the hell away from his customers during the day, but that I could do as I pleased after hours.

So there I was, surrounded by bottles of bleach and drain clog remover with an upended pallet box for a desk, a cordless phone, and a lamp shaped like a palm tree that I'd found in a dumpster. But I was in business, the difference between Mexican wrestling and American wrestling notwithstanding.

See, Mexican wrestling is all about reaction, not choreography. The wrestlers, or, *luchadors,* have pat responses to certain moves, sure, but there's no set order. You don't know who's going to throw what, when. That means Mexican wrestling is less about fakery and more about how well you react to a hit.

3.

The wrestler I recruited first called himself El Pared, which means The Wall. He was about my age, late forties, and big as the monolith in that science fiction movie. He had enough power packed into his massive frame to toss some *chilango* and his extended family from Tijuana to Mexico City, never mind that it was nearly three thousand miles away. He wore royal blue trunks, blue knee boots and a blue silk mask with holes for his dark eyes and brutish lips. His shoulders and chest were covered with a forest of black, wiry hair and his hands were the size of boxing gloves. On the broad canvas of his belly was a stretched and faded tattoo of people cheering as a section of the Berlin Wall came down. The scene wasn't meant to show the strength of the Berlin Wall itself, but the strength of the freedom behind it. Trust me, the rationale sounds even more goddamn impressive when it's explained to you in a thick, noble accent. And barely visible below his gut was a thick, blue vinyl belt with a gold metal buckle that had the outline of Mexico stamped onto it.

To see what The Wall could do, I invited an established wrestler named Golden Conquistador over to the gym for a one-on-one bout. Golden Conquistador looked just like you'd expect—gold mask, gold trunks, gold cape, gold boots. The whole get-up. When the bell rang, Golden Conquistador climbed to the top of a corner post and leapt at The Wall as the hairy bastard stood in the center of the ring, arms crossed, like he didn't know the match had started. I yelled for him to move, but he ignored me as Golden Conquistador flew at him. For that terrible, mid-air moment, I saw Golden Conquistador transformed into a screaming bird of prey, capable of tearing any creature limb from limb—until he bounced off The Wall like a pigeon hitting a high-rise window and flopped onto the mat unconscious. The Wall grinned at me triumphantly then, as if he'd proven the goddamn fortitude of freedom.

The Wall could have been his own team if not for one problem: Tequila. The bottle called to him more sweetly than a dirty back room of *putas*. He'd smuggle a flask into the ring by tucking it under his belt, and then sneak a swig while other wrestlers were showboating or after he'd pitched an opponent over the ropes or whenever else he could. As a result, about halfway into a match, The Wall would crumble all on his own.

The second member of my team was Cucaracha del Diablo, or Devil Cockroach, a twenty-two year old kid who came from a long line of bug exterminators. Growing up, his father regaled him with stories of how cockroaches avoided traps and sprays with an aptitude that belied their speck-of-sand-sized brains. You could say that Devil Cockroach's family hunted cockroaches in much the same way that American Indians hunted buffalo: with great respect and because their survival depended on it.

Devil Cockroach wore a brown mask with thick black circles around the eyeholes and a brown unitard with two stuffed roach legs hanging from the middle. Each stuffed leg was the size of a baseball bat with black pipe cleaners stuck into it to represent hairs. On a gold chain around his neck hung a roach encased in Lucite—a big brown fucker the size of a business card that he kissed for good luck before entering the ring. The Devil part of his name referred to the red, yellow and orange hellfire emblem embroidered on the back of his costume by his grandmother to strike holy terror in Catholic opponents, which in Mexico is pretty much everybody.

Devil Cockroach relied on hit and run tactics, executing Roundhouse-Clothesline combos so fast you could barely tell the moves apart. He would have been a scurrying force to reckon with if not for those goddamn stuffed legs. If left too long in the ring, he would inevitably get tied up in them. Once he tried to execute a Side Rolling Leg Scissor Takedown and thanks to the stuffing, ended up pinning himself. When I suggested he rip off the legs and paint them on instead, he looked at me like I wanted to put his mother in a donkey show. I didn't push the issue because I knew how important cockroaches were to him and his family.

Our errand boy was the gym owner's grandson that I mentioned earlier. He was a 16-year-old midget who did our scut work—laundered clothes, emptied the spit bucket, that sort of thing. He turned out to be a decent kid and knew every wrestler and every wrestling statistic by heart. We called him Chihuahua not because he was small or came from the town of Chihuahua, but because he took Ritalin on account of hyperactivity. Even with the drug, he trembled and stared at you in that weird sidelong way that real Chihuahuas did. On busy days, I hid his prescription bottle so he'd rev up and get more done.

I split the take we earned from matches evenly among the team. The Wall, Devil Cockroach and Chihuahua each got ten percent, and I got the remaining seventy percent, which makes sense when you think about it.

4.

And that was pretty much the way things went: The Wall would let opponents wreck themselves against him until he got too drunk to stand, and then Devil Cockroach would deliver a quick finish, usually before he pinned himself with his stuffed legs. We did so well in doubles matches that we qualified for trios matches—three against three—which were the final step before going to the championship.

That meant I needed a third wrestler, so I paid a couple guys seventy-five cents each for the day to paper windshields and storefronts with fliers. The first person to respond who wasn't a *borracho* looking for a place to piss was only a foot taller than Chihuahua and introduced himself in a squeaky voice as Jorge, el Ratón Volador.

"Wait, don't tell me," I told The Wall, who acted as interpreter during the interviews. "El Ratón Volador means The Vicious Raptor, right?"

The Wall gave me a look. "No, my friend. It means The Flying Mouse."

The Flying Mouse was dressed in a snug-fitting cowl made of dark gray fur that covered his face down to his nose, and a black body suit with red fabric wings that stretched from his arms to his sides. He was barefoot too with the longest, narrowest toes I'd ever seen. Stupid name aside, the guy didn't smell like Tequila, have two extra extremities, or tremble like a spaz, so I decided to give him a chance in the ring against The Wall.

When I rang the bell, they entered the ring at opposite corners. The Wall took his place at center, arms crossed, as usual. The Flying Mouse leaped to the top rope as easily as you'd step onto a street curb, using his long narrow toes like fingers to grip the rope and bounce like he was on a trampoline—low at first, then higher as he flapped his red fabric wings. Once he really got going, he let go of the rope and soared until he was lost in the rafters a good forty feet in the air, then reappeared a second later diving like a goddamn fighter jet.

He hit The Wall full force and bounced off—as I expected—but The Wall rocked back a step as The Flying Mouse somersaulted and landed on the top rope again, unharmed. Until then, nobody had moved The Wall after he was set. Nobody.

Chihuahua was so excited that he did back flips and had to calm down with a handful of pills. And me? I was happy as a drug cartel mule whose condoms hadn't burst in transit. I was sure I'd found the wrestler who'd take us to the championship.

I couldn't have been more goddamn wrong.

5.

The trios matches were held the following Thursday through Sunday at the Auditorio Municipal down the block from the gym, with teams winning the most of four matches moving on to the championship. The Auditorio smelled like piss and jock itch, and held five thousand roaring fans, six thousand if you ignored fire code, so let's just call it six thousand. The ring was new with bright red ropes, shiny black corner-posts, and the Auditorio Municipal monogram printed in blue ink on the white, spring-mounted mat.

Chihuahua and I sat ringside behind a waist-high, grated-metal partition that separated the fighters from the crowd. The Wall, Devil Cockroach and The Flying Mouse stood directly in front of us inside the team's designated starting area on the arena floor. The rules were simple: All members of your team had to enter the ring at least once; action that took place out of the ring was a free-for-all; you had to pin every member of the opposing team to win.

Our opening match was against Los Patriotas. Each member of their team wore a satin mask, unitard and cape that corresponded to a color of the Mexican flag. If you ask me, that sort of public pandering really cheapens the sport of professional wrestling.

The Wall and Señor Verde entered the ring from opposite corners. Señor Verde stood on the second turnbuckle and bellowed the first verse of the Mexican national anthem to the crowd— *Mexicanos, al grito de Guerra / El acero, aprestad y el bridón, / y retiemble en sus centros la tierra. / Al sonoro rugir del canon!* —as The Wall stood in his usual spot with arms crossed and waited.

The bell sounded and Señor Verde, still singing, charged and struck The Wall hard across the chest with a Shoulder Smash. The Wall didn't even flinch as Señor Verde's shoulder dislocated with a hollow pop that echoed all the way to the nosebleed seats. Señor Verde hollered, arm lolling like a hooked cow carcass. The crowd went ape-shit with appreciation. Devil Cockroach and Chihuahua went nuts, too, hopping up and down, but The Flying Mouse stood absolutely still, not making a goddamn sound.

At that point, Señor Verde could execute only Head-Butt/Toe Stomp combos, which The Wall calmly endured while covering his mouth with both hands as he pretended to yawn. I knew exactly what the monolithic drunkard was up to and kept a close eye on him as he returned the flask to his belt.

Pretty soon, the frustrated Señor Verde tagged Señor Blanco who bounded into the ring with a Jumping Spin Kick. As he flew through the air, Señor Blanco sang the anthem's second verse— *¡Guerra, guerra sin tregua al que intente / De la patria manchar* —until The Wall blocked with a forearm that sent him headfirst into a corner post. Señor Blanco was stunned, but I could see that The Wall was starting to waver. I called to him and he lumbered drunkenly to the edge of the ring where he tagged one of Devil Cockroach's stuffed legs.

Taking his cue, Devil Cockroach kissed the vile bug around his neck, and then scurried under the lowest rope just as Señor Blanco recovered and began singing again. He spun around so Señor Blanco could see the hellfire emblem, and when the man dropped his guard to cross himself, Devil Cockroach struck with a Whirling Roundhouse Kick to the chest. Señor Blanco pitched into the ropes, then bounded back helplessly, at which point Devil Cockroach took him down with a brutal Clothesline across the throat. After that, he simply fell across Señor Blanco's inert body for one, two, three counts, earning the pin.

Devil Cockroach then flung himself through the ropes at the injured Señor Verde in what should have been a beautiful outside-the-ring Suicide Splash had it not been for those goddamn stuffed legs. As he sailed through the air, they whipped around to cinch his arms at the elbows, causing him to miss Señor Verde and smack face-first on the arena floor. Now it was a free-for-all.

Señor Verde and Señor Rojo converged on the twitching Devil Cockroach for the pin when the crowd's roar suddenly rose an octave. There was The Flying Mouse holding onto the top rope with his long toes, flapping his red wings and bouncing away. When he let go, a hush rippled through the crowd. He sailed up to the lighting grid—which was a good thirty feet higher than our gym ceiling—hung motionless for a split-second at the top of his flight arc, and then plunged into a dive. Señor Rojo was so mesmerized by the spectacle that he didn't evade as The Flying Mouse swooped down on him. The bone-jarring impact sent Señor Rojo spinning underneath the ring where he remained unconscious for the rest of the match.

Señor Verde cowered as The Flying Mouse stood and dusted himself off. But instead of going for the easy pin, The Flying Mouse returned to the team's designated area. I just about pinched a burrito right there. Señor Verde got a look on his face like he couldn't believe his luck, and then picked up a metal folding chair with his good arm and smashed the still-struggling Devil Cockroach with it repeatedly as though it were the heel of some enormous shoe.

"Go help Cockroach, goddammit!" I yelled as the metal chair slammed down with a hollow *whang!* That was when The Flying Mouse looked at me with the blankest eyes I'd ever seen on a person without a mullet and squeaked, "El ratón sólo vuele en la noche."

"What did he say?" I asked The Wall who was standing nearby in a miasma of Tequila fumes.

"'The mouse flies only at night,'" The Wall slurred.

I stared at The Flying Mouse in confused disbelief. "It is nighttime! Now get over there before Cockroach gets squashed!"

Again, The Flying Mouse didn't move and repeated, "El ratón sólo vuele en la noche."

The shock of The Flying Mouse's insubordination hit me like an Open Hand Chop to the throat. I felt a strange, almost overwhelming fear unfurl inside my gut and flood my muscles with jittery adrenaline.

The Wall must have sensed my mental short-out because he took it upon himself to help Devil Cockroach instead. In his condition, he couldn't have pinned a goddamn corsage but Señor Verde didn't know that. When the guy saw The Wall lurching toward him, he dropped the chair and ran out of the arena, green cape flapping behind him like it was waving goodbye.

That was it; we'd won the match. As after every match at Auditorio Municipal, the air became thick with hurled tortillas. Chihuahua explained that the tradition started a few years back after a wrestler was killed by a tossed beer bottle, tortillas being much safer. I'd be lying if I said I didn't hope something more dangerous than a tortilla might hit The Flying Mouse after the stunt he pulled. But I took a deep breath to calm myself and realized it was the little guy's first match with a new team and he was bound to be nervous, so I let the matter slide. Soon after, my panic passed.

6.

Later that night, we were back in the gym eating dinner on a card table set clear of the ring and weight racks. Devil Cockroach had brought in chicken tamales handmade by his grandmother. No matter how loud we smacked our lips over those savory wonders, The Flying Mouse wouldn't join us. He stayed perched on the top rope of the ring like a goddamn parakeet and watched us eat. Come to think of it, I never saw him eat the whole time I knew him—or drink, or take a dump, or sleep, for that matter.

He also never took off that red-winged body suit and, frankly, it was getting ripe. Keeping his mask on, that I understood. Thanks to Chihuahua, I knew the mask gave a wrestler the freedom to express himself in the ring. It was a sacred symbol of identity, a projection of the soul. Take off the mask in public, and he loses it all. He has to literally reinvent himself. So I understood why The Wall and Devil Cockroach still had their masks on, pushed up to their noses to facilitate tamale eating. But they'd also changed into the white robes I'd swiped from the hotel next door.

As strange as it was, though, I saw The Flying Mouse as a sort of hapless child who belonged to us despite his weird utterances and oily costume. If I got rid of him because of a simple goddamn mistake, I'd be doing all of us an injustice. But I wanted to know what the team thought, so I asked them in a lowered voice when Devil Cockroach broke out flan for dessert.

The Wall replied, "Each wrestler has the freedom to fight in the manner he wishes."

"Even though he almost lost us the match today?" I followed up, frowning.

"We have the freedom to lose, as well."

"This would have never happened if he was a cockroach," Devil Cockroach interjected. "In a colony, every member protects every other member to insure survival. I say we replace him."

"Freedom is survival," The Wall said. "Each man defines freedom in his own way, then reaps the benefits or suffers the consequences."

"Oh yeah?" Devil Cockroach said. "Maybe I should give you guys the freedom to fend for yourselves."

This wasn't good. The Flying Mouse's attitude was starting to affect the rest of the team. I had to act fast to break the tension. "What do you think, Chihuahua?" I asked.

"Well," said Chihuahua thoughtfully, pressing a Ritalin tablet into his flan with his index finger before taking a bite, "when Javier Sanchez and Blue Cobra replaced their third teammate Tierra y Fuego with Mr. Rio Grande in 1943, they went on to win the championship. However, when El Loco Padre and Chupacabra fired Pelayo Marquez in favor of La Criatura Del Dolor in 1956, the team vanished mysteriously, never to be heard from again..."

Leave it to Chihuahua to convolute an issue with too many facts and chatter. I tuned him out, then remembered we were talking about The Flying Mouse when he was actually in the room a mere fifty feet away. I got up, loaded a couple tamales onto a paper plate, and brought them over in the interest of conducting an experiment.

"You should eat," I told him.

"El ratón sólo vuele en la noche," he squeaked, which was apparently his motto now.

"You'll need your strength tomorrow," I said, raising the plate.

He stared at me.

"Come on, Devil Cockroach's grandmother made these special for us."

I was about to give up when he stretched out his leg and grabbed a tamale with his goddamn foot. I leapt back in disgust because that was the first time I got a really good look at his toes. They were the color of sausages with blue-veined nails that looked chewed to the quick and smelled like queso manchego.

The Flying Mouse was unmoved by my reaction. He stayed balanced on his perch and brought the tamale slowly toward his mouth only to mash it against his chin.

I'd intended to toss him from the team if he refused my order to eat, but a tremendous fatigue came over me like I'd been in a dozen wrestling matches—and with that fatigue came the jittery wave of fear I'd felt earlier. Before that wave could crest, I hurried away, telling myself that I didn't have the energy to enforce my intentions. The fear began to subside as I returned to the group.

Devil Cockroach shook his head as I sat. "We're going to pay for keeping him around," he said. "You wait and see."

7.

I figured Thursday would be the end of the weirdness, but Friday got even weirder.

Devil Cockroach was still groggy after his encounter with the folding chair, so I figured I'd put The Flying Mouse in the ring after The Wall. This time we were fighting Los Diputados Especiales, a trio of muscled bruisers clad in khaki jumpsuits like local cops. Instead of traditional masks, they wore mirrored sunglasses with blue bandanas hanging from the frames to hide their faces.

The Wall did his usual immovable-object routine, but when it came time for The Flying Mouse to tag in and finish the job, the little winged bastard stayed in the team's designated area. The only thing I could figure was the change in order confused him.

"Mouse! Get in the goddamn ring!" I yelled, and wouldn't you know it, he looked at me with the same dim expression and gave me the same goddamn line, "El ratón sólo vuele en la noche." The little twerp's defiance hit me like an Underhook Face Breaker and I felt the same, undefined sense of dread flood my body.

The Wall stood drunkenly with his dinner plate-sized hand outstretched for the tag until a Deputy delivered a Two-Fisted Rabbit Punch to his kidneys. The blow pitched The Wall over the ropes onto the arena floor. The crowd let out an ecstatic howl—and still The Flying Mouse did nothing.

I was on my feet now, pacing frantically behind the partition. It didn't matter how exhausted the Deputies were—The Wall and Devil Cockroach weren't in any shape to take them on. But if nobody took the ring we'd be disqualified.

And then the crowd started to boo. They wanted action and they wanted it now. From the corner of my eye, I saw Devil Cockroach plant a wet one on his Lucite roach. I stretched over the partition to grab him but it was too late. He scurried into the ring, and angled his back to display the hellfire emblem as the Deputy bore down on him, but apparently he was fighting the only atheist in the entire goddamn country.

Without missing a beat, the Deputy lifted him overhead and smashed him, tailbone-first onto the mat for the pin while The Flying Mouse continued to watch from the designated area. Only when it was his usual time to wrestle did he leap onto the top rope, but by then too much dead time had passed and the referee called the match.

The only thing that stopped me from collapsing in total panic was the revelation that The Flying Mouse must be feeling the same way I was to be acting like this. He was afraid, poor little guy. And how could I yell at him when I was afraid, too?

Turned out I should have said something to him because Saturday's match was even more of a goddamn disaster. I don't even remember who we fought it went so badly. This time, the Flying Mouse refused to enter the ring at all, even when all he had to do was dive and pin the last guy. Instead, when I was screaming at him to tag in, he looked at me calmly from the designated area and said … you guessed it.

But I had a contingency plan. I leaned over the partition and told The Wall that The Flying Mouse felt nervous and needed help with his signature move.

"I'll give The Flying Mouse freedom to overcome his fear," he replied with breath pungent enough to ignite.

The Wall lifted The Flying Mouse over the top rope so that the small of his back rested against it, and then pulled until the rope stretched past the mat to the arena floor like a giant slingshot. Even though The Flying Mouse must have known what was going to happen, he didn't cry out or struggle. On the contrary, he went goddamn limp.

The Wall let go and the rope whipped The Flying Mouse high into the air. He soared straight up, arms and legs flopping like a beanbag doll, until his head clipped the lighting grid and he went cart-wheeling into the crowd. He didn't get so much as a scratch—little spud was tough as an old tire—but since he didn't actually touch the mat, we were disqualified.

8.

That night was too hot to sleep, so I took a red cab to the gym, hoping to come up with a plan that would insure victory on Sunday. Since we'd lost two out of three matches, we needed to enter a mask-versus-mask bout to win a wildcard spot or we'd be out of the finals. Wrestlers avoided these bouts like used steroid needles because losers had to give away their masks to winners in the ring. That meant losers revealed their identities to the public, which was like throwing away who they'd been for years. The risk was huge, but I was willing to take that risk for a shot at the championship and getting my life back.

I let myself into the gym and walked past the ring to my office. Moonlight streamed through the windows and created long shadows on the floor. A creak drew my attention to the corner rafters. I peered into the darkness and saw the silhouette of something hunkered there like a buzzard.

I ran to the office and fetched the .22 pistol that I used to shoot rats in the alley, then positioned myself directly under whatever was lurking in the rafters and fired a single shot. I missed, hearing the bullet thunk wood, but the shot had a profound effect nonetheless. The thing shifted heavily and knocked a rain of objects from its perch. Nibbled-on tortillas slapped the floor around me and sent dust swirling; a rusty spittoon bounced with a *clang!* and sprayed a fan of what looked like dried guano; and a copy of *National Geographic* (Spanish edition) dropped open to the centerfold photo of a flying squirrel, the pages stiff and wrinkled like something wet had dried on them.

"Goddammit, Mouse!" I yelled, flipping on the gym lights. "I know it's you."

I heard the scritch-scritch of toenails on wood before The Flying Mouse jumped down from the rafters onto the floor. He was wearing his oily costume, as always. I didn't care that he was living in the rafters. I just wanted to know what his problem was in the ring.

"Why the hell aren't you diving anymore?" I asked.

He said nothing as an errant breeze caused his red wings to flap gently against his sides.

"Are the guys giving you trouble? I can talk with them if they are."

Still no answer.

"Look, Jorge, you have to pull your weight. It's only fair. How about making another move your new specialty if diving is a problem? Say, Airplane Spin Toss instead."

He shook his head.

"Okay, how about Reverse Monkey Flip?"

He shook his head.

"Pumphandle Argentine Back Breaker?"

He shook his head.

"Belly to Belly Suplex Turnbuckle Smash?"

He shook his head.

"Overhead Face First Powerbomb Ring Rope Clothesline Calamity?"

He shook his head. My entire body ached and I felt pinned to the mat as the familiar fear flooded my brain. Try as I might, I couldn't understand why The Flying Mouse had this effect on me.

"Goddammit, you have to do something," I stammered.

"El ratón sólo vuele en la noche," he squeaked, and that's when I finally lost my temper.

"I didn't run over three thousand miles from New York to let a goddamn flying mouse fuck up my life again!" I yelled. "If you screw up the match tomorrow, I'll fire you on the spot! Got that?!"

I don't know if he got it or not because he stood there, quiet as always. I was about to storm out when a final thought occurred to me, a last ditch effort to remedy whatever problem existed between us. "Mouse," I said with the kindest tone I could muster under the circumstances, "do you want to crash at my place until you find a place to live?"

"El ratón solo— "

I held up my hand to stop him, and then walked away, trembling, resigned that I'd done all I could.

9.

Sunday morning came too fast and not fast enough. Too fast because I wasn't sure we'd win the mask versus mask bout and the consequences of not winning were too horrible to contemplate. Not fast enough because I wanted to get on with the championship and on with my life.

I'd told the team to be at the auditorium an hour before fight time so I could give them a pep talk. I'd made sure to tell The Flying Mouse again when I saw him last night. But when I arrived, only The Wall, Devil Cockroach and Chihuahua were there. The Wall and Devil Cockroach were stretching in the team's designated area while Chihuahua was folding clean, white towels for use after the match. They each worked slowly, heads hung low. Even Chihuahua had a less spastic spring in his step. They knew what was at stake today, how much they each had to lose.

"Where the hell is Jorge?" I asked Devil Cockroach who was adjusting his stuffed legs. He glared at me like our dismal record in the trios matches was my fault, which it was for the most part, but it was far better for the team if I avoided blame and focused on the problem at hand.

"Wall, do you know where Mouse is?" I asked.

"He is where he is," The Wall said.

The auditorium doors opened to let in the public. The thunder of footsteps and roar of anticipation was almost deafening. The crowd knew all about mask-versus-mask bouts. The bloodlust in the air was palpable.

I was nearly frantic. If The Flying Mouse didn't show by opening bell, we'd be disqualified. I clutched Chihuahua by the shoulders and pulled him aside.

"I need you to find The Flying Mouse," I whispered urgently.

"He's not here?" Chihuahua gasped, and started to shake. He dug into his pocket and yanked out his prescription bottle, but I snatched it away and pitched it deep into the crowd.

"Go!" I yelled. Wide-eyed with the onset of hyperactivity, Chihuahua bolted down the concourse toward the exit.

I clenched my teeth as the fear struck again, sharp and sudden. I didn't know if it was because I hoped The Flying Mouse would or wouldn't be found. At that point—and I can't explain why—I felt like fate brought him to the team. Despite my anxiety attacks, I felt like there was some divine purpose at work, something I didn't understand and wasn't meant to understand. Who was I to argue with the goddamn Man Upstairs if he had a plan?

"We should have recruited another member of the insect family," Devil Cockroach hissed while The Wall kept repeating, "We have the freedom to win or lose … win or lose …"

A short time later, our opponents entered their designated area: a team called El Día del Muerto dressed like skeletons. And then, too soon, it was time to enter the ring.

The Wall and a portly skeleton took opposite corners when I spotted Chihuahua running back down the concourse all sweaty and red ... and alone.

I grabbed his arm when he got close. "Where's The Flying Mouse?!"

"Dead," Chihuahua said, panting. "I went to the gym and found a note from Grandpa saying that he'd found The Flying Mouse living there and had him arrested. He was fine when the cops put him in his cell..." Chihuahua swallowed hard, his tiny Adam's apple bobbing frantically, "...he was lying on a cot with his eyes rolled back, his mouth open, his knees drawn up to his chest. He was dead. Dead as dead can be." Chihuahua's expression went dark and the hyperactivity drained from his body like oil from a ruptured tanker. He looked at his shoes and mumbled, "You know, The Flying Mouse is the first wrestler to die in police custody in the entire history of Lucha Libre wrestling."

I took a deep breath and tried to calm the screaming panic inside me. The Flying Mouse was dead, which was tragic. But just as bad, we'd lost the match and that meant...

I turned away from Chihuahua, climbed over the partition into the designated area, and gestured for The Wall to come join Devil Cockroach and me on the floor. I waited as he lumbered over the ropes and took his place on my right side, his massive frame shading us from the bright arena lights. Then I gave them both the news.

Devil Cockroach couldn't believe we'd lost the match without throwing a single move and scurried around in tight circles before sitting heavily, his stuffed limbs crushed beneath his real legs. The Wall nodded slowly for several moments, then retook his place in the ring. The skeleton must have sensed the forfeit because he backed up to give The Wall room.

And then, before I realized what I was doing, I yelled for The Wall to run because I knew what had to come next. I yelled for him to get his big-as-a-monolith Mexican ass out of the ring and run to save his identity, run to save his goddamn life, but he ignored me and stood there, strong as always, and hooked a thumb under the edge of his mask below the chin.

The crowd went quiet, but I was still yelling, fueled by guilt and panic, my voice echoing off the walls and ceiling. Flashbulbs began to pop which meant The Wall's face would be plastered on the front page of every goddamn piece-of-shit tabloid between stories of alien abduction and miracle weight loss plans.

I kept yelling until my throat was raw, but The Wall never wavered. He pulled up the mask slowly to reveal his brutish mouth in full and then weathered cheeks turned ruddy by Tequila and a nose pressed flat by who knows how many punches and elbow jabs. Next came his dark, wizened eyes and a forehead corrugated by pink scar tissue. The wounds were self-inflicted by a razorblade, no doubt, from when he had to draw blood to excite a crowd, long before he earned the right to wear a mask. A pallet of black hair was revealed last when he pulled the mask free of his head.

The Wall held up the blue mask, gripping it by the top so the crowd could see its face, and then passed it to the skeleton who accepted it reverently with a bony hand. The Wall had spent years building his reputation and identity in the ring, yet here he was, handing over his mask without loss of pride in himself or the sport.

And that's when my panic disappeared. As I watched The Wall surrender, the feeling crumbled away into nothing inside me, just like that. For a moment, I felt hollow and alone without the panic, like I'd been abandoned by a close and familiar friend. But then the emptiness was replaced by something that felt lighter. Felt good. Felt *free*.

I sagged to my knees, weak with relief. I looked up at The Wall who stood in the ring with his arms crossed. The crowd applauded and he soaked up the adoration humbly, a big smile lighting up his face. Still smiling, he looked down at me.

His smile told me that I shouldn't feel guilty about our loss. It told me that we were all responsible for what had happened, and that everything was going to be okay. It proved to me once and for all the fortitude of freedom.

If I was the type of guy who rolled around with his feminine side, I could make all sorts of parallels here. But I'm not, so you can draw your own goddamn conclusions about what happened.

And then it was over.

The match. Our identities. My panic.

All of it.

10.

I left Tijuana a few days later after apologizing to the team for my significant role in the fiasco. Devil Cockroach (who had blond hair, blue eyes and a roach tattoo on his forehead) grudgingly accepted my apology, while Chihuahua jumped up and down, excited that he'd been a witness to history.

And The Wall? He shook my hand and reaffirmed what I saw in his smile that day in the ring. He also told me to consider the loss a blessing since guises held too long can do more harm than good. Trust me, the rationale sounds even more impressive when you hear it in a thick, noble accent.

I don't consider Tijuana a squalid shithole anymore. Sure, the place lacks polish, but that's because only artificial things have polish and Tijuana is anything but. It's a place that's organic and alive and doesn't offer air-conditioned cubbyholes to help you hide from yourself.

I'm keeping the new way I see Tijuana in mind now that I'm heading back to New York. I plan to talk with the GM about our unresolved issues in a cool, calm and un-adulterous way if he can see clear of siccing his goons on me. I owe him that much. Our falling-out aside, he's always been a sort of father to me.

Needless to say, I owe The Wall, Devil Cockroach and Chihuahua a lot, and in a profound and dysfunctional way, The Flying Mouse too.

The Flying Mouse wasn't scary to everyone, but he was to me, and in the end, that was really all that goddamn mattered.

Hulk Hogan Jesus

Hulk Hogan Jesus
wears his crown
of gold and thorns
around his waist
to preserve his bandana.

Hulk Hogan Jesus
performs his scripture
directly into the mic.

Hulk Hogan Jesus
enters Jerusalem
to "I Am A Real American,"
confusing all who look on
who cheer wildly anyway.

Hulk Hogan Jesus
does the sign of a cross
bent in half with arms
miraculously enhanced.

Hulk Hogan Jesus
lays a hand to his ear
and cures himself of deafness
from thunderous applause.

Hulk Hogan Jesus
holds his last supper
by the announcers' ringside.
The Judas is the one
who moonsaults the table.

When on the brink of falling

Hulk Hogan Jesus
will convulse with invulnerability
to converse with his lord
who consistently does not
forsake him to die.

Hulk Hogan Jesus
has as many resurrections
as his contract allows.

Hulk Hogan Jesus
will rise from his grave
on the second day.

Hulk Hogan Jesus
never stays down
for a third count.

WCW^2

so much depends
upon

a turned hulk
hogan

prepped to give
leg drop

to macho man
savage.

Muscle Memory

The wanna be tough kids from little Italy
came to Saint John's red eyed and bitchy
the morning after Bruno Sammartino lost
the bronze WWF strap to the Russian Bear.
I tried to hide my unbridled glee three
weeks later when Pedro Morales
won the title for us barrio bums
but I let it slip while buying a Pepsi,
bazooka bubble gum and some wrestling
rags at a bodega that I was proud to be
a Spanish kid now that one of ours
was the champion of the world.

Senor Ramirez, the shop owner,
boxed my ears and pointed to
a picture on the back wall of his son,
Nestor, who was killed in Vietnam.
"Pendejo, my boy got murdered in
a swamp. This is why you should be
proud to be Spanish. That wrestling
shit is fake anyway. Grow up, pendejo."
I bought the magazines anyway
and hid them under the mattress
where my big brother, Benito, used to
stash his Playboys, rubbers and smack.

He was built and badass before the horse
started fucking with him and though five
years older and fifty pounds of muscle heavier
we always wrestled at least a half hour every
day and after a ton of slapping punches,
full nelsons and knee drops he'd airplane spin
my ass like a runaway tilt a whirl before the grand

finale of a body slam and I'd be sore as shit
but he always raised my hand in victory at the end.
I found his barbells and exercise books in the closet
and I started pumping iron and I swore my biceps were
growing faster than my 13 year old morning hard-ons.

A few weeks later I snuck into Madison Square Garden
and saw Pedro beat Blackjack Mulligan and for one
glorious night I forgot about Benito overdosing in
an abandoned building full of rats and parasite junkies.
Morning came in cold without my bro there to tell
about the matches and I was like fuck Senor Ramirez
for I had my own hole in heart and I realized learning
the ropes on the street would be more agony than ecstasy
so I took to the heels like George the Animal Steele,
Killer Kowalski and Freddie Blassie to school me
some nasty to marry the muscle to carry the weight
of this lonely ass world my brother left behind.

Stinger

Faces turn ugly and heels remain so
as they all look the other way even
as the red haired ring rat wanna be
rips the collar of her Hulk Hogan
t shirt to bust out some cleavage
but B cups won't work in this wicked
crowd as the ghost of Hatpin Mary
fuels her desire to stick a sewing needle
up the hard asses of gods blind to her
brand of bad girl heat home schooled
in a bedroom wallpapered with wet
dreams and XXXI WrestleMania posters.

From Parts Unknown

The spine
where nerves
became energy.

The ropes
where welts
became character.

The hell
where fear
became fury.

The ring
where dreams
became reality.

229

EACH JAPANESE WRESTLER WAS
ASSIGNED A TRAINEE.

BENOIT MADE $50,000
AS A TRAINEE.

YEN
MONEY

BENOIT ARRIVED IN JAPAN
WITH 6'6 300 LB. DARRYL
PETERSON.

THEY WOULD BE THE FIRST
TWO NON-JAPANESE WRESTLERS
TO TRAIN IN THE DOJO.

THEY HAD LITTLE IDEA OF
THE ABUSE THEY WERE
ABOUT TO ENDURE.

WRESTLERS ACTUALLY
DIED HERE.

②

230

ON ONE OCCASION, WRESTLER KENSUKE SASAKI, FELT HIS TRAINEE HIROMITSU GOMPEI WAS BEING LAZY.

HE BEAT UP GOMPEI BUT WENT TOO FAR AND GOMPEI DIED RIGHT IN THE RING.

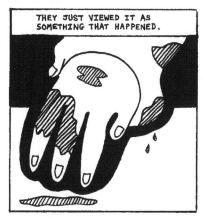

THEY JUST VIEWED IT AS SOMETHING THAT HAPPENED.

THIS WAS IN 1995, YEARS AFTER BENOIT HAD FINISHED HIS TRAINING AND THEY HAD ACTUALLY BECOME MORE LENIENT!

WRESTLER KENZO SUZUKI FLED JAPAN FOR THE U.S. AND THE WWE AFTER HIS TRAINEE TAKAYURI OKADA DIED UNDER HIS SUPERVISION.

JAPANESE WRESTLING WAS CONTROLLED BY THE MAFIA, SO THESE SORTS OF THINGS WERE JUST SWEPT UNDER THE RUG.

ONE WRESTLER, BIG VAN VADER, WHO WAS A HUGE STAR IN JAPAN AS WELL AS IN THE U.S. WAS ONCE TORTURED WITH RAZOR BLADES.

VADER TIME

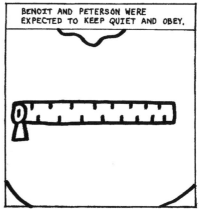

BENOIT AND PETERSON WERE EXPECTED TO KEEP QUIET AND OBEY.

THE JAPANESE WRESTLERS WERE TOLD TO BE AS MEAN AS POSSIBLE TO THE TRAINEES.

IGNORING THEIR EXISTENCE

BENOIT WAS REPEATEDLY INTENTIONALLY PUNCHED IN THE EARS AND PUT IN HEADLOCKS.

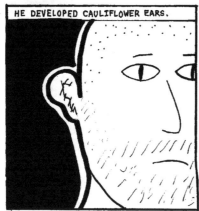

HE DEVELOPED CAULIFLOWER EARS.

THEY WERE WOKEN UP EARLY IN THE MORNING "MILITARY STYLE".

RISE AND SHINE LADIES. DROP YOUR COCKS AND GRAB YOUR SOCKS! 4

TRAINEES WERE EXPECTED TO DO
EVERYTHING FOR THEIR WRESTLER
INCLUDING DOING HIS LAUNDRY,
SHINING HIS SHOES, AND
WASHING HIM IN THE SHOWER(!).

IN RETURN THE WRESTLER WOULD
TEACH THE TRAINEE WRESTLING.

THEY HAD THEIR HEADS SHAVED
AND WORE THE SAME UNIFORMS.

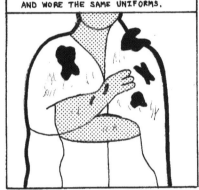

AFTER THEY AWOKE THEY WERE
MADE TO CLEAN THE DOJO AND
PUNCHED IF THEY DIDN'T DO
IT RIGHT.

THEY RECIEVED SMALL MEALS OF
FISH, SEAWEED, AND RICE
WHICH LEFT THEM STARVING.

GRUMBLE

MANY YEARS LATER A TRAINEE WAS
SODOMIZED WITH A BANANA AFTER
HE COMPLAINED ABOUT THE FOOD.

5

233

ONE TRAINEE WAS FORCED TO EAT UNTIL HE THREW UP OVER AND OVER AGAIN.

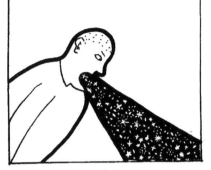

TRAINEES WERE FORCED TO MASTURBATE INTO A JAR AND DRINK IT.

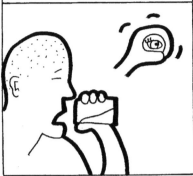

AT 10:00 A.M. THEY BEGAN THEIR WORKOUT WITH AT LEAST 1,000 HINDU SQUATS AND 500 PUSHUPS.

HOW TO DO A HINDU SQUAT

WRESTLERS BEAT THEM AS THEY DID THIS.

THIS IS HOW I TEACH HIM. OTHERWISE, HE BE AN IDIOT HIS WHOLE LIFE.

IRONICALLY, WHEN BENOIT WAS IN WWE HE MADE SHAWN DAIVARI (A FORMER MCAD STUDENT) DO 1,000 HINDU SQUATS WHEN HE FELT SHAWN HAD DISRESPECTED ANOTHER WRESTLER. SHAWN ENDED UP HOSPITALIZED.

BENOIT DID THEM RIGHT ALONG WITH HIM AND WAS FINE.

IF THE TRAINEES WERE IN PAIN THEY WERE MADE TO DO IT AGAIN AND AGAIN.

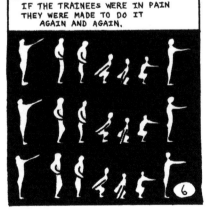

AFTER THAT THEY DID CALESTHENICS, JUMPED ROPE, AND WERE TRAINED IN AMATEUR WRESTLING DRILLS WHILE BEING BEATEN.

THERE WERE THREATS OF TORTURE AND EVEN MURDER.

I'LL KILL YOU!

THERE WERE THREATS TO SEND THEM HOME. THEY MADE THE TRAINEES BEG TO BE ALLOWED TO STAY.

THEY WOULD BREAK THEM DOWN PSYCHOLOGICALLY.

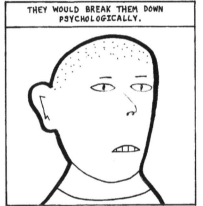

THE IDEA BEING THAT A WRESTLER PUSHED TO HIS BREAKING POINT WOULD LOOK LIKE HE WAS REALLY FIGHTING FOR HIS LIFE WHEN HE GOT IN THE RING.

THEY WERE TORTURED WITH WRESTLING HOLDS AND MADE TO BEG FOR MERCY.

7

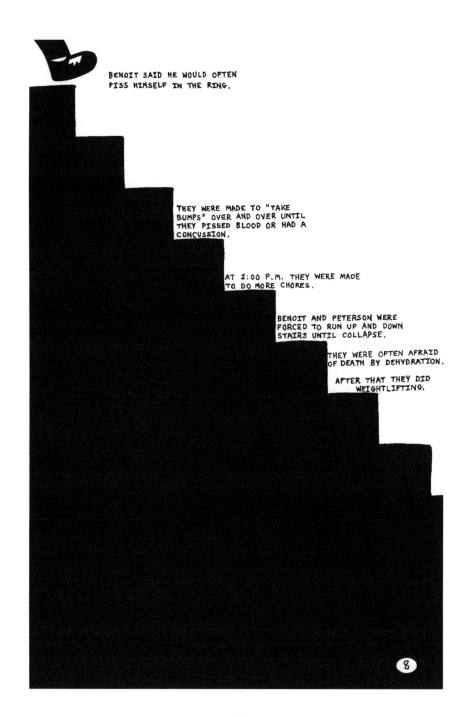

BENOIT SAID HE WOULD OFTEN
PISS HIMSELF IN THE RING.

THEY WERE MADE TO "TAKE
BUMPS" OVER AND OVER UNTIL
THEY PISSED BLOOD OR HAD A
CONCUSSION.

AT 2:00 P.M. THEY WERE MADE
TO DO MORE CHORES.

BENOIT AND PETERSON WERE
FORCED TO RUN UP AND DOWN
STAIRS UNTIL COLLAPSE.

THEY WERE OFTEN AFRAID
OF DEATH BY DEHYDRATION.

AFTER THAT THEY DID
WEIGHTLIFTING.

8

DINNER CONSISTED OF A
REVOLTING CHICKEN AND
VEGETABLE STEW THAT
SUMO WRESTLERS ATE TO
BULK UP.

BEDTIME WAS MIDNIGHT.
THEY WERE OFTEN WOKEN AT
2:00 A.M. FOR A SURPRISE
WORKOUT.

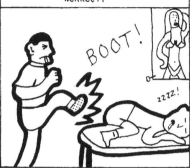

BENOIT MADE A BRIEF TRIP
BACK HOME TO CANADA.

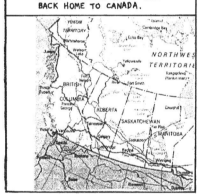

AFTER TALKING WITH SOME
FELLOW WRESTLERS HE
REALIZED THE PRESTIGE OF
GRADUATING FROM THE DOJO.

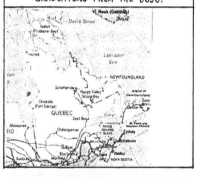

HE FELT IT WAS A SACRIFICE
HE NEEDED TO MAKE.

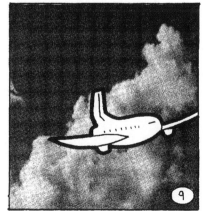

HE WAS GIVEN SOMEWHAT BETTER TREATMENT THIS TIME AROUND.

ON 1/2/87 BENOIT MADE HIS NJPW DEBUT AFTER FIVE MONTHS OF TRAINING AT THE DOJO. BENOIT DID NOT LOSE HIS FIRST MATCH. IT WAS A DRAW. (NEITHER MAN WON) THIS WAS VERY UNUSUAL AND SPOKE VOLUMES ABOUT THE FACT THAT THEY SAW TALENT IN BENOIT. HE DID LOSE MOST OF HIS MATCHES THOUGH. IN AUGUST HE WAS SENT HOME.

⑩

WHEN HE RETURNED IN NOVEMBER HE WAS NOW A FULL-TIME MEMBER OF THE ROSTER,

SUDDENLY HE WAS SLEEPING IN FIVE-STAR HOTELS, AND TRAVELLING ON LUXURY BUSES MAKING $5,000 TO $20,000 A WEEK,

(11)

239

HE WAS SENT BACK TO CANADA
TO PAY HIS DUES AND PERFECT
HIS CRAFT AND PROMISED A
SPOT AS A TOP STAR WHEN HE
RETURNED.

DURING HIS TIME AWAY HE
STARTED USING STEROIDS.

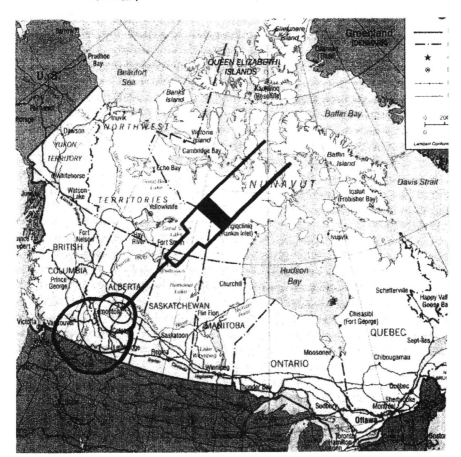

WHEN HE RETURNED HE WAS
MAKING $300,000 TO $400,000
WORKING TWENTY WEEKS A YEAR.

(12)

HE WOULD WRESTLE IN BOTH THE U.S.
AND JAPAN OVER THE NEXT SEVERAL YEARS.

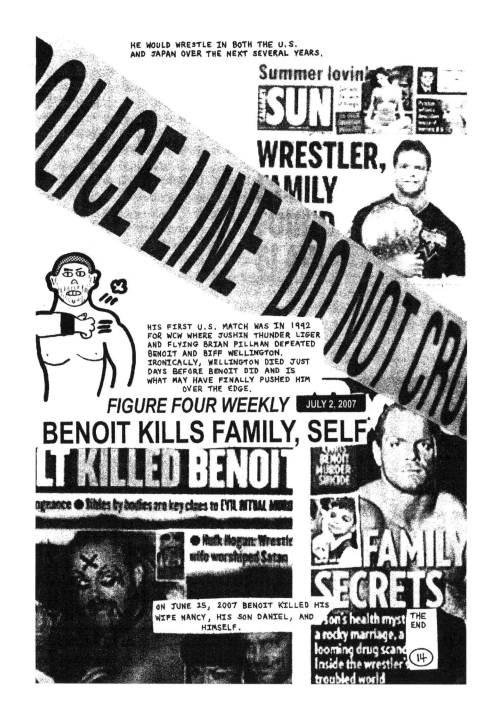

Summer lovin'

SUN

WRESTLER, FAMILY

HIS FIRST U.S. MATCH WAS IN 1992
FOR WCW WHERE JUSHIN THUNDER LIGER
AND FLYING BRIAN PILLMAN DEFEATED
BENOIT AND BIFF WELLINGTON.
IRONICALLY, WELLINGTON DIED JUST
DAYS BEFORE BENOIT DID AND IS
WHAT MAY HAVE FINALLY PUSHED HIM
OVER THE EDGE.

FIGURE FOUR WEEKLY JULY 2, 2007

BENOIT KILLS FAMILY, SELF

LT KILLED BENOIT

grance ● Bibles by bodies are key clues to **EVIL RITUAL MURDER**

● Hulk Hogan: Wrestler
wife worshiped Satan

FAMILY SECRETS

ON JUNE 25, 2007 BENOIT KILLED HIS
WIFE NANCY, HIS SON DANIEL, AND
HIMSELF.

son's health myst
a rocky marriage, a
looming drug scand
Inside the wrestler's
troubled world

THE
END

14

242

Chasing The American Dream: A Chubby Fan(atic) Recalls His Favorite Professional Wrestlers

Professional wrestling has been my favorite thing since I was five years old. I grew up near a small town (Madison) in the foothills of the Blue Ridge Mountains of Virginia. My nearest friend lived 10 miles away and being an only child, I was obliged to spend my summers throwing sticks at trees while pretending to be a medieval knight or a cowboy. Sometimes I would play ping-pong against the wall for hours, and you can still see the ruts in my parents' 1963 pool table from the stock car races that I would have on the green felt with my Matchbox cars. My dad worked for the telephone company and would take me fishing or play catch with me on the weekends, but most weekdays, he was at work from 6 am until 6 pm. My mother grew up in a large, evangelical family and much of her day revolved around obsessively cleaning our house (the most significant thing that she ever owned). She would periodically stop doing the housework long enough to bring me a soda and a Fruitpie-the-Magician fruit pie, but her lessons generally involved a sermon detailing the devilish agenda of the bugs that I would soon be tracking into her clean house.

I can't claim to have had an epiphany (as a first grader) the first time that I saw professional wrestling on TV; however, nothing in my life has ever been the same. So what is the psychological attraction of professional wrestling for me? Why did I beg my long-suffering parents to take me to over 150 matches (including family vacations to North Carolina and Florida) when I was a child? Why do I love professional wrestling? The answer lies in avoirdupois. When I was a kid, professional wrestlers were the only fat people on television. I was overweight and insecure, and the wrestlers were everything that I wanted to be (i.e. strong, smart, and cool). I was a fat kid and they were my only role models. I wanted to be Dusty Rhodes (the self-proclaimed "chubby plumber's son from Austin, Texas"). Dusty Rhodes weighed well over 300 pounds and spoke with a lisp, yet when he claimed to have "wined n' dined with kings n' queens" and to have "slept in alleys, ate pork n' beans," I desperately wanted to believe him.

In second grade, my friends and I would turn a card table upside down, attach twine to the legs, and have matches with our Johnny West action figures (no one ever referred to them as dolls). In fourth grade, we pretended we were the wrestlers and would have tag-team matches with the sofa cushions executing moves likes the pile driver and the figure-four. We had our own entrance music on the 8-track (usually Hank Williams, Jr. or David Allan Coe) and sometimes my mom would let us borrow a couple of her older/rattier robes to add to the spectacle. In some of our more heated matches with the sofa cushions, we would even take our shirts off and expose to the world (i.e. my parents' basement) a fat, hillbilly kid's sense of "twisted steel and sex appeal." In sixth grade, my friend, Allen and I made "Mid-Atlantic Tag-Team Championship" belts in his garage and wore them for the entire school year. We would have matches at recess with my mother serving as special referee; she would always cheat so that we would win. In eighth grade, we gave everyone in our town a professional wrestling code name, so that we could talk smack about them without their knowledge. My dad was "Harley Race" (because of his 1970's style sideburns) and our school principal was "Ray 'The Crippler' Stevens" (because he was old, grumpy and walked with a slight limp).

I think everyone remembers cranking their favorite music while driving in their first car. Well, if there's ever any doubt that I was a bigger fan than you (a key component in a true fan's love of professional wrestling), just know that instead of listening to The Clash, I played tape-recorded wrestler interviews in my 1976 Chevy Nova. My parents eventually sent me to boarding school for reconditioning, and I can't say that was my finest hour, especially since the tuition was more than half of my dad's total salary for the year. I was also the son of the school switchboard operator and that meant that I was 3rd string on the social pecking order. I was 3rd string on the football team and 3rd string class clown. Of course, rich adolescents like professional wrestling too, but in my case, it became part of my white trash persona along with country music and chewing tobacco. College was more to my liking, especially since you were judged by how many beers you could shotgun as opposed to your dad's salary; therefore, my appreciation of professional wrestling re-emerged. My friends and I dressed in 3-piece suits (as was the style of the "classier" wrestlers of the period) and headed for the Richmond Coliseum to cheer on the Four-Horseman any time they were in town. Perhaps one of my favorite college memories is that of my roommate Opie, stopping two 13-year-old girls as they scrambled down the aisle to get an autograph and exclaiming, "Girls, if you're looking for Ric Flair, he's right here" while pointing at his own chest.

Professional wrestling has lost a bit of its luster over the years and is something of a niche market in 2012 (thanks in part to the fact that WWE owner, Vince McMahon admitted in court that professional wrestling was scripted). I haven't been to a live match in over 10 years, and I generally only tune in for the first and last 10 minutes of the weekly TV shows. As I look back on my life though, I can't deny the impact that professional wrestling has had on the man that I have become. I'll readily admit that I'm something of a fool, but I believe that much of my sense of humor (as well as my sense of masculinity) can be traced back to the heavyset, southern, smack-talking professional wrestlers of my childhood. With this in mind, I think the best tribute that I could do for the idols/icons of my youth is to assemble a "who's who" list of my favorite wrestlers with a short description of their role in my growth and development. I guess I should warn you that I'm a mark for the old Mid-Atlantic Championship Wrestling (the one with Bob Caudle and David Crockett) and that even as a child, I thought that the WWE was corporate and choreographed. I also realize that the true fans of professional wrestling will want me to qualify my criteria for picking my favorite professional wrestlers as it relates to mic skills, popularity, and actual wrestling ability. Well, *Pro Wrestling Illustrated* always used to qualify their fan voting with the disclaimer, "if you could watch the matches of only one wrestler, who would it be?" and I think that definition will work just fine for me.

Cactus Jack: It's Ok to Be Ugly

As a young adult, I read about Cactus Jack Manson in the pages of *Pro Wrestling Illustrated*. Cactus Jack (aka Mick Foley) was usually presented as a mentally deranged schizophrenic who enjoyed pain (such as pulling out clumps of his own hair) and who constantly shrieked (usually for his mother) throughout his matches. One of the most memorable matches of my childhood (ok, I was really 25) occurred in Munich, Germany in 1994 when Cactus Jack took on Big Van Vader for the World Championship Wrestling Title. During the course of the match, Cactus Jack's head became tangled in the ropes and his right ear was torn completely off. The match continued for another three minutes (Cactus Jack eventually lost) with the referee simply handing the torn ear to a ring attendant. Cactus Jack was in good spirits after the match with no damage to his hearing or balance. Reports were that Cactus Jack would take a few months off for reconstructive surgery, but it never happened and his ear (hole) appears the same today as it did in 1994.

Since his retirement, Mick Foley has begun a writing career and his *Have A Nice Day: A Tale of Blood and Sweatsocks* has become a *New York Times* bestseller. Not only does the book describe Foley's wrestling career, it delves deeply into his family and personal life. Often, the audience only sees wrestling as entertainment, but Foley exposes it as a full-fledged business, with employees and decisions, with economic implications for each show. What is most memorable about the book is Foley's descriptions of some of his most gruesome matches. This section is accompanied by 16 color photos with detailed descriptions of the numerous injuries the author suffered throughout his career, including a broken nose and dislocated jaw in his very first professional bout. Foley is an unlikely hero, but is nevertheless a good example of what hard work and determination can get you in life. This is ultimately the message of Foley's book as well as the majority of other professional wrestling biographies.

More importantly, Mick Foley is fat, ugly and missing teeth (he sometimes claims to have swallowed them during an untelevised match with Steve "Sting" Borden, but it was really the result of a car accident in the late 1980's). To tell you the truth, Mick Foley isn't really much of a technical wrestler, but he sure knows how to take a bump. Over the years, critics have referred to Foley as a "glorified stuntman" (hence the classic Ric Flair line: "sitting on a thumbtack in a bingo parlor don't make you Ric Flair"), but those qualities are ultimately part of his mystique/charm. Mick Foley is everyman—-he's living proof that an awkward gym teacher's son from New Jersey can grow up to be the heavyweight champion of the world. There was a time when I would have called Cactus Jack my favorite wrestler, but somewhere along the line, I think Mick Foley started reading too many of his own WWE press clippings. That being said, Mick Foley is the only wrestler on my list that reached me as an adult. I'm not from New Jersey and I've always hated the WWE, but Mick Foley made it ok for another lost generation of kids to dream.

"Rowdy" Roddy Piper: It's Ok To Be a Man and Wear a Skirt

There's a framed wrestling poster in my childhood bedroom from 11/22/81—live from the Culpeper Junior High School gym. The main event was Ric Flair v. Greg Valentine for the United States title, but Johnny Weaver v. Roddy Piper stole the show. I was only 13-years-old, but I already knew that dudes didn't wear dresses (or kilts) in Culpeper, VA on a Saturday night in 1981 (or 2012 for that matter). And Roddy Piper coming to the ring surrounded by a screaming mob that I'll affectionately refer to as my "home people" was as electric as anything that I've ever witnessed in my entire life. I don't remember who won the match that night, but I knew Rowdy Roddy Piper was destined to be a star. The dog collar match with Greg Valentine where Piper's eardrum was shattered was impressive as well—and we drove all the way to Richmond to watch it on closed circuit TV. More recently, while Hulk Hogan was blathering on to Larry King about "Hulkamaniacs needing to buy his new grill," Roddy Piper was calling for universal healthcare for all professional wrestlers.

Roddy Piper claimed to be from Scotland (hence the kilt he wore to the ring), but he was actually from Saskatoon. As an adolescent (and fan of professional wrestling), I was keenly aware of the reaction of my hometown to the variety of personas adopted by the performers and Piper's "dress" received the biggest "pop" of all. It seemed to me that every adult male (the farmers, the high school athletes, the volunteer firemen) all seemed to love-to-hate Piper. They told Piper that "his mama dressed him funny" and asked "what was under his skirt." They called him other things too, but I think you get the point. The thing is, the crowd's reaction to Piper (as "Scotsman") was somewhat different from their reaction to the "nature boys" (wrestlers with long hair and frilly robes who were perceived as egotistical and feminine). They hated nature boys with a passion, but even "Nature Boy" Ric Flair didn't have the courage to wear a skirt in the junior high school gym. It's hard to explain, but the crowd seemed to appreciate that Piper was somehow messing with us on another level. It would be nice to believe that my home people actually learned something from the manner in which Piper subtly tweaked their sexuality, but ultimately I think we just liked the way he talked. Even my dad would look up from his newspaper (that he would carry into whatever arena in whatever town) when Roddy Piper made his way to the ring in anticipation that something unscripted was about to happen.

Jimmy "Boogie-Woogie Man" Valiant: It's Ok To Be Poor

Jimmy Valiant may very well be the most REAL person on this list. And I realize that "real" is relative when it comes to professional wrestling, but I'm almost certain that Jimmy Valiant wasn't just playing a trailer park hillbilly on TV. If I could have any video that has ever existed, it would be the 1983 clip of a down and out, Boogie Man drinking Mad Dog 20/20 on the streets of Charlotte with a group of homeless people—you know, the one where Big Mama (Boogie's old lady at the time) steps out of a limousine and calls out to him: "Hey Boogie Man, let's go party!" Boogie's response: "No, Big Mama, Boogie Man down. Boogie Man hurt." WWE owner Vince McMahon didn't fly in some off-Broadway actors to play the street people—the people were really homeless and I like to pretend that their pay for the day was a few more bottles of Mad Dog 20/20. And if this skit wasn't "real," I think it was about as close as professional wrestling will ever get. I actually met Jimmy Valiant at a mall in Blacksburg around 1993 when he was collecting money for juvenile diabetes. Our three-minute chat turned into a three hour conversation and after it was over, The Boogie Man gave me a free autographed poster and tee-shirt. I returned the favor by going back to my apartment and bringing back tee-shirts for Boogie and his new old lady, Angel (and Boogie refused to comment on what happened to Big Mama because Angel was always listening). Boogie also invited me to come down and try out for his wrestling school in Shawsville, but mama said "no."

When I reflect on what The Boogie Man meant to me as a child, I think it has more to do with economics than masculinity. Valiant's handlers never referred to him as being homeless, but I think that was the implication. Boogie dressed in what could be described in 2012 as "dumpster chic"—stained spandex tights, thrift store tees, bandanas and boots. He had long, crazy hair and an even crazier, rubber-banded beard and he danced and clapped his hands whenever he spoke—much like a homeless person who was trying to talk you into giving him money, but who had done too many drugs or spent too many nights on the street to really care if you did or not. Boogie had something of a biker's edge to him as well—hence the 30-40 tattoos and the ubiquitous "old lady" (Big Mama in 1982 and Angel in 2012) in the background. He also had a crazy uncle quality to him, but I think social implications go even deeper. I may not have understood what being rich truly entailed when I was 12-years-old, but I think most of us assumed that since the wrestlers were on TV that they had to be millionaires. There was just something about Jimmy Valiant that made me think that I lived a nicer life—-that my parents' brick ranch house out in the country was somehow nicer than Boogie's shack. One of the highest compliments that I can give a peer in 2012 is to say that he/she is "of-the-people" (i.e. not elitist) and Jimmy Valiant's homespun philanthropy certainly got through to me. I may not necessarily dance and yell - "have mercy, daddy!" whenever one of my students makes a point in class, but Boogie's lesson on humility remains crystal clear.

"The American Dream" Dusty Rhodes: It's Ok To Be Fat

Dusty Rhodes has "wined n' dined with kings and queens/has slept in alleys, ate pork n' beans/he's the need you want, the want you need/he'll make your back crack, your knees freeze, your liver quiver/if you don't dig that mess, you got the wrong address/while everyone else is in the back room laughing and joking/Big Dust is out front, cookin' and smokin'/."[5] What can I say about the American Dream? I think he'd be #1 on my list if not for the fact that he spent most of my childhood in Florida instead of the Carolinas. In a nutshell, Dusty Rhodes made it ok for all of us to be fat. If you've never seen a photograph of Dusty Rhodes, let me paint the picture: 330 lbs., kinky hair, a large, red birthmark on his stomach, and a speech impediment. Yet he grew up to live the American Dream. I'm not going to tell that I used a red magic marker to give myself a red, splotchy birthmark when I was in sixth grade, but I will you tell you that whenever I'm in a really good mood now and realize that no one is looking, I'll take off my shirt and dance around the mirror like I was about to give someone The Dream's signature bionic elbow.

No doubt, Dusty Rhodes is my American Idol. Much like Mick Foley, Rhodes' success in the world of wrestling is more about heart and determination than actual athleticism. Dusty Rhodes could have passed for a fat, Texas truck driver (albeit with dyed blonde hair and a lisp), but instead, he was selling out Madison Square Garden and hanging out on tour with Willie Nelson. He was the first fat person that I ever saw on TV (and there were plenty of them walking around my hometown even if Hollywood leads us to believe that they've always been kept in a zoo). Dusty Rhodes did national television commercials for Goody's Headache Powder and I can't think of another overweight celebrity (outside of a Jenny Craig spokesperson) that does that in 2012. How big of an influence was Dusty Rhodes in my life? I sent my mom out to buy Goody's Headache Powder even though I didn't have a headache and I didn't really know what Goody's Headache Powder was. The American Dream was larger-than-life for a lot of people back then— he spoke for a generation of "chubby plumbers' sons" who otherwise would have had no one to tell their stories. Civil rights have changed a lot over the last 30 years, but you and I both know that fat people are the ones headed to the back of the bus in 2012. For the cynics who don't believe in The American Dream, I would encourage you to search "Dusty Rhodes" + "hard times" on YouTube. He speaks of what we were and who we have become better than I ever could.

"Nature Boy" Ric Flair: To Be the Man, You Have to Beat the Man

Do you remember where you were when you heard the news that John Kennedy had been assassinated? Do you remember the first time that you heard the Beatles? Do you remember what you were doing on 9/11? Well, the first time I turned on the television in 1973, "Nature Boy" Ric Flair was on WTVR out of Richmond. When I turned the TV off after his retirement speech in March 2008, I realized that there had never been a moment in my life that The Nature Boy hadn't been a part of it. (Mercifully, Flair came out of retirement in the spring of 2009 and is now a part of TNA Wrestling on Spike TV). If I'm telling the truth, Ric Flair is Alpha and Omega to me. I don't care about your politicians and I don't care about your movie stars. I'm not ashamed to say that Ric Flair is the most important icon of my entire life. The Nature Boy was always there for me and always made me feel better about my life (if only for a little while). I hid under the table between my dad's legs in that Raleigh restaurant in 1976 when Ric Flair and Greg Valentine (with rings on every finger) came in for lunch. I haven't seen my Aunt Nora in five years, but the next time I see her (probably at someone's funeral), I'll ask for the story about the time Ric Flair ran over her mailbox in 1978. She claims that he called her a "fat bitch" and she called him a "blonde-haired SOB" as she chased him down a Louisa County dirt road trying to get his license plate.

Ric Flair is considered by many to be the greatest professional wrestler of all time in a career that spans over 40 years. Flair currently works for Total NonStop Action Wrestling and is noted for his tenure and highly decorated world title reigns with the National Wrestling Alliance (NWA), World Championship Wrestling (WCW) and the World Wrestling Federation (WWF). Flair is officially recognized by *Pro Wrestling Illustrated* as a 16-time world champion, but the actual tally of world championship reigns varies by source (and Flair considers himself to be a 21-time world champion). During the course of his career, Flair has survived two plane crashes (the first of which in 1975 took the life of the pilot and paralyzed fellow wrestler, Johnny Valentine). Flair broke his back in three places and was told by his doctors that he would never wrestle again. Flair returned to the ring after just six months, although the crash did force Flair to change from the brawling style that he used early in his career to the "nature boy" style which became his trademark. Flair has been honored by Congress for his service to the state of North Carolina and in 2008, it was announced that the sequin covered robe that he wore at WrestleMania XXIV would be placed in the pop culture section of the National Museum of American History in Washington, D.C. Of more significance to my Aunt Nora was the day in December 2005 when Flair was arrested for a road rage incident in Charlotte, NC after he allegedly got out of his car, grabbed a motorist by the neck, and kicked in the doors of the man's sports utility vehicle. She also seemed quite pleased when it was announced (post-incident) that Flair had lost his gig as North Carolina's Anti Drunk Driving Spokesperson.

Ric Flair is as much a part of my life now as he was in 1978, but then again, I'm old-school. Most of the "boys in the back" (i.e. the faculty lounge) rely on e-smoke and mirrors, but I still wade into the crowd like it was 1982—-clapping my hands and challenging the kid in the back who's watching cars go through the Hardee's drive thru on his iPhone (instead of listening to me) to connect his actions back to Richard Rodriguez's "The Achievement of Desire." I think the "fans" are a little tougher to win over in the information age than they were when professional wrestling only aired once a week on local stations, but it's still doable for the lonely, fat kid who always dreamed of being a superstar. Case in point, whenever one of my students appears to be more interested in updating their Facebook status than listening to my lecture, I'll kick into my Ric Flair impersonation (complete with strut) which goes a little something like this: "Facebook, I think I might go to Taco Bell for lunch—-woooooo! Facebook, I think I might order a Beef Meximelt and a Coke—-woooooo! I'm walking down the hall—woooooo! I'm opening the door—wooooo! I'm walking out to my car—woooooo!" And what do my students say when they see me in Taco Bell after class? They scream, "woooooo" and ask me to retell the story of the time that "The Nature Boy" Ric Flair ran over my Aunt Nora's mailbox.

Working Stiff

He was the face
the good guy
the boy next door
with his soap opera looks
and chiseled physique
he was a natural

Some said he was the best
ever to grace the squared circle
Even his critics said
he was at least all right

He only listened to the fans
roaring as he dragged his opponent
around the ring
a ricochet off the ropes
an exchange of forearms
teeth flew
souvenirs
for a lucky ringsider

The magic
always making the violence
look real

but now a new illusion
added to the act
not just Good Vs Evil
but the living grappling the dead
Shakespeare could not
have scripted it better

His masked opponent

universally reviled
but a proven money maker
the one the fans love to hate
and now three weeks cold

The trick to the passion play
wrestling mortality
avoiding the clench
submission is forever

Just like the poster said

The Reaper Vs Johnny Victory
for the all the gold
Texas Death Match
Winner take all

The Brute Responds to His Fan Mail

Dear Brute,

Why did you double-cross Reverend Wrath in your tag-team championship match against the Low-Riders for the Kentucky-Fried Tag-Team Title Belts?

Confused and Disappointed in Bucksnort, TN

(P.S. you guys were the best tag-team ever!!!)

Hello Confused,

I'd be disappointed too if I lived in a shit-hole like Bucksnot. The reason I double-crossed the righteous Reverend could be counted on more than one hand but I will summarize for you. I know they don't value arithmetic much in Bucksnot.

1. He stiffed me with the check on consecutive weeks at Ma's Home Cooking and All-You-Can-Eat Restaurant.
2. He stiffed me with the tab at Big Jim's Tavern more times than I can count on two five-fingered loaded black gloves.
3. He stiffed me on the two rats turned strippers turned escorts we picked up at The Silk and Lace Gentlemen's Club the Wed. before.
4. The straw that broke the camel's back was coming back to a shared hotel room after dining at Ma's Home Cooking and All-You-Can-Eat Restaurant and attempting to use the hotel's bathroom only to see the commode filled to the brim and stinking like King Kong had taken a dump courtesy of the Reverend. And I mean stinking. And that's why I double-crossed his nicotine-stained-fingers, cheap-whiskey-breath-smelling, never-washed-his testicles, socially-retarded, no-neck, no-good, low-down snake of a human being. Thou shall flush the crapper or get your sorry assed whipped. And he did. I whipped his ass all across the Bluegrass state. Sure championship belts mean a bigger payday and always impress the skirts but sometimes a man just has to make a stand.

Hey Brute,

Why did you destroy Jurassic Mark's priceless sabretooth tiger-skin robe?

High in Houston

Hey High,

That Alley Oop wannabe. Priceless? He bought that robe at a garage sale in Waxahachie, TX for ten bucks. I should been have given a medal by the EPA. Damn thing was only held together by the cum-stains. I had to get a penicillin shot after I shredded it. And if you don't like it, the Hell with you.

Dear Brute,
Why did you bitch-slap referee Ian Ladd during your chain match with the Golden Boy
Chipp Smooth.
Curious in Evansville

Dear Curious,
The reason I bitch-slapped that yellow-striped referee was because of alleged backstage mistreatment of my good friend, the King Kong Kid, the world's best midget wrestler. Bar none. Nobody's gonna mistreat one of my pint-sized friends but me. I do not tolerate size-discrimination. Ask all the fat chicks I've fucked. And like I'd ever take orders from some sap named Ian. That slap earned me a 15 day suspension and a $500 fine by the Commission. Money well spent.

Dearest Brute,
Do you recall having sexual relations with a bleached blond (curtains matched the drapes) named Sandy at Big Dick's Half Way Inn just off Interstate 75 in Mudflap, KY? She's my mom. Hello Daddy.
Your Long Lost Loving Daughter

Dearest Long Lost,
I do recall Sandy. She had the longest nose hairs I've ever seen on a broad. Me and the rest of the boys referred to her as the Human Vacuum. I say that with much respect as she could suck a mean dick. Shit on a good night, she can handle a half dozen and answer the encore. Sadly, I never had intercourse with your mom. After one blowjob, I hit the sack. One and done. However, I would advise you seek out Reverend Wrath. I was personally on hand to see him wear out your mom's ass (talk about a dark match) and other holes on several occasion. And like the Reverend after-hours, catch-phrase went, "No condom needed."

The Brute is a nationally recognized pro-wrestler, holding titles all over the USA, including Texas Brass Knux Champion, Mason-Dixon Champion, Stars and Stripes Champion, Wrestler-Most-Likely-To-End-Your-Career by Pro-Wrestling Insider Magazine three years in a row and the El Paso Chili-eating

Champion. He is the roughest, toughest, meanest, son-of-a-bitch ever to lace up a pair of boots. If you don't believe it, you tell him.

Everyone Has a Price

If I told you that the big contract had nothing to do with my signing, I'd be lying. It made the future secure for my family. Don't get me wrong, every pro wrestler dreams of this moment, of getting called up by the WWE - but that kind of thing comes with a price - usually everything that made you special in that ring... it all has to go.

They control everything. Your name. Your gimmick. They want to be able to take credit for putting your face in the minds of their millions of viewers. Want to take credit for you.

I had all that in the back of my head as I stared down at that piece of paper - the last in a monstrous stack of documents detailing in fine print all the terms and conditions of my new life. In so many words, these papers explained that in exchange for accepting my new identity, they would pay me a designated amount. Lot of numbers. A figure ending in more zeroes than I'd ever seen.

Part of me wanted to look that silver-spoon-licking asshole in the eyes, tell him right to his face that he could take that contract and shove it up his ass.

But I worked hard to get to this point. And my wife and son were waiting in the lobby downstairs, so anxious for me to come out and tell them Daddy was FINALLY gonna be a Superstar. So I grabbed that pen in my trembling hand, squeezed out a little bit of ink, and I did it.

I made the future secure for my family.

And old Vince...Vince McMahon...he got this smug-ass smile, and stuck his hand out for me to shake.

And I took it.

Because my hand was now his.

Labyrinthine Poem

Though many men have felt the lure of the squared circle,
only a few will be called *wrestler:* men with bodies

best described as specimens, their broad shoulders, thick thighs
and tiny waists fit for feats of strength but flexible enough to part

the air with grace and ease, always landing where they should
(and if they don't not letting on); men who understand the art

of arm-bars, sleeper holds and suplexes in all their many forms
(wheelbarrow, belly-to-back, slingshot and super); men willing

to wear clown suits or polka-dotted trunks, paint their faces,
shave their heads or don a mask and seek revenge on enemies

who once were friends; men who will sneer and swagger
through a hostile crowd, will cheat and taunt and threaten,

roll out of the ring to keep from being pinned or clutch the ropes
and beg for mercy they never deserve, and who, having run

their course as heels, can reinvent themselves as babyfaces
(upright, loyal, true) and charm fans into cheering even louder

than they booed; men who know how to hide their blades,
whose hands are deft and sure, skin easy to saw through;

men who make their dates despite torn tendons, broken ribs
and raging staph, snowstorms that strand their cars, nights spent

on sagging cots in jails and cheap motels, despite sick kids
and wives who want divorces when the belt is up for grabs;

men who do their jobs with minimal complaint, are well-liked
in the locker room and generous in bars, who help the new boys out

(but not too much); men who honor and respect the long tradition
of the ring, whose heroes passed away in unsung poverty,

their scarred foreheads and frozen joints the only proof
of how loved they once were; for because this ancient,

noble sport means more than any single grappler can or will,
it requires men whose fondest wish, always and ever,

is to sacrifice themselves for what they serve: fans, promoters,
brothers-in-tights, the business bigger than them all.

Revelation: Jake Roberts

Jake "The Snake" Roberts's 1996 face turn as a bible-thumping preacher was derailed by his real-life struggles with alcohol and drugs.

My father never told us wrestling wasn't real,
so we bought everything he sold, the neck brace
he wore home for storyline, how he couldn't quit

because he had our mouths to feed. When I
joined him in the ring, he said he was ashamed
of how I worked, so I swore I'd be better

than he ever was—bigger, meaner, more beloved.
My motel rooms always have two things:
a Bible in the drawer and the pills I take for pain,

for waking up and slowing down, getting my head
right for a show. Christ spent years spreading
his word to crowds that sometimes booed

and threatened riot, sometimes stood so close
he couldn't breathe. On the worst nights
no one came, or they did but didn't listen,

let themselves be moved. To get their attention,
he must've made Heaven sound better, Hell hotter,
the blood he'd spill—his own—more precious

every night. My dad hated snakes, said such
a stupid gimmick would never catch on. When I
worked out my character, how to be a perfect heel,

I thought of my dad conceiving me in rape, saying
his fists were all our fault, that my sister deserved

her murder. I understand why Christ cursed

that fig tree just before he died. Because he could.
Because he was tired, angry, scared and sick
of feeling anything at all. I'd make a lousy prophet

because I keep seeing the same things: the road,
the ring, doors to the past I can't keep closed,
the pills and smoke and booze I need to make

my shows. In the end, it didn't matter how
Christ felt about his death. He knew his fans
would be outnumbered, but he came anyway.

The Jobber

A jobber is a wrestler who is consistently booked to lose matches.

The art of losing takes a lot of time to master,
a lot of practice in the gym, a lot of wrestling
dark matches in arenas that only fill part way.
The biggest names don't always work

that well. They might give good interviews,
have their gimmicks down, but they're technically
unsound, unable to adapt to make sure
they get over. The basic moves are still the same—

suplex, piledriver, chokeslam and sleeper,
but you have to deliver them with style,
give your opponent something to sell fans.
I like a guy who's not too good to take a bump,

win by inches or decision. I don't have to be
the general every time, but if my opponent
panics or gets hurt, shows up too drunk or stoned
to remember what we said backstage,

I'll call the moves till it's time to go home.
I won't get squashed in front of crowds I know,
won't take potatoes without giving a receipt,
but if the other guy blows up I'll wrestle myself,

the ref, an empty chair and make us all
look good. I'll make my opponent look like
he deserves the pin, leave my fans believing
next time might be mine. I don't have to win

the match to know I'm honoring my craft.
I always come prepared to do my job.

The Fabulous Moolah

Born in 1923, Mary Lillian Ellison was the first woman to wrestle in Madison Square Garden.

I didn't give a rat's behind what girls
did in the dark as long as it never came
to light. Half trainer, half mother hen,
I carried hairspray, handkerchiefs
and safety pins, cupped my hand
under their chins so they could spit
their gum. My girls didn't smoke
or swear, date male wrestlers, leave
the gym without lipstick and powder,
scarves over their hair. Promoters
told me what they wanted—blondes,
redheads, dimples, straight or curved—
and that's what I sent. I never told my girls
how far to go if they were asked
for something extra. They could say no
if they wanted, but they still owed my fee.

When the Garden made what I did a sport
and not a sin, I was 49,
but I still kept my hair teased high,
could cinch and squeeze into my tights.
Even in my 70s I booked
a bra and panties match. It felt good
to be under the lights, feel the buzz
against my skin. The best thing about getting
so old is no one wants to know
if I have sex, how often or with who.
Folks probably think that Mae moved in
so we can knit and drink each other's tea.

I may have married at 14, left my child

behind when I realized I could wrestle.
I may have started with a slave girl gimmick,
been ring candy and a kissing valet,
had to dodge the hands of men
I thought were friends, left my second
husband when he asked me to stay home.
I may have fought to keep my title
when I should've passed the torch,
may have pushed my girls too hard
to be like me. But I was Fabulous before
it was my name, a Goddess and a Diva
on exactly my own terms. I was Queen
of the Ring because I earned the crown.

Hunger: Haystacks Calhoun

On the road I'd eat until my jaws
were tired: eggs, bacon, biscuits, ham,
red-eye gravy boiled in cast-iron,
two kinds of pie. Boys set
on keeping slim would push away
their plates, let me finish what
they'd left. I could never find a scale
with numbers high enough to get
my weight, but I knew I was losing.
When I tightened up my galluses
before a match, dark lines marked
where the buckles used to be.

It's beneath a big man's dignity
to hurry. I'd let my opponent
bounce around, warm up the crowd
before I showed off my long reach,
the speed no one expected. Back when
I was working out my splash—
600 pounds falling like judgment
just before the pin—I got sued for busting
a guy's lung and my career took off.
Fans always wanted more of me,
but guys my size were known division
killers. Because we couldn't lose,
if we stayed in one place we'd hurt the gate.

When doctors told me to lose weight,
I'd rattle off some *Aw, shucks* talk
about the farm and all my favorite cows,
horse whose shoe I wore
around my neck. If I didn't eat more
than I wanted when I had the chance,

hunger struck when I was sleeping,
just before a match or on a highway
with nowhere to stop: the early twinges
turning into pain, then sickness
rising in my throat, panic that made
my knees and fingers twitch. To keep
myself alive till my next meal,
I carried crackers and canned meat,
rolls saved from hotel suppers.

A big man can't afford to cringe or cower,
ignore an insult or risk seeming small.
There were nights I felt my shadow
shrinking underneath the lights,
nights I hit the mat and wanted
to stay down. No one understood
how fast I burned through fuel, how frail
I felt at less than my full weight.

Marty Jannetty Buries Shawn Michaels

Shawn says everything we did
was his idea: high-spotting off
the ropes, doing moves in tandem,
tagging in and out too fast for guys
to follow. We changed the way
that tag teams worked, but he
complained I held him back,
said he carried me in every match.
He forgot the times I saved
his life backstage, protected him
from his own mouth, boys
pissed he didn't show respect.

Shawn says he went astray because
he wanted to belong, blames me
for his mistakes. I admit
I went to work unfit, threatened
to quit till I got fired. I punched
a cop in his smug throat,
put a sleeper on my ex, broke
a jobber's neck because my leglock
slipped, ignored my lawyer's
warnings and ended up on house arrest.
Shawn had better luck and a more
honest face, but we behaved
the same. When I see him
invited back as a guest referee,
hear him brag about the Hall
and all his belts, I want to reach
through my TV and break his nose
for real instead of storyline.

Every couple years he calls

to say he hates how we left off.
First he brags how good
we were, how every night
we blew the boys away,
had girls screaming at our door.
Then: how bad he felt
when I got fired, how it was never
his idea and I should let
my grudges go. If he thinks
he's losing me he says my name,
first high and questioning,
then low and sharp, the way
we signaled in a match.
I never say I'm hanging up,
just *click* and toss the phone
aside. Whatever hold he had
on me, I broke it years ago.

Poem Ending in Disqualification

Laid out on the mat,
I hear the crowd suck in
its breath, feel my opponent's shadow
cross my face as he comes flying.
Exhausted, my right arm
cradling my injured left,
I stagger to a corner, pull myself
to the top rope, then pause,
lungs heaving in my chest.

They say my talent's been erased
by my tattoos, drugs I've built
my body with. They say
the weight of my last name
is more than I can lift. I admit,
a thousand main events
have scorched the core of me.

My opponent lunges to his feet,
locks arms around my waist,
forces me to feel the mat again.
I arch my back
to keep my shoulders clear,
reverse his hold to take us home.
He stretches, flails, frees
one leg before I snatch it back.
Trapped, he's seconds away
from tapping out,
but I want something more.

Cording my neck to signal strain,
I give the camera
my most famous face—

eyes narrowed to slits,
stubbled cheekbones sharp as blades.
Then my teeth meet the muscle
of his thigh, hold on till my ears ring
with the closing bell.
Somewhere far away,
a voice announces my defeat.

Dear C.M. Punk

Spring 2014

Dear C.M. Punk, where did you go? You helped us
make a cult of you, then ran away when our love
was too much. In Chicago, your hometown fans
can't stop chanting your name. They need you
to sit cross-legged on the mat, tear down
the big machine you hate but use to pay your bills.
You're only 35, and while I halfway hope
you won't come back, cheapen the grand exit
that you've made, I know how hard it is
for guys to stay retired. When I miss you the most,
I replay the night you faced Paul Heyman
and his protégé, Heyman calling you a son
he'd made and come to hate, his spit flying
in your face when he over-pronounced *Punk.*
The next time you were on TV: two black eyes,
stitches in your hair, your red-starred hoodie
riding up to show the welts and bruises
on your back. I doubt that single match explains
why five months later you walked out, but to me
the narrative makes sense. I wonder if the wrist-tape
you wear to the ring—straight-edge Xs drawn
across your hands—brings your anger on
or holds it in. Like you, I rely on irony and innuendo,
threaten to punch the world's face to hide
that I'm afraid. When you call your fans fickle,
you want them to prove they aren't. C.M. Punk,
if you stay away from wrestling for good, we'll just learn
to follow someone else. I worry you're the one
who won't be able to let go, that you can't live
without the love you've been pretending to resist.

Two Wrestlers Touring the Musee D'orsey

Paul Cezanne's "Pommes et Oranges."
Earthenware dishes. A jug with a flower motif.
Draped cloth harkening back to 17th century
Flemish still lifes. Combining modernity and
sumptuous beauty, Cezanne creates a
complex spacial construction.

SPINNING HEADLOCK ELBOW DROP!
SLIDING FOREARM SMASH!
TIGER FEINT KICK!
LEG LARIAT!

Edouard Manet's "On the Beach."
Summer, 1893, a family getaway to
Berck-sur-Mer on the Mediterranean.
His wife poses for him. His brother.
There is sand mixed in with the paint.
The two triangles formed by the figures
stabilize the composition but the figures
are absorbed in their own worlds.
The painting – a world of melancholia.

DIVING DOUBLE AXE HANDLE!
MOONSAULT DOUBLE FOOT STOMP!
DIVING SPEAR!
PHOENIX SPLASH!

August Renoir's "Dance at Le Moulin de la Galette."
It is one of Renoir's most famous paintings.
It is one of the most important paintings in all of
Impressionism. The form, the shimmer. The
vivacious and joyous atmosphere in Montmartre.
Bathed in natural and artificial light, the Parisians

seem to be moving within the static of the frame.

LEG SWEEP!
WHEELBARROW ARM DRAG!
COBRA CLUTCH BULLDOG!
INVERTED STOMP FACEBREAKER!

"Excusez-moi." The wrestlers stop. "Vous aurez a batter ailleurs."

Excuse me. You will have to wrestle elsewhere.

POWER BOMB! DOUBLE KNEE BACKBREAKER COMBINATION!

"…" Paramedics arrive. The museum guard is taken away.

Two wrestlers touring the Musee D'Orsey.

Alexandre Falguière's 1875 painting - oil on canvas. "Wrestlers."

Short Poems by Wrestler Poets

William Carlos "The Thief" Williams

I have given you
the five moves
of doom

You were hoping
for a cleaner
finish.

Forgive me,
but you had to be
destroyed.

Emily "Titan" Dickinson

If I can stop one heart from beating,
I shall not have wrestled in vain;
If I can crush this man I'm meeting,
or cause him serious pain,
or pile drive this sucker
into the earth again
I shall not wrestle in vain.

Maya "Too Much For You" Angelou

Your skin all bruised
mine like bronze.
One bleeds beginning
the match's end.
The other, laughing
at your pathetic effort.

Edna "Captain Fillet" Millay

My fists burn
at both ends,
You will not last the
night;
But oh, my foes, and oh, my foes –
They end every fight.

Sappho "The Mad Lesbian"

Cry, my sacred vanquished foe;
cry, let my tilt-a-whirl cross body
accompany your tears

"Smasho" Basho

The double foot stomp
Coupled with the dragon whip.
I laugh at your grave

Bump

In the art of professional wrestling, the process of falling on your back properly without injuring yourself is called 'taking a bump.'

It's been said that taking a single bump in a wrestling ring is the equivalent of getting rear-ended at 15 miles an hour.

There is no secret trick to making a bump hurt less.

The only thing you can do is get back up,

Take another bump,

And repeat this process until your back becomes calloused

Until it becomes second nature.

Until you can take a bump on anything.

Until you can't feel the pain of a bump anymore.

If I've learned from taking bumps it's that:

Life is full of bumps, whether they be physical, emotional or mental.

And it's much easier to get up from physical bumps than the others.

But you've still gotta get back up.

Because you're here to be a wrestler.

And wrestlers take bumps.

That's just the way it is.

Andre the Giant

He held an ice tray out and cracked it into one
of his hands and then extended his arm palm up
holding all sixteen of the ice cubes at once.

I grabbed a tray myself
worked the cubes free with both hands
and used my right to release
the cubes into my left
half of which crashed to the ground
Then turned to him with the eight
cubes that I caught.

He said "You can hold eight ice cubes at once."
"That's wonderful!"
And then both of us laughed and laughed.

The Child Killer

for Chris Benoit

When the toothless aggression comes a calling,
you have to pay the rabid wolverine his toll.

After I heard that Eddie Guerrero died,
it was difficult for me to watch wrestling.

On the RAW where they memorialized you,
while listening to William Regal talk
Matt noticed that something was off.
There was a hole in the story.
An injury no one wanted to mention
because their spot is more important
than their health.
That is the mentality you have to have
to make it to the top of mountain.
This is how you conquer the brass rings.

A winged horse flies across the sky.
The Pegasus Kid crashes to the mat,
a headbutt to the fools who stand in his way.
Even if causes blackouts
between the shine and the finish,
try to ignore it and get your heat.

When the crippler almost became the crippled
like the Dynamite Kid,
did he think of Sabu
and the altar to the extreme revolution
they had "broke in" their bodies on.
Did he worry about ever being able to put butts in seats?
Did he think that when he left

that Tony Schiavone would bury him
from the announcers chair?

In the storm of confetti,
looking down from the elevation
that the main event rises to
was it hard for you and Eddie
to not think of all the miles
and bumps it took
to earn the right
be the champion.

From the distorted harmonic of your entrance music,
I popped like a good mark should.
You were a hero for those of us
who didn't have the Hollywood face.
You showed that if you were willing to be the best,
then you could achieve the impossible.
Even if the fame isn't worth
the paychecks it's printed on.
Even if the sacrifice and the addiction
isn't worth the millions and millions at home
cheering you on
as you pinned your sanity
lost your legacy.

When the news broke
and there you were
a murderer,
another dead wrestler,
another child killer,
the hero who could do nothing
but become the villain.

The company did what they thought was necessary.

You were just left out of the story.
You name became censored.
You were just to be forgotten
but the fans
we don't forget
and we forgive too easy
the heinous things that wrestlers have done.
Steve Austin beating his wife,
Jimmy Snuka possibly murdering a woman.
We forgive a little too much.
But, it is always difficult when someone truly was
the best and could back it up
night after night
the memory becomes deep.

But let's not be fools,
there is still a boy who will never grow up
and a mother who will never see that son grow
so let's not forget them
in our forgiveness which only
immortalizes the legend
and forgets that the greater the hero,
the greater the flaw.

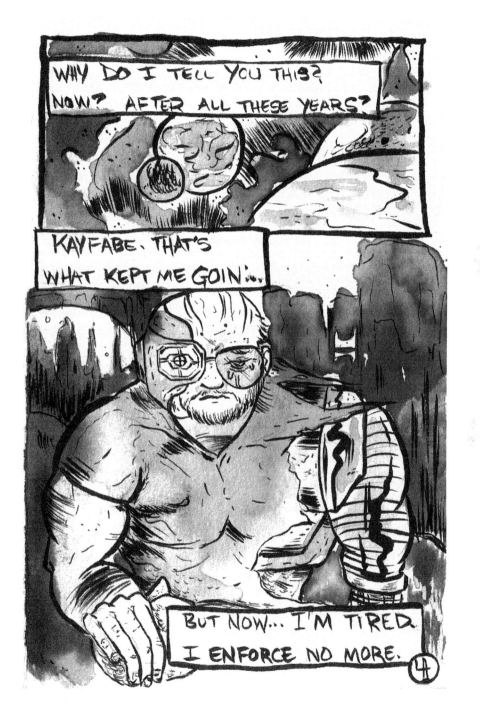

The Ode Not Taken

for Dennis Stamp and all enhancement talent everywhere

I would be there but I wasn't invited, he says,
and a man who set people on fire in Japan
grovels and pleads for his presence at the event
because he knows this man's worth.

While his peers travelled the globe
barreling through explosives and razor wire
Dennis stayed at home, waiting for the territory system
to come back. He stayed in shape. His job
was to do the job.   To receive the violence of other men
whose names are bright enough on the marquee
to put asses every 18 inches. The problem
with being a jobber is that no one ever gives you credit
for playing your part to perfection.
It's like being such a good desk jockey in *Serpico*
that your every reaction makes Al Pacino look like
the toughest cop on the beat.

They should call Dennis Stamp a great salesman
but instead they call him a *jabroni.* A jobber.
At least in the old days hands like him were called
carpenters. More respectful, that term,
an acknowledgement that no event occurs
without everyone working together
to help build it.

The Lie

and then the truth and then the other lie

you don't have/to retire/
you don't have to/
you don't have to drop/
you don't have to drop the belt/
you/have/creative control/
you don't have to drop the belt in montreal/
in montreal/you don't have to/
you know/you have/control/
you don't have to drop/montreal/
you can retire it on tv/
you don't have to/retire/control/
we/have/to let you go/
to retire/you/
we/swear to god/we/don't have/control/
you/have/reasonable/creative control/
you can/still be champion/
you can/still/have control/
you/don't have
don't have to/be/reasonable/

we/don't have to/
have/reasonable/tv/
we/have/you/in montreal
we/have control/
you don't/

(i/swear to god/i
didn't/know)

Antisocialist

for CM Punk

One day you went to take out the trash
and someone was waiting there
for your autograph.
You're a prick
when you won't take a picture with a fan
at an airport
at 2AM.

I am not mad at you for walking out
on the action figure and video game money.

You threw yourself into so many glass ceilings
and came back still bleeding, still broken,
not whole. But they needed you, they said.
They needed you and the pop that eclipsed
the static and Vernon Reid guitars
crunching out of the speakers.

You were never a fan of going through the motions.
You saw your opponent's knees crumble bump by bump,
men you traveled down the road with
lose feeling in their arms when their necks
betrayed them.   It was impossible for you
to be the body you were before.
All the changes you were told would be made
were printed on t-shirts and shrank in the wash.

They could have at least come through on the ice cream bars.

So it's okay if you want to enjoy
what being a fighting champion brought you:

a lair in the heart of your stomping grounds.
A flourishing new marriage. A chance to breathe
for the first time in years.
Blackhawks season tickets you can actually use.

Never say never is the song on every wrestler's playlist.
You remixed it on a red carpet, screaming
never /ever/ ever
and your cult of personality wobbles.
If you listen through the edits,
your name echoes through Rosemont,
hoping they can conjure you from the gorilla position.

I wish you walks on the beach
that aren't broadcast one still shot at a time.
I wish you find that spark
that makes you want to put on kickpads again,
to come out from behind a fist clutching lightning,
to shout Ben Grimm's battlecry from bended knee.

Now is the time for you to put away all your luggage.
To learn what it is to be a fan again.
If you never return, we understand.
But we will never stop chanting your name.

The Bray Wyatt Motivational Seminar

Chapter One: Follow The Buzzards

I see you, man, running around the maze
with all of the other little rats. You've been spoon-fed
just enough half-truths and sugarcubes
to keep you soft and bloated. You click on buttons
and the pictures floating in front of your bleary eyes
hypnotize you into staying numb. But you keep hitting
that button. Click-click, click-click.
Have some more pictures. Eat some more sugar.
This maze you run goes nowhere
but for you, there's something pretty to look at,
and mmmmm, the sugar is so, so sweet.
I'm here, man, to pluck you out of the maze
and watch what happens when you scamper
into the forest for the first time. Where there are no
easy rewards, where everything in front of your eyes
has been watching you from places you never thought
to look. Are you scared, little rat? What will you do
when you hear something crackle in the distance?
When you no longer have the protection of the maze,
when all the things you taste are suddenly sour or bitter?

You need someone who can keep you safe
from all the monsters who will swipe at you,
the predators who will see your exposed belly
and salivate at the tasty little morsel you've become.
So soft and slow. So so sweet. I can offer you a place
under my wing. You need the shelter of a guide who knows
what the bloodlust tastes like. I've been there,
man, deep in the thickness of these woods,
vines strangling all life that tries to struggle.
Trees that look like thick, ancient prison bars.

This is the real world, man, and it's not a place
where your pictures and sugarcubes can help you
from being consumed. Time to join an army
that will train in you in the art of survival. You need
a strong brotherhood that knows what miracles
can occur when you learn how to believe. You need
a family like us. We will sharpen your claws. Teach you
how to use your teeth. I will keep you safe in the
darkness if you follow my light. Or you can refuse
to accept my truth and get eaten by this world.

Take your time. I'll be here waiting.

Time is on my side.

Memoirs of a would-be Wrestler

In September 1984 I started grade 6, and was the year I went from normal wrestling fan to hardcore die-hard wrestling fan. Hulk Hogan was the heavyweight champion of the world and had been for almost a year, since defeating The Iron Sheik at Madison Square Garden a mere 9 months prior. I like most kids my age was a "Hulkamaniac" and I was convinced Hogan was invincible. The Hulk had faced opponent after opponent 9 straight months now and nobody could defeat him!

I had already found my own strange connection between rock n' roll and wrestling the first time I saw The Road Warriors wrestle, and they entered the ring to Black Sabbath's "Iron Man" but there was now a whole new movement starting to unfold that would prove to be the biggest boom for wrestling... It was known as "the rock n' wrestling connection"

It all started when wrestler/manager Captain Lou Albano was on a flight and he met Cindi Lauper, an up and coming female singer. The two hit it off on the flight and Lauper asked Lou to be in her video for "Girls just wanna have fun" portraying the role of her father. Lauper soon appeared on Rowdy Roddy Piper's talk show segment "Piper's Pit" where Lou (who was a heel or bad guy) insulted Lauper, resulting in her issuing a challenge. Each of them would select a female wrestler of their choice to represent them.

MTV broadcasted "The brawl to end it all" which saw Cindi's pick, Wendi Richter going up against Lou's pick, The Fabulous Moolah who had a boastful 28 year run as the WWF women's champion. Lauper hit Moolah with "the loaded purse of doom" and we had a new women's champion! Lauper continued her collaboration with the WWF and Lou appeared in more of her music videos along with other wrestlers such as Roddy Piper and The Iron Sheik just to name a couple. Rick Derringer composed a song for Hulk Hogan entitled "Real American" and the next thing you knew all the wrestlers, mainly the heels, followed suit and made their own songs which spawned "The Wrestling Album"

Meanwhile over in the AWA, The warriors were still bashing skulls to Black Sabbath, and the company itself was releasing a lot of promotional videos that were accompanied by rock music. Some of the AWA wrestlers even made their own songs and videos, including The Midnight Rockers and my boys The Road Warriors. I was really liking the way things were shaping up in life, two of my most favourite loves were on top of the world and it seemed like it couldn't get any better.

Wrestling was booming yet sadly all the independent territories were being absorbed by Vince McMahon who was "liquidating" them all into his company the WWF. Cindi Lauper was still on the scene in Wendi Richter's corner. The former champ Moolah brought in a new protégé Lelani Kai, who won the title from Wendi at "The war to settle the score" Richter regained her title at the inaugural WrestleMania, which in itself was the greatest wrestling event ever held at that point in time

It was the Super Bowl of wrestling. Sadly back in those days there was no pay per view nor any restaurants with closed circuit TV airing it except perhaps stripjoints. Unless you had tickets or a satellite dish you were shit out of luck. I was left to wait patiently for Coliseum Home Video to release it on VHS. If I remember correctly my dad ended up getting us a copy from a guy at his work. WrestleMania destroyed my senses it was that good, or at least it seemed. Looking back now a lot of the matches were forgettable to say the least. Quite a few celebrities were involved including Muhammed Ali, Liberace, and even my first role model Mr. T was a part of the magic.

WrestleMania was a huge success and wrestling was the newest, hottest commodity in sports. Hulk Hogan appeared on the cover of sports illustrated and was billed as the 3rd highest paid athlete in all of professional sports. NBC saw the explosion and jumped on board. They started randomly airing "Saturday Nights Main Event" in place of Saturday Night Live, which consisted of pay per view quality bouts as opposed to all the squash matches you'd normally see on weekend afternoon programming.

There was also a cartoon show launched called "Hulk Hogan's Rock n' Wrestling" that aired Saturday mornings in the toon rotation. It wasn't the greatest cartoon by any means but it had little skits between commercials and what not, that were filmed in live action with the wrestlers themselves in the flesh. That was pretty cool in my books. I can remember just videotaping those clips of the show specifically, as it was really the first time I was seeing wrestlers outside of wrestling.

I had tons of wrestling VHS tapes as I used to tape matches every Saturday afternoon and the occasional Saturday night when SNME was on. I had started collecting wrestling magazines in grade 7 so by this time my collection had grown quite large. Wrestling figures were also in abundance inside my toy box and I'd virtually wrestle with whatever type of action figures I could get my hands on, be it G.I. Joe or He-Man.

My obsession with wrestling grew and grew, I knew everyone's stats, dates of historic title changes and so on. Things got to the point where I didn't even want to be a rock star anymore, I was determined to be a wrestler. Our school had a wrestling team so I decided to join, from there on I had a brief stint with the amateur wrestling team at school until I decided to use a vertical suplex one day and that was the end of my amateur wrestling career.

Not to be bested I decided to start my own wrestling promotion, the BWF. As far as I know the BWF could have possibly been the first ever backyard wrestling organization in Brampton, my home town where I grew up. My friends and I made up the small roster and we had matches every day on lunch, created title belts, declared champions and kept stats. Wrestling was also influencing my artistic side, as all I was creating through grade 8 were wrestling comics and animated flip books of wrestling.

The BWF was getting bigger and we had a new kid who invited himself into our organization regardless of the fact that we blatantly didn't consider him a part of it. His involvement and annoyance would lead to an epic historical day close to the end of the school year.....a hair vs hair/ title vs title match between him and yours truly. Grade 8 was winding down to a close, all in all it was a fun, mischievous, music filled year. Towards the end of the year this kid named Bob started wrestling with us in the BWF. None of us liked him so we came up with a scheme to rid him from our fed.

One of our buddies agreed to team up with him and we started having tag team matches, all of which saw Bob as the legal man being double teamed for the entire match without ever tagging in his partner. We ran this angle for about a week and it finally culminated in Bob's tag team partner going berserk due to the fact his partner kept losing their matches. In a fit of rage he joined the opposing team, which consisted of me and my partner, in stomping Bob to a pulp and torturing him with every submission move under the sun. Bob realized this was for real and got the fuck out of dodge before he was seriously injured.

Over the next week or two Bob completely ignored us, until one day in class he came up to us claiming he had started his own fed, the BWA (Brampton Wrestling Association) which he boasted was a superior product in comparison to our BWF. We quickly grilled Bob about who he had on his roster to which he retorted "Bob the barber beefcake, the macho man bob savage" and other wrestler names with "Bob" worked into them in an un clever manner, his roster was nothing more than him as multiple characters....or personalities.

My friends and I were in hysterics as we made fun of Bob and his imaginary wrestling federation, to the point where he snapped and actually manned up for once in his life, issuing a challenge against your humble narrator. Bob demanded a title vs. title match. My BWF title belt against his BWA title belt, which we were sure was also imaginary. The bout would have a one hour time limit, and would take place on lunch hour, during the final day of the grade 8 semester. I quickly agreed to Bob's list of demands with a cocky laugh, which he tried to cut short by adding one final stipulation...the loser would have his hair cut off by the winner.

There was no way in hell I was losing my hair! I knew Bob had no chance of beating me, yet the thought of my locks being cut off filled me with feelings of anxiety and worry. I had to come up with a fool proof plan to assure my hair would remain unscathed. All my friends had their own ideas to prevent me from losing but I liked my idea the best so we rolled with it.

My plan was simple, I would only wrestle defensively and let Bob make the moves. I knew I could stimey and reverse anything he threw at me so I decided to just keep shutting him down, proving to him I was the superior wrestler. Then when there were mere minutes remaining in the time limit, my boys would pull a run in which would result in a no contest and we'd both keep our titles respectively. Nobody would lose their belt and nobody would lose their hair....or at least that's what the plan was.

The day of the big match arrived and so did the end of grade 8. I excused myself from whatever class I had before lunch minutes prior to bell time so I could go suit up. My wrestler persona was "Killer Kevin Piper" an amalgamation of my two favorite singles wrestlers at the time, Rowdy Roddy Piper and Jason the Terrible (Karl Moffat) My gear consisted of my high top Adidas sneakers, some colorful "jam" shorts or skateboarding shorts with one of my mother's kilts over top, my "hot rod" shirt I bought at a WWF event that year at Maple Leaf Gardens, and the coup de gras..... A hard plastic street hockey goalie mask donated to me by my good friend Jay Poole.

I knew Bob would immediately try to remove my goalie mask, so being the master of head games I decided to start the match off with one offensive move. I still had whippersnappers left over from my Boston trip, so I used masking tape and attached a few to the mask. I then exited the side doors of the school and made my entrance onto the soccer field with my bag of tricks and radio blasting Black Sabbath's "Iron Man". Bob and I now stood face to face as the ref checked us over for illegal objects. As soon as the bell sounded I quickly head butted bob repeatedly causing the whippersnappers to explode on contact, which resulted in numerous small burns on his forehead. As expected Bob pulled the goalie mask off and tossed it aside.

We locked up. Stalemate. We locked up again but this time Bob went for a quick arm bar, which I easily reversed and broke. Another lock up, Bob puts me in a hammerlock. I spin around behind him putting his arm in a hammerlock then I pushed him to the ground. He makes a shoot for my legs while he's down, but he can't get me to the ground. Back to his feet now, he rushed in for yet another lock up. This time he applied a side head lock, which I ended up pulling out of, and again shoved him from behind forcing him to the ground once again. I could see the frustration starting to build inside of him. Bob couldn't keep one hold on me nor could he fathom why I wasn't attempting any moves of my own. Confused, he kept attempting moves and holds which I kept escaping or reversing, generally resulting in Bob on the ground.

On his feet again, he came in for another lockup. This time he quickly scooted in behind me and applied a full nelson. Bob was applying the pressure hard and asking the ref to check if I wanted to submit. Obviously not. The move was synched in deep. Generally I could escape this move with ease but I had to give him credit, he was locked in for dear life. I threw my head back attempting to smash my skull into his face but he had his head down, our skulls collided and dizzied us both. I stomped on his foot a few times so he readjusted his legs so I couldn't stomp any more. I threw a few kicks back at his shin and groin, which

293

connected but he didn't break the hold, I made comments about how he must have no balls seeing as the groin kicks didn't affect him. I put my arms straight up and attempted to slide down, a textbook escape from the nelson, but Bob knew of this trick and he lowered his body with mine. I was now sitting on the ground still in the hold with Bob behind me on one knee and one foot.

I was starting to run out of gas by this point so I was actually happy to be on my ass and getting some rest. For the next 20 minutes or so Bob kept asking the ref to check if I was ready to give up. Hell no. I told Bob he may as well break the hold and try something new, as there was no way he was going to submit me. He refused and held onto the belief that this would be his finisher. We sat on the ground for what seemed like an eternity until the time keeper announced there was only 5 minutes left in the time limit. This was the cue to signal the final part of the plan.

My buddy Chris ran in and drop kicked Bob square in the side of the head, which broke the hold and caused the ref to end the match due to interference. Technically I had lost by disqualification but the last laugh would be all mine. Before Bob could collect his thoughts another wrestler ran in and threw a bag of the mysterious "white powder" in Bob's face. It was actually a bag of flower from my mother's pantry. Now blinded and dazed, we all started laying the boots to Bob. Someone put him in a Boston crab and another kid applied a camel clutch. The combination of the two submission moves simultaneously caused Bob's body to resemble the letter U.

Now folded in half and screaming in pain, it was time to end this once and for all. I reached into my bag of tricks and pulled out the scissors. Bob had a haircut similar to Tony Hawk at the time, a skater cut, short with a side part and long bangs. I frantically started snipping away at his bangs as well as the hair on top of his head, making sporadic cuts which resulted in him looking like he had a fight with a lawn mower. The bell sounded to end lunch, so we all ran off laughing and yelling victoriously. Bob was so humiliated that he got up and walked home, instead of returning to class for the second half of the day. With my hair still intact and title around my waist, I declared the BWA was officially dead. I shouted out "long live the BWF" repeatedly and my chant was joined by the entire roster. We all cheered as we marched back into the school. No one ever heard from or saw Bob again until the first day of grade 9, where he acted like he had never known or met any of us before...WIN!!!

I had previously been black listed from amateur wrestling in middle school, but now that I was in a new high school I was able to try out for the school wrestling team. The tryouts were announced fairly early into the fall and I was all over it like stink on doodoo. The tryouts were held after school but they were not in the gymnasium. Our school had a fitness room on the second floor that contained exercise bikes, weight machines, and other work out equipment.

When I got there on the first day of tryouts there were thin blue mats laid out in a large square, the same kind of mats you would see in pro wrestling on the outside of the ring. There were a group of males sitting in a circle on the mats so I went and joined in. I was a bit surprised to find out there weren't even any teachers present, as the class was being taught by three senior students from the wrestling team, all of them clean cut, cocky, preppy jocks...the type of guys I loathed.

We started out with some stretching then we went into some simple drills. As the drilling went on they became much harder and harder. The smallest of the three instructors was maybe 5'3 at best and he had the biggest mouth and attitude of the group. As the drills went on he proceeded to start singling me out and pushing me harder than the rest of the group. I immediately assumed that since I was the biggest grade nine at the tryouts he was looking to make an example of me while making himself feel better about his short stature. I'm sure the fact that I had a long flowing mullet just encouraged the target that was now placed on me.

As the weeks went on so did the bullying and abuse from the one instructor. When we finally got into learning holds he would constantly pick me as his volunteer to show the rest of the class the moves we were learning, and he always made a point of really applying the pressure to me and stretching my body to its limits. I can recall him putting me in a reverse hammerlock while I was face down on the mat with him straddling me, he then instructed me to try and break free. Every time I tried to get lose he would tweak my arm harder and harder, to the point where it felt like it was about to break.

Defeated by the pain being inflicted on my bad arm I had broken years prior, I just lied there and gave up, which made him even madder. Blinded by anger now his voice raised as he demanded I try to get free or he was going to break my arm, then he applied the pressure harder than ever. Something snapped in me and I saw red. Before I even knew what I was doing, I violently jerked my body in the direction of my free arm and rolled. Now he was back down on the mat with me on top of him, my back facing his front, the hold was still slapped on good and I'm pretty sure he was legitimately trying to break my arm. I thrusted my head back and our skulls collided, dazed he let go of my arm and I flipped over, my knees now pinning his shoulders to the mat. I heard a hand slap down on the mat declaring a pin and a cheer erupted from the grade nine lackeys.

I got up and raised my hands in victory, the so called "teacher" jumped to his feet in dispute, his face red with embarrassment. Humiliated, he charged at me with a crazed look in his eye trying to start a fight with me. The two other "teachers" had to grab onto him and hold him back. I felt great about besting him but there was no way I was going to be a part of this wrestling team, so I grabbed my stuff and left. After that whenever I passed him in the halls he would give me dirty looks but he never tried to start anything with me. A few weeks later a friend of mine in grade nine who was being bullied by the same guy decided to fight back one day which resulted in the grade 12 wrestler getting his nose broken, and his ass kicked in general. After that I never heard much out of him again and he didn't even make eye contact with me anymore. It looked good on him.

The next day at school I was telling some of the older metal guys about the happenings at the wrestling try outs. They all had a good laugh about it and gave me some proverbial pats on the back. One of them informed me that him and a few of the guys had been doing their own wrestling training at the school during evenings in the same fitness room on the 2nd floor of the high school. He told me I should come check it out and assured me there were no jocks, no instructors, and no teachers supervising, but there was a record player and we could bring our own records to listen to.

The sessions started at 7:30pm and I found it strange that a bunch of kids could have the run of the school so late in the evening with no teachers in sight. In fact I think the janitorial crew were the only adults in the building. I showed up with my gym bag packed with records and a change of clothes to work out in. I knew one of the guys John loved AC/DC to death, so I opted to only bring their records as opposed to my new thrash albums. When I showed up it was just a very small crew of guys, maybe five tops, all of whom I had known since the days of grade school.

Everyone was just kind of doing their own thing, riding exercise bikes, lifting weights, jumping elbow drops off of gym apparatus onto crash mats, all while our vinyl records blasted the sound track for the evening. I can remember thinking "how am I supposed to learn anything here?" There was nobody to teach or train me and nobody here had any form of training, it was merely a bunch of guys just fucking around and imitating wrestling moves they had seen on television. I kind of stepped back and appraised the situation then thought to myself "I've been backyard wrestling a few years now, I've got a bit of amateur experience, and I'm very well versed in emulating the moves off TV without seriously injuring people"

As far as I was concerned I didn't really need any professional training, all I needed to do was hit the weights hardcore so I could be the size of the Hulk Hogans and Randy Savages. By today's standards I may have stood a chance as a cruiser weight, but in the 80s it was all about having a weight lifters physique. I hit the weights nightly for a week or two and started eating like a champ. Unfortunately I have a high metabolism and can eat and eat without so much as gaining a pound. Without weight gain I could not get bigger muscles, this ended up being very frustrating.

As the weeks went on our "training sessions" turned into a gong show of Tom foolery. Now with my own metal band in full motion and my new found love for partying, I decided to give up my dreams of pro wrestling and continue to pursue my art and my music. Wrestling was still very close to my heart and one of my passions in life, but realistically I knew I'd never make it to the big stage unless it was as an announcer or a ref, but to be a wrestler... I did not have the discipline. Unbeknownst to me however, I would get to live out my boyhood dream over a decade later. But that is another story...

Jesus Was His Tag Team Partner

They fought the Freebirds,
Harts, Von Erichs, and
Funks in every town
along the twenty.

They smashed six packs
starting sundown
in Shreveport
to brunch in Dallas.

They'd been cheated,
almost been champs,
and forever challengers.
Then the booker said
they'd feud through the Fall.

It was a trail
of no quarter, no repentance.
Jesus was the white meat
babyface. The pro-wrestler
was cast as the cowardly heel,
boots of silver.

They brawled and bled in nightly
cage, lumberjack, and dog-chain matches.
No new opponents until Easter.

They knew the outcome,
knew the crowd,
Jesus got the pop.
the wrestler got the heat.

From The Turnbuckle

Once in a while even
adrenalin stops despite
a redhead in the
second row, a bottle of Oxycodone
backstage, and a crowd
so eager, they'll wait to be popped.

The pro-wrestler balances with unlaced
boots on the top rope. It's as
sturdy as garden hose
painted red, white in the center
and blue on the bottom rope.

In the moment he balances
sweaty, hated under a name,
not his own.

He is the carny.
He is the un-perched gargoyle
transcending the hero's
bad dreams, if he makes this jump
his knee will graze against temple,
nothing more.

But before his legs relax
his lungs take in the scent
of sweets and popcorn and
brews stewed in a cigarette
smog, flickering under
old light bulbs in a colossal arena.

Americana jammed
down every side,
tonight the villain wins.

Gimmick, pt. 2

The pro-wrestler tried on a mask,
a neon green cloth
that laced around his skull
with crimson cardinals perched
on twisted red-eyed serpents,
embroidered around the temples
entwined down into Aztec
chains around his chin.
The slits of eyes
weren't even child size,
he relied on his rivals
and other senses.
His fluorescent tights
beamed throughout dark venues
in the Southwest territory.
Mostly, they loved him,
the promoter insisted he holler
Yo soy el rey de un mundo!
before each bell.
Crowds from Nogales, El Paso,
Santa Fe, and Phoenix applauded wildly.
But where the big money is made
in Tijuana and Laredo
the crowds would
not cheer, would
not throw pennies, trash,
or beer to a conquering gringo.

Shinsuke Nakamura

Like Shinsuke Nakamura
dancing from the locker room
to the wrestling ring,
I want to swagger into 7-11,
a generic J-pop guitar riff scoring
each strut, every note
encouraging the pomp and stutter.

I want to shift my shoulders,
one hand across heart
the other pointing sideways
to the security camera over the counter.
Nakamura, the storyteller,
I don't understand the plot
but love the way he says it,
Nakamura, the king of strong style!
And me, guy craving
a Dr Pepper.

I will grab hold of the spill tray
at the Big Gulp station
bend my knees hard
so horizon and back are flat, body
flailing to the reaction
and roars of fans.

I will cast eyes, slowly, around the shop
the smell of convenience store coffee
passes as the stench of sweat,
scent of blood and nickels,
this evening's prior violence in the air.

When I approach the clerk

who keeps order in the store
like a crooked referee
I'll look at the dollar bill clutched
in my hand as I would the IWGP
Title, reluctantly handing over.

And when it's time to leave
my foot will tap impatiently,
its rhythm a haiku about a heartbeat,
until I charge the automated doors
with a running Boma Ye flying knee,
destroying the dinging sensor,
in a shower of fragmented glass
and neon lights.

Tonight I coronate myself
Gaijin of strong style!

WrestleMania III

For months, I begged mom to let me tag along with Mike
to his friend's house in Potwin,
that old, grand neighborhood, so alien
among the clapboard buildings around Topeka High.
I'd been dreaming of Hogan: what six-year-old
wouldn't? He was everything a Midwest 80s boy
wished he could be, tanned, strong, able to charm
a crowd like those snake-charmers
on old movies. Mike said Andre would break him
like a twig, but back then I still believed in heroes.

We gathered in the massive rec room.
I sat in the corner, promised not to talk. I entered thinking I was Hulk,
and left whispering Steamboat
like a mantra. For fifteen minutes, he'd battled with Savage,
and then, in an instant, he'd gone from half-dead on the mat
to rolling him up. 1, 2, 3, in the Small Package,
and he was champion. After that, Hulkster's strength
couldn't compare. We walked home.
The lights of Potwin gave way to the dirty yellows
of 6th Street. It was March 29th, 1987. I'd seen the decade
peak, though I didn't know it. The next day Danny
and I would wrestle in his backyard.
Six years later, Andre was dead, the first of many.
That was after Danny's walk down
to the river. The long 1980s were half over,
and I thought, that night, that the future spread before me
like Steamboat, frozen forever at the height of his leap
from the top rope.

Contributor Bios

Mark James Andrews is currently hawking a flash fiction collection, *Compendium 20/20* (Deadly Chaps) and a poetry CD, *Brylcreem Sandwich* (with Tom Brzezina). He continues to live and write just outside the Detroit city limits most of the time.

Benjamin Anthony is the cartoonist formerly known as Bernie Crowsheet. He's an indie game developer, pizza enthusiast, dad, and yeah, he has been jammin: http://turbostab.com/.

Colette Arrand is a poet, essayist, and critic living in Athens, Georgia. Her work has appeared in a number of literary journals, including *The Atlas Review*, *CutBank*, and *Hobart*. She writes about wrestling constantly through a number of forums: The website *Fear of a Ghost Planet*, the tumblrs *Date with a Wrestler* and *Wrestling Fashion*, and the online webcomic, *Wrestling School*, which is drawn by Scott Stripling. She lives her life by three words: Hustle. Loyalty. Respect.

Brian Baumgart is the director of the Associate of Fine Arts in Creative Writing program at North Hennepin Community College just outside Minneapolis, and he holds an MFA from Minnesota State University-Mankato. He recently taught his son and daughter how to use a power sander and a hatchet; he's amazed he still has all of his fingers. His son adores mythological monsters, and his daughter has learned to croak "Redrum" while angling her finger at strangers. He will gladly accept responsibility for these children. His writing has been published in various journals, including *Ruminate*, *Sweet*, and *Cleaver Magazine*.

ed blair is the current editor of *PWF*, a zine devoted to charting the emotional landscape of professional wrestling. he also runs the holy demon army zine distro, the only zine distro devoted to zines about pro-wrestling. he co-writes *black metal of the americas*, and is a repeat contributor to *the atomic elbow*.

Eric Lloyd Blix lives in Minneapolis. His writing has appeared in such journals as *Western Humanities Review*, *Caketrain*, *Paper Darts*, and others, and it has been reprinted at *Longform.org*. He teaches composition and creative writing at Minnesota State University, Mankato.

Ryan Bradley has previously published work in *The Missouri Review*, *The Rumpus*, *Pinball*, the anthology *Drawn to Marvel*, and others. He contributes writing regularly to *Action Figure Fury*. Most recently, he won the JP Reads flash fiction contest. He is working on his first novel. He will receive an MFA in Fiction from Emerson College this May.

Peter Burzynski is a third-year PhD student in and Graduate Assistant Coordinator of Creative Writing-Poetry at the University of Wisconsin-Milwaukee. He holds a B.A. from the University of Wisconsin-Madison, a M.F.A. in Poetry from The New School University, and a M.A. in Polish Literature from Columbia University. In between his studies, he has worked as a chef in New York City and Milwaukee. In addition, he works as a Teaching Assistant and an occasional adjunct. He is an Assistant Editor for *the cream city review*. His poetry has appeared or is forthcoming from *The Best American Poetry Blog*, *Thin Air*, *Prick of the Spindle*, *Thrush Poetry Review*, *Your Impossible Voice*, *RHINO*, and *Forklift Ohio*, amongst others.

Glendaliz Camacho is a Pushcart Prize nominee, 2015 Write A House Finalist, and currently a recipient of a Lower Manhattan Cultural Council Workspace residency. She has been an artist in residence at Jentel, Caldera, Kimmel Harding Nelson, and Hedgebrook. Glendaliz is a proud VONA/Voices alum. Her work appears in *The Female Complaint* (Shade Mountain Press), *Soulmate 101 and Other Essays on Love and Sex* (Full Grown People) and *All About Skin: Short Fiction by Women of Color* (University of Wisconsin Press), as well as *The Butter*, *Saraba Magazine*, and *Kweli Journal*, among others. She is currently working on a short story collection, novel, essays, and a musical. It still took her twenty minutes to recover from meeting Jay Briscoe. Learn more about Glendaliz at becomenzando.com.

Ricardo Castaño IV watched wrestling back when he was smaller than one of the Hulkster's 24-inch pythons, and has carried a flame for it since. Now he writes about funny movies and works as a copywriter with a flair for the dramatic, so check him out at *RicksWriting.com*, brother.

Michael Chin was born and raised in Utica, New York and is currently an MFA student in creative writing at Oregon State University. He won the 2014 Jim Knudsen Editor's Prize for fiction and has previously published fiction in journals including *Bayou Magazine*, *The Rappahannock Review*, and *CaKe: A Journal of Poetry and Art*. He writes a weekly wrestling column for 411mania.com, called The Magnificent Seven. You can visit him online at miketchin.com and follow him on Twitter @miketchin.

A.V. Christensen is a queer, feminist pro wrestler and creator of *Femmezuigiri* - a publication dedicated to highlighting women in pro-wrestling and subverting misogyny within the culture. She comes complete with a "Macho Man" Randy Savage tattoo and obsession for flashy ring gear and over the top promos. More information can be found at: www.femmezuigiri.com, @femmezuigiri, and @mynameisacacia.

Benjamin Drevlow was the winner of the 2006 Many Voices Project and the author of a collection of short stories, *Bend With the Knees and Other Love Advice From My Father* (New Rivers Press, 2008). His fiction has also appeared in the *Fiction Southeast, Passages North*, and *Hot House Magazine*. He is the fiction editor at *BULL: Men's Fiction*, teaches writing at Georgia Southern University, and lives both in Georgia and online at <www.thedrevlow-olsonshow.com>.

Brian Alan Ellis edits the journal *Tables Without Chairs*, and is the author of *The Mustache He's Always Wanted but Could Never Grow, 33 Fragments of Sick-Sad Living, King Shit* (with Waylon Thornton), and *Something Good, Something Bad, Something Dirty*. His writing has appeared, or is forthcoming, at *Juked, Hobart, Crossed Out, Zygote in My Coffee, Monkeybicycle, Literary Orphans, DOGZPLOT, Lost in Thought, Sundog Lit, Connotation Press, Vol. 1 Brooklyn, That Lit Site, Heavy Feather Review, Diverse Voices Quarterly, Out of the Gutter, NAP, Electric Literature, The Next Best Book Blog, Entropy, Revolution John*, and *Atticus Review*, among other places. He currently subsists on the air of combat in Tallahassee, Florida, where nightmares are generally the best part of his day.

Joseph Feeney III is a freelance writer and a student, currently pursuing a Master's Degree in Creative Writing, and the host of the Creative Control podcast. His writing and reviews have appeared in *Alternative Wrestling Magazine*, and on The Place To Be Nation, B-Sides On Air & Online, Creative Control World, The Wrestling Observer, 1Wrestling.com, and the Pro Wrestling Torch. He is a lifelong pro wrestling fan, and a regular attendee of events, especially in the ECW Arena. He currently lives in Pennsylvania with his beautiful, patient wife Emily, and their four cats.

Craig Firsdon is a poet and artist from Holland, Ohio. He has been published in numerous publications including *Red Fez, Rusty Truck*, and *Zygote In My Coffee*. He has also published his chapbook *Opiate Dreams* and been a reader at poetry events including Zygote In My Fez, 100 Thousand Poets for Change, Snoetry and Toledo Art Walk. Craig is also a paint and charcoal artist who has had a local showcase for his art. In 2010 journalist Lorraine Cipriano called him the "Toledo renaissance man" in an article for the *Toledo Poetry Examiner*. Currently Craig still writes and creates art without letting his disability stop him.

Kyle Flak is just another random dude from Michigan. His newest and tiniest poems are on a website called *Cacti Fur*. He likes vegetables, long walks, and Basho.

Wred Fright is the author of the novels *The Pornographic Flabbergasted Emus* and *Blog Love Omega Glee*. More of his work can be found through Wredfright.Com.

Michael Frissore has completed his first novel, *Dead Wrestlers, Part I*, and is currently writing *Part II*. He hopes to publish both in 2016 or '17. His poems in *Working Stiff* previously appeared in his chapbook *Long Blue Boomerang* (Heavy Hands Ink). He's published a lot of stuff in a lot of places, but he's most happy being Reference #14 on the "Toothbrush moustache" *Wikipedia* page. Mike was at the Mass Transit Incident in Revere, MA and often sits on his porch, smoking a pipe and stroking his beard, whilst telling the tale to neighborhood children. Also, his wife tells him he giggles like a five-year-old when The New Day are on TV.

Kelly Froh is a comic artist who lives in Seattle, WA. She is also the co-founder of Short Run Comix & Arts Festival. She misses going to ECCW matches in Vancouver, BC, Canada. It was there where she saw her first lumberjack match, and she fell in love with the brutality and passion of Minor League wrestlers. Find her work here: www.cargocollective.com/kefroh and www.shortrun.org.

Keith Gaustad is the author of *High Art & Love Poems* (Broken Bird Press) and one third of the world's only non-ironic Polka Hip Hop band The November Criminals. He lives in Milwaukee where he edits *Burdock Magazine* once a year, volunteers at riverwestradio.com on the board of directors and co-hosting There Goes The Neighborhood. His favorite wrestlers are Mick Foley, Bryan Danielson, Bret Hart, and Dean Ambrose. His favorite match (seen live) is Danielson vs. Moxley at The Miramar Theatre.

Michael "Mad Dog" Goscinski spends most of his days stylin' and profilin' in Upstate New York. Occasionally he wrassles his way into a small press zine … *Zygote, gutter eloquence, Red Fez, Otoliths* and many others have felt the fury of his 5 knuckle shuffle!! He's currently makin' a comeback, and "you can believe dat, sucka."

Michael Grover is a Florida born poet. He now lives in Toledo, OH. He has been published all over the small press. Over the years Michael has released over a dozen chapbooks and released his first novel

Lockewood/The Wolves Of Lockewood available on Hiptiy Scotch Press. Michael is currently the head poetry editor at *Red Fez*.

Born in Detroit, **Steven Gulvezan** has worked as a journalist and a library director. His stories and poems have appeared in *Ellery Queen's Mystery Magazine*, *Red Fez*, *The Ann Arbor Review*, *Literary Orphans*, and many other publications. A collection of his poetry is *The Dogs of Paris*.

Amorak Huey is author of the poetry collection *Ha Ha Ha Thump* (Sundress, 2015) and the chapbook *The Insomniac Circus* (Hyacinth Girl, 2014). A former newspaper editor and reporter, he teaches writing at Grand Valley State University in Michigan. His poems appear in *The Best American Poetry 2012*, *The Cincinnati Review*, *The Southern Review*, *The Collagist*, *Menacing Hedge*, and many other print and online journals.

This **Alex Jones** does not have a radio show or the truth about 9/11. Instead, he has a BA in English from the University of Detroit Mercy, publication credits that include *Chorus* and Detroit's *Metro Times* newspaper, and the distinction of being the only person in his elementary school carpool to have not received a Tony Award nomination.

JT Wilkins (JTW) has been creating mini comics since his pre-teens but started doing comics seriously in 2004, when he self-published his first comic zine *Lunchbox*. Since then, he was part of the Local DC Conspiracy comic scene in which his work can be seen in the *Magic Bullet Comic Newspaper*. He has labeled his technique in coloring and effects as "Hi-Octane".

W. Todd Kaneko is the author of *The Dead Wrestler Elegies* (Curbside Splendor, 2014). His poems and prose have appeared in *Bellingham Review*, *Los Angeles Review*, *Barrelhouse*, *The Normal School*, where "The Manly Arts" first appeared, *[PANK]*, *The Collagist, and* many other places. A recipient of fellowships from Kundiman and the Kenyon Review Writers Workshop, he is co-editor of *Waxwing* magazine and now lives in Grand Rapids, Michigan, where he teaches in the Writing Department at Grand Valley State University.

Janne Karlsson is an ultra-productive artist from Sweden. His dark edgy work is widely spread over the world. When this wine sipping madman isn´t busy drawing he's just sitting somewhere, impatiently waiting for you to buy his books, chaps and stuff through amazon, Epic Rites Press or his website www.svenskapache.se.

Pat King has had stories, essays, and pop culture articles published here and there on the web and in print. His novel *Exit Nothing* is available on Amazon and Kuboapress.wordpress.com.

Misti Rainwater-Lites lives in San Antonio where she sucks the occasional cock and writes the occasional novel. She took her brother to see Stone Cold Steve Austin once. It was fun watching the wrestler douse himself with beer.

Eric Lyden is the maker of the zine *Fish with Legs* that has not had a new issue in a while, but he's constantly working on it. He also reviews zines for *Xerography Debt*. Contact him at Eric.Lyden@gmail.com, friend him at Facebook.com/Ericfishlegs and maybe follow him on Twitter @FakeEricLyden even though he rarely tweets. He also finds it corny when writers comment on how weird it is to be writing about themselves in the third person, but is still compelled to do so.

Dan Mancilla lives in Grand Rapids, Michigan where he teaches writing at Kendall College of Art and Design and at Aquinas College. He holds a Ph.D. in Creative Writing from Western Michigan University. His work has been published in such journals as *Barrelhouse*, *The Chicago Tribune*, *The Malahat Review*, *The Saturday Evening Post*, and *River Styx*, among others. His fiction has won numerous awards and distinctions including the 2014 *Madison Review Chris O'Malley Fiction Prize*, the 2012 *Washington Square Review Flash Fiction Award*, and finalist for the 2009 *Chicago Tribune Nelson Algren Award*. Dan's professional wrestling-themed novella, *The Deathmask of El Gaucho* (Little Presque Books/Passages North) and his debut short story collection, *All the Proud Fathers* (Dock Street Press) are forthcoming in 2016. You can read more about Dan and his writing at danmancilla.com.

Lavie Margolin is the author of several best-selling career books including *Winning Answers to 500 Interview Questions*. He has slipped several wrestling references into his professional writing as well as written a few book reviews on behalf of WrestlingObserver.com. The first match he remembers watching on television was The Mega Powers against The Twin Towers. The first live even he attended was Hulk Hogan against The Canadian Earthquake at Madison Square Garden. He once purchased a two-pak of The Godwinns WWF Wrestling figures by Jakks.

Catfish McDaris' ancestors were from the Aniwaya Clan of the Cherokee Nation. He was in jail once for punching a pitbull that bit him in the ass, when he used his one call, his girlfriend told him to take a flying fuck and put the dog on the phone. His newest novella is at: http://weeklyweirdmonthly.bigcartel.com/product/naked-serial-killers-in-volkswagens-by-catfish-mcdaris

In the cruel stadium of high school gym class, **Leopold "The Great White Waif" McGinnis** was once pitted in a wrestling death match against Muhammed "Middle Eastern Stick Boy" Muhammed. The evenly pitted fighters grappled for nearly half an hour in pursuit of the 'Second Weakest Class Featherweight' Championship, much to the delight of the class. The sadistic coach refused to call a tie, in total disregard for the five-minute time limit, and eventually Leopold was pinned to the mat in an exhausted heap. Leopold went on to author 3 independent novels (*Game Quest*, *Bad Attitude*, *The Red Fez*), two books of poetry (*Poetaster*, *Zeus and the Giant Iced Tea*) and currently heads up the amazing greatness of redfez.net. The further journeys of Muhammed Muhammed, however, have been lost to the mists of time…

Mister V is the author of nine graphic novels, twenty-seven mini-comics, and the weekly comic strips Them There Hills and Life is Grand, both published in Kremmling, Colorado's The Grand Gazette. He lives in Granby, Colorado with his beautiful wife and smelly dog. Most of his comics can be read for free at his website www.arborcides.com.

D. O'Brien is a mother of five and a grandmother of one who refuses to grow up, who owns too many clever t-shirts, and who can usually be found photobombing people at wrestling shows unintentionally. Her work has been published in *Pro Wrestling Feelings #1* and at her own wrestling blog, thestretchplum.tumblr.com.

Brian Oliu is originally from New Jersey and currently teaches at the University of Alabama. He is the author of three full-length collections, *So You Know It's Me* (Tiny Hardcore Press, 2011), a series of Craigslist Missed Connections, *Leave Luck to Heaven* (Uncanny Valley Press, 2014), an ode to 8-bit video games, & *Enter Your Initials For Record Keeping* (Cobalt Press, 2015), essays on NBA Jam. *i/o* (Civil Coping Mechanisms), a memoir in the form of a computer virus, is forthcoming in 2015. His works in progress deal with professional wrestling and long distance running (not at once).

Josh Olsen is a writer, teacher, father, and librarian. He's written two collections of flash fiction, he's a card-carrying member of the WWE Fan Council, and he's the editor of *Working Stiff*.

A former journalist, **Marc Paoletti** holds a master's degree in fiction, and writes copy for advertising agencies and corporate clients. He is the author of *Scorch*, a thriller that draws upon his experiences as a Hollywood pyrotechnician, and co-author of *The Last Vampire* and *The Vampire Agent*. His acclaimed short fiction has appeared in numerous anthologies. Visit him online at marcpaoletti.com.

Chad Parenteau is the current host and organizer of the Stone Soup Poetry series now based in Cambridge MA at the Out of The Blue Art Gallery. He has had work recently published in *Off The Coast*, *Amethyst Arsenic*, *Incessant Pipe*, and the anthology *Multiverse*. His first full-length poetry collection, *Patron Emeritus*, was released by FootHills Publishing in 2013. He serves as Associate Editor of the online journal *Oddball Magazine*.

Tony Pena's poems are often times like a biopsy of one's soul put under a microscope. Not always a pretty specimen but it is vibrant, passionate and diverse as life itself. Over the years some of his specimens have found homes in *Full of Crow*, *Slipstream*, *Poetic Space*, *Underground Voices*, *Third Lung Review*, *Gutter Eloquence*, *Zygote in my coffee* and *Chronogram*. He has also had three pieces of fiction published in *Red Fez*. His first chapbook of poetry, *Opening night in Gehenna*, is available now. Some of his performances can be seen at www.youtube.com/tonypenapoetry.

Aaron Poliwoda is from your girlfriend's bedroom. He stands six foot seven three inches from heaven. He weighs three-oh-five and can whip any man alive! He is an autistic cartoonist who has published 76 issues of Low Blow comics (mostly about autism and wrestling) as of this writing.

Carl Robinson is an associate professor of English at a small college in the Midwest. He is the author of *Fat on the Vine*, *Bloodreal*, and *Rogue Holler Blues*. He would trade the entire 2015 WWE roster for Bruiser Brody and a horseman to be named later.

Brian Rosenberger lives in a cellar in Marietta, GA (on the outskirts of Bad Street) and writes by the light of captured fireflies. He is the celebrated author of *As the Worm Turns* and three (that's right three) poetry collections. Rumor has it he once terrorized the squared-circles of the Mid-West as the King Kong Kid, the world's tallest midget grappler, before retiring to terrorize the literate. Connect with him via www.facebook.com/HeWhoSuffers, because he does, in fact and practice, suffer for your sins. Brusier Brody remains his all-time favorite wrestler and constant inspiration. Dig it.

Jenny Seay earned her MFA in Creative Writing from Columbia College Chicago. Her work has appeared in *Punk Planet*, *Swink*, *TimeOut Chicago*, *Venus Zine*, and *Hair Trigger 27*, among others. She is currently at work on her first novel, which, much like the piece in this anthology, indulges her life-long love of professional wrestling. She has also taken a body slam from A.J. Styles.

Carrie Shipers's poems have appeared in *Crab Orchard Review*, *Hayden's Ferry Review*, *New England Review*, *North American Review*, *Prairie Schooner*, *The Southern Review*, and other journals. She is the author of *Ordinary Mourning* (ABZ, 2010), *Cause for Concern* (Able Muse, 2015), and *Family Resemblances* (University of New Mexico, forthcoming) as well as two chapbooks.

Jonathan Shipley is a freelance writer living in Seattle. His writing has appeared in such varied publications as the *Los Angeles Times*, *Meatpaper*, and a German trade publication for welders.

Evan Slambroze (b. 1995) is a poet who has only authored one chapbook, *Probably* (Writing Knights Press, 2013), and has transitioned his main form of art from the pen and paper to the squared circle, performing as "Weird Body" Evan Adams for Absolute Intense Wrestling in Cleveland, Ohio. He will probably stick with the latter, but still plans on dabbling in the former from time to time.

Matthew Sradeja lives in Toledo, Ohio with his wife and two cats. Matthew has worked in the glass and automotive industry. He began attending open mic poetry readings in 1999. Matthew has been published in print in *Broadway Bards First*, *every reason zine*, *CFDL*, and *This is Poetry Vol. 2 Mid-West Poets*. You can find his poems online at *Red Fez*, *Full of Crow*, *Rusty Truck*, and *Foliate Oak Literary Magazine*. "I find energy in poetry and I am always learning how to create it and or use it."

Nathan Steinman was born in Oklahoma in the Eighties, and his father joined the military after the oil bust. His family moved around to government whims, then back to Oklahoma where he started writing poetry at the age of seventeen. Now, 14 years later, still writing, he is married and has a degree in Music Education. He hopes to discover truth in the music of words.

Scott Stripling is a cartoonist who works and publishes under Shoot the Moon Comics http:// shootthemooncomics.tumblr.com who has been drawing comics since he could hold a crayon. He was recently accepted to SAW (The Sequential Artists Workshop) in Gainesville, Florida, and does a weekly wrestling comic strip with Colette Arrand at http://wrestlingschool.tumblr.com.

Rob Sturma is the curator and editor-in-chief of both the pop culture poetry journal *FreezeRay* and its print offshoot FreezeRay Press. He began his love affair with nerd poetics by editing the anthologies *Aim For The Head* and *MultiVerse* for Write Bloody Publishing. His own work can be seen online currently at *The Harpoon Review, Drunk In A Midnight Choir, Borderline, and Ghost House Review*. He lives in Oklahoma City, OK, where he co-hosts the Red Dirt Wayward Poets open mic and dreams of making more dope books.

Kevin Michael Theodoropolus, better known by his stage name Kabal, is an underground rapper & producer from Bramalea, Ontario Canada. He is also an established tattoo artist, special effects artist, as well as a former amateur/indy pro wrestler, & senior wrestling official for UWA Hardcore Wrestling. Full bio can be found at: www.kabal.webstarts.com

Jerry VanIeperen lives in Utah with his wife and two children. He briefly considered writing manifestos from a dark, windowless cabin in the heart of the Rocky Mountains, but felt his beard was not quite Nordic enough for such endeavors. He received an MFA from the University of Nebraska and is a founding editor of the poetry journal *Sugar House Review*.

Israel Wasserstein is a Lecturer in English at Washburn University. His first poetry collection is *This Ecstasy They Call Damnation*. His poetry and prose have appeared or will soon appear in *Crab Orchard Review, Flint Hills Review, Prairie Schooner*, and elsewhere. He owns too many pro-wrestling themed t-shirts.

64739911R00183

Made in the USA
Charleston, SC
02 December 2016